transition

Portrait of Eugene Jolas by André Masson, 1941, which arose out
of a series of discussions between Jolas and Masson on the writer
Novalis and the subject of night

transition

The History of a Literary Era
1927-1938

by

Dougald McMillan

CALDER AND BOYARS
LONDON

First published in Great Britain 1975
by Calder and Boyars Ltd
18 Brewer Street London W1R 4AS

© Dougald McMillan 1975

ISBN 0 7145 1016 5 Casebound Edition

Typeset in Great Britain by Gloucester Typesetting Co. Ltd.
Printed by Whitstable Litho, Straker Brothers Ltd.

CONTENTS

ACKNOWLEDGMENTS

I would like to thank Richard Ellmann for starting me on my way with this book, and Ernest Samuels and Northwestern University for helping me to obtain a research grant to continue.

I would also like to thank the friends of *transition* who answered my many questions and shared their recollections with me. They are an extraordinary group of people. I remember with pleasure and gratitude my meetings with Samuel Beckett, Marcel Brion, Stuart Gilbert,★ Carola Giedion-Welcker, Lucie Noel,★ Maeve Sage, Philippe Soupault, Francis Steloff, and Laurence Vail.★

Most of all I want to thank Maria Jolas, who embodies so well her generation's remarkable combination of revolutionary spirit and uncommon graciousness and generosity. My family and I could not have asked for a kinder or more helpful reception. From the first she offered invaluable assistance in ways ranging from providing un-published materials to correcting details of the text.

I also feel special affection for Barbara Toffolo, Gloria Stephenson, and Fran Dressman who helped me in my struggles with the manuscript.

★now deceased

LIST OF ILLUSTRATIONS

List of Illustrations

(The photographs of Eugene Jolas, Maria Jolas and the Joyce family, the André Masson portrait of Eugene Jolas, as well as all the material which appeared in *transition*, are reprinted by the kind permission of Maria Jolas)

INTRODUCTION

transition was the most important of the American expatriate 'little' magazines. For Americans at home (and for a smaller number of English intellectuals) it came to stand for all that was new in contemporary writing. Over one thousand of them subscribed in hopes that at least some of these developments from Paris could get by the rigid customs officers. Others bought it at centres of avant-garde enthusiasm like the Gotham Book Mart, which became, in 1928, the official American agent for *transition*.[1] Most people never saw a copy but nodded in agreement as book review pages of newspapers pronounced it unintelligible or laughed as *Life* magazine satirized it in a cartoon as the quintessence of expatriate extremism. Even today it remains in many minds synonomous with the now legendary 'Lost Generation' of Americans who enlivened Paris in the twenties.

In fact *transition* did not begin publication until 1927; it is more a magazine of the thirties than the twenties. And during these years it was not Americans like Ernest Hemingway and F. Scott Fitzgerald or even Ezra Pound and T. S. Eliot who were animating Paris and setting new trends in literature. In these years Paris was the center of a wave of neo-romantic, irrationalist thought that created new interest in German expressionism and dadaism, and culminated in surrealism and its offshoots. This was the major intellectual current that *transition*'s editor, Eugene Jolas, decided to transmit to America.

By the time Jolas began *transition* in 1927, the outstanding success of

1

their own kind of modernism had largely separated English writers from the neo-romantic movement, which had influenced continental literature so strongly. Both continental and English-speaking authors had begun the century with attacks on a common enemy—the bourgeois mentality and its accompanying didacticism and shopworn rhetoric. Dadaism, expressionism, and surrealism had moved rapidly toward greater verbal freedom and the unmediated presentation of the subconscious. In English no significant tradition of presenting interior material directly for its own sake had developed. English authors were still largely concerned with depicting characters in traditional fictional modes. The best young writers of the twenties (Sherwood Anderson, F. Scott Fitzgerald, Sinclair Lewis, John Dos Passos, Ernest Hemingway) continued to exploit and perfect the methods of conventional realistic fiction. Those writers who were dealing so successfully with interior experience (D. H. Lawrence, Eugene O'Neill, Virginia Woolf, Katherine Mansfield, and even the Joyce of *Portrait of the Artist* and *Ulysses*) had, for the most part, used mental phenomena as motivation for characters still firmly grounded in external reality.

The dominant attitude toward language in English also ran directly counter to the overriding interest in verbal experience and innovation on the continent. In English, the attack upon rhetoric had grown into a fundamental distrust of language itself and the rejection of the 'merely verbal'. The attitudes of the imagist movement pervaded the works of the best poets of the language—even those not directly involved in its manifestoes and publications. Yeats, Ezra Pound, T. S. Eliot, William Carlos Williams, Wallace Stevens, and Robert Frost, to name only the best, all contrasted the concision and 'hardness' of the image with the 'soft' inadequacy of words. They spoke metaphorically of poetry as if it were constructed out of a non-verbal visual or tactile medium. In prose, the stark reticence of Hemingway and his imitators grew out of a similar distrust of words.

The major achievements of these writers left little feeling among the writers themselves or the public of a need to participate in apparently peripheral continental movements. In this context it was a remarkable accomplishment to bring the work of Kafka and surrealism to readers attuned to imagism, Hemingway, Sherwood Anderson, and the stream-of-consciousness novel. To bring together those few but important writers in English with attitudes more like those of their French and

German contemporaries was an even greater service. Because of his unique cultural background, Eugene Jolas was able to do both.

Between 1927 and 1938 *transition* published portions of André Breton's 'Mad Love' and 'Nadja', his 'Introduction to a Discourse on the Dearth of Reality', and the surrealist manifesto 'Hands Off Love'. It introduced Kafka to English readers with works like 'The Sentence', 'Metamorphosis', and 'Letter to his Father'. It provided examples and explanations of dadaism by original dadaists like Hans (Jean) Arp, Hugo Ball, and Kurt Schwitters.

More significantly *transition* welcomed important works that other English editors had dismissed or ignored. It published much of Joyce's *Finnegans Wake* as 'Work in Progress' and a great deal of Gertrude Stein's work including 'An Elucidation', 'Four Saints in Three Acts', and a re-publication of 'Tender Buttons'. It published portions of Hart Crane's 'The Bridge', early poems and stories by Dylan Thomas, and Samuel Beckett's earliest works.

In spite of numerous editorial statements and a consistent editorial policy which produced no issues which were simply eclectic, the aims and achievements of *transition* have, with a few exceptions,[2] been misunderstood. Even sympathetic and relatively informed accounts of *transition* like that of Samuel Putnam in *Paris Was Our Mistress* have tended to exaggerate its sensational aspects.

Putnam acknowledges that *transition* was important. It has, he says, a 'unique place in the literary history of the period and cannot be overlooked by any future critic or chronicler. ... It was *transition* that really awakened the broader circles of the American intelligentsia to the fact that something was going on in Europe among our expatriates.'[3] He also recognized the seriousness and ability of Eugene Jolas and even understood the importance of German influences like expressionism in helping to shape *transition*'s programme. These observations, however, are overshadowed by Putnam's emphasis on *transition* as a part of the highly romanticized, consciously nonconformist expatriate life in Paris. After pointing out the importance of *transition* and reassuring his readers that Jolas was 'a very discriminating editor ... and did not ... accept anything for its sensational value,' Putnam continues, 'Still there were some amusing stories.' Among them is a description of Lincoln Gillespie. According to Putnam, Eugene Jolas is supposed to have heard that Gillespie appended '*J'espère que non*' to the end of each phrase in an hour-long narrative which he delivered at the Dome and to have exclaimed, 'Why the man is a genius! We must have him for *transition*!' Putnam comments that the anecdote is 'charmingly apocryphal no doubt, but there was a feeling that it could be true'.[4] Despite the earlier laudatory comments and the admission that the anecdote is apocryphal, one is left with the impression that Jolas had an inordinate respect for eccentricity.[5]

Putnam discusses the 'Revolution of the Word Proclamation', a manifesto which grew organically out of the editorial statements of *transition*'s first year, similarly as a part of Paris café life. The manifesto is quoted but not discussed; instead, the emphasis is upon the conversations it evoked in Montparnasse and the counter-manifesto, 'Direction', which Putnam and others wrote 'around a café table'.

Putnam's treatment of *transition* is not intentionally biased, but the emphasis on the aspects of the magazine which make his memoir entertaining leads away from understanding *transition* rather than toward it. An era too much described in ready-made phrases and stereotypes like 'expatriate', 'the twenties', 'the lost generation', 'the Montparnasse crowd', and 'the group in the Place de l'Odéon quarter', is already in danger of being misunderstood, and when the tendency toward sensationalism and oversimplification is bolstered by first-hand accounts like Putnam's, further misunderstanding is inevitable.

The memoirs of Malcolm Cowley, Matthew Josephson, Sisley Huddleston, Ernest Hemingway, and others have also helped to keep alive the picture of *transition* as the work of a small group of dedicated but idiosyncratic people who carried out an indiscriminate war on clear writing from some almost secret headquarters in the Rue de l'Odéon.

The disparity between *transition*'s reputation as the work of an extremist clique and its long list of distinguished contributors has been stated most bluntly by Marvin Magalaner and Richard M. Kain in their work *Joyce, the Man, the Work, the Reputation*. 'Why did [Joyce] not dissociate himself from the more blatant extravagances of this admittedly plucky magazine?'[6] The question applies as well to the other contributors. The answer lies in a full understanding of the literary revolution *transition* set about to accomplish and not the sensational details surrounding the manifestoes and pronouncements.

The history of that revolution involves some of the same kinds of complexities that surround a political revolution—the situation from which a call for renewal arises, the theory that defines new goals and methods, the men who lead, the followers they are able to attract, the opposition they evoke from within and without, and the new forms they establish. And beyond these concerns where the literary theoretician might stop, there remains, for anyone trying to grasp the feeling of this revolution, the story of the personal attachments which grow out of the common struggle.

transition's contributors were not a close-knit literary cabal, but a loose alliance of writers whom Eugene Jolas attempted to bring together under the aegis of a theory partly imported from European movements, partly derived from the practice of important English-language innovators, and partly simply asserted out of the exigencies of his own personal background. The authors who appear in the magazine are a little like the brigades that came in the thirties from all over Europe and America to fight in the Spanish republican cause. They came with varying levels of commitment to theory and to those who called for them to come, but they came to assert the right to common liberties. Even while they were joined together, they maintained a nearly incompatible independence of doctrine and method. Their diversity forces us to consider individually their relationship to the men and ideas that brought them together, but their importance lies in their common attitudes. Together the contributors of *transition* define an important wave of literary thought and practice that passed over Europe and America in the late 1920s and '30s. It was *transition* that proclaimed the poet's right to more direct presentation of the unconscious, greater linguistic experimentation, and freer development of personal mythic structures. And it was primarily *transition* that re-established the importance of 'the word' which had suffered so much in the exaltation of the image in the first quarter of the century.

Notes

1 One of these enthusiasts, James Laughlin IV, later dedicated his *New Directions* series to the readers, editors, and contributors of *transition* for successfully carrying out the 'Revolution of the Word'.
2 The accounts in Frederick J. Hoffman, Charles Allen, Carolyn Ulrich, *The Little Magazine* (Princeton, 1947) and in Kay Boyle

and Robert McAlmon, *Being Geniuses Together* (New York, 1968) are notably more balanced than other presentations.

3 Samuel Putnam, *Paris Was Our Mistress* (New York, 1947), pp. 219–20.

4 *Ibid.*, pp. 223–4.

5 The account is completely apocryphal. Gillespie originally brought his own unsolicited works to *transition*'s office where Elliot Paul, and not Jolas, accepted them.

6 Marvin Magalaner and Richard M. Kain, *Joyce the Man, the Work, the Reputation* (New York, 1957), p. 245.

Part 1

JOLAS AND THE MOVEMENT

Eugene Jolas in New York, 1915

I

GETTING INTO PRINT

When he returned to Paris in the summer of 1926 Eugene Jolas was thirty-two, a little-known poet without a critical following. He was probably best known for the literary column he was writing in the Paris edition of the *Chicago Tribune*. He had no money except his salary as a newspaper reporter (which ceased before the first issue appeared) and a small income from his wife's holdings in America. His greatest assets were his background in three linguistic cultures and his personality.

Jolas's special mixture of European and American experience and his practical knowledge of journalism made him uniquely suited to bring together the important neo-romantic literary movements of the continent with the most innovative writers in English. Jolas was, as he said, 'a man from Babel'.[1] An American citizen born of immigrant parents in New Jersey, he had grown up in his father's native village of Forbach in Lorraine where the family had returned when he was two years old. As a child of linguistically and culturally divided Lorraine, he had learned both the Rhenish German of his mother and his father's French. But his heritage was not simply bilingual. The cultural conflict between the French and the Germans in Forbach produced in Jolas a sense of 'millennial' struggle and what he called 'frontier anguish'. His attempts in *transition* to find a stratum of experience and a language deeper than the surface differences of national literatures were in part an attempt to reconcile the cultural conflict which had troubled him from his childhood.

The romantic striving for the absolute which became an important part of *transition* was also the product of his European boyhood. Encouraged by his devout Catholic mother, Jolas developed a deeply religious nature. At first it appeared that his religious concerns would take the form of orthodoxy. In 1908-9 he attended the seminary at Montigny near Metz with the idea of becoming a priest. Though he did not take vows and later rebelled against the church, he never entirely left it. His later work and theory both reflect his almost medieval belief that poetry is a means of experiencing a transcendental state which is essentially religious. He found confirmation of this belief in the works of the German romantics (Adalbert Stifter, Ludwig Tieck, Brentano and the brothers Grimm) which he read first as a child and returned to later in life. Jolas saw *transition* as a modern day continuation of the search for transcendent experience which had marked the early romantics.

If Jolas's early life in Lorraine shaped the background and temperament which would give much of *transition*'s unique flavour, his later American experience left an equally strong mark upon him and led directly to the founding of the magazine. As a child Jolas had read James Fennimore Cooper, Harriet Beecher Stowe, and Karl May. Stimulated by these melodramatic authors, a trunkful of souvenirs from the family's stay in New Jersey, and his parents' hopeful talk of a return, he began to build a personal fantasy of America as a land of fulfilment.

In 1910, when he was barely sixteen, a loan from his aunt in New York allowed him to emigrate. At first he found a part of his vision confirmed. The sense of growth and activity and the lighted cubes of the New York skyline suggested that America was a totally new world. Soon enough, though, he also experienced the problems of a young immigrant struggling to find a job, lose a foreign accent, and make his place in a modern city. In his first job as a delivery boy for a German grocery, even the skyscrapers took on a negative aspect. For him the narrow shafts of the dumb waiters leading up to rich apartments came to symbolize the distance between what Dos Passos later called the two Americas.

Jolas's experience in America was an almost archetypal climb through a succession of shabby lodgings and menial jobs to bookstore clerk, then night school, then to Carnegie Libraries where he read about Joseph Pulitzer, the poor immigrant become publisher, and finally to a career as a newspaper reporter.

At first he was still confined to the periphery of American life by his position on the German language *Pittsburgh Volksblatt*, but he learned his trade well and moved rapidly into the world of American journalism when he took the newly created position of 'automobile reporter' for the *Pittsburgh Post*. In the job he learned the romance of the machine first-hand from salesmen, drivers, and mechanics. In spite of his reservations about the impact of technology, both his own poetry and his magazine were later to reflect the changes in language which occur when the romantic temperament is confronted with the machine.

While he was learning the journalistic skills which were to be so helpful to him in founding *transition*, Jolas was also assimilating modern American poetry and writing poems of his own. His first large effort at poetry came after he was drafted in 1916. As secretary to an Army psychiatrist he was moved by the inner experiences of the patients which he recorded to write a series of poems, published under the collective title 'Ink' by Oscar Williams in his magazine *Rhythmus* in 1924.

After his discharge in 1920, Jolas's life and poetry began more and more to be marked by the conflict between the spirit of change and renewal in America and the oppressive growth of technological culture. One sign of the country's search for new forms to contain the modern experience was the tabloid newspaper. When he was accepted as a reporter for the New York *Daily News* Jolas was excited but he soon developed second thoughts. In their stories about 'bootleg queens' and other colourful figures, the reporters of the *Daily News* thought of themselves as 'mythmakers in the industrial chaos'. But as Jolas concluded in his autobiography, 'we were simply echoing the epoch's anarchic individualism . . . of the mercantile philistine. . . . We were chiming the collective belief in unending progress and perfectibility, the triumph of the machine.' 'Ink' expresses the tension Jolas felt between the brutal surface of life as reported in the daily press and the spiritual calm for which he longed.

Seeking relief, Jolas left the *Daily News* for what he hoped would be the quieter world of the Waterbury Connecticut *Republican*. In the smaller offices of the Connecticut paper the noise of telephones, typewriters, presses, and the passing traffic was even more oppressive. They became for Jolas the 'figures of diabolical instruments that had but one aim: to despiritualize the life of the individual. Against this mechanization of the human spirit I posited the catalytic powers of poetry and art.' In many ways *transition* reflects this same urge to counteract the abrasive elements of modern life through art. His prodigious reading of American poets at this period was an important part of his preparation for the magazine.

In Waterbury his belief in America had received a temporary setback. His response was to return in late 1923 to his family in Forbach. He was beginning on the path that would lead to *transition*, but it could hardly have appeared to him then that anything so positive was in store for him. He came home to his family with the same trunk he had taken with him. The worn clothes, disorderly manuscripts, and few books which it contained revealed how few of his hopes had materialized during the twelve years he had been gone. Although the quiet of Forbach and the leisure to reread Novalis and the other German romantics and the newer expressionists like Georg Trakl were at first pleasant, a return to the old ways of Europe was not the answer he was looking for. By now he considered himself American in spirit and could not be satisfied with the retirement of provincial life in Lorraine.

In the spring of 1924 a job on the Paris edition of the *Chicago Tribune* gave him the first chance to begin the kind of intercontinental literary journalism for which he was so well suited. He moved rapidly in a few months from the night cable desk, to reporter, to city editor. In that position he gave unusually close coverage to intellectual and cultural developments.

The literary section of the Paris *Tribune* was at that time under the direction of Ford Madox Ford, primarily a novelist, and David Darrah, the editor of the paper, wanted a trained newspaperman to handle the section. Jolas was at first awed by the fame of his predecessor and was hesitant to accept the job. Darrah insisted and Jolas agreed to assume the literary section on a trial basis, which very quickly was changed to a permanent arrangement.

He began a series of weekly articles called 'Rambles Through Literary Paris' for the Sunday edition. At a time when American knowledge of French literature seemed to have stopped with Anatole France, he interviewed people like Jean Giraudoux, André Gide, Philippe Soupault, André Breton, Valéry Larbaud, and Paul Eluard. He also talked with foreign writers like Ernest Hemingway and Hans Arp who had made their way to Paris after the war.

The column was not the usual discussion of books which had just

Cover of *transition* 25, 1936, by Jean Miró

Eugene Jolas, 1929

Maria Jolas, 1936

appeared but a collection of interviews with people who were writing books or taking part in literary movements. Often it included discussion of works which were going to appear but were not yet published. A regular feature of the column was the discussion of each new issue of the French reviews like the *Nouvelle Revue Française, La Revue Européenne, Le Navire d'Argent, La Révolution Surréaliste* and *Les Nouvelles Littéraires*.

Several subjects dominated the column: Joyce's *Ulysses* and the interior monologue; the births, deaths, and activities of 'little magazines'; and the militant revolt of the newly-formed surrealist group. It is not difficult to see the background of *transition* in 'Rambles Through Literary Paris'. The names of many of the writers whom Jolas interviewed appear later as contributors to *transition*. The idea of a fundamental extension of consciousness which the surrealists fostered became the keynote for Jolas again in 1927.

'Rambles Through Literary Paris' caught the eye of a young music student, Maria McDonald, from Louisville, Kentucky. They met at a party in May 1925 and liked each other at once. He invited her to accompany him to the annual meeting of the P.E.N. Club. She went with him and was introduced to James Joyce, who later became a close friend. As Jolas said in his column the following Sunday, he found the meeting, chaired by John Galsworthy, stiff and formal and not a very good way to promote international understanding among authors. It was not, however, a bad way to start a courtship; Jolas and Maria McDonald decided almost immediately that they would be married.

Interested in literature, proficient in both French and German, she found little difficulty in entering into the literary circle that grew up around *transition*. Eventually she contributed significantly to *transition* in many ways—as office manager, translator, and most importantly as unnamed but ever-present consulting editor. On occasion it was she who undertook the demanding work of taking the copy of an issue to the printer and seeing that it got through the presses without major errors.

The wedding was planned to take place in New York in January 1926, so Jolas left the *Tribune* to return again to America with the idea of remaining there. After a brief stay in New York where the bohemianism and bath-tub gin of Greenwich Village quickly tired them, they moved on to New Orleans where he became feature reporter for the *Item Tribune*. Out of his experiences in New Orleans, it became clear to Jolas that he could accept neither Europe nor America by itself.

Among the people the Jolases met in New Orleans were Sherwood Anderson and his family. Both Jolas and Anderson were consciously American. Despite the dark pictures Anderson's stories gave of life in small American towns, he had a lyrical faith in America and often talked to Jolas about it. Jolas, in turn, was elated when Anderson read the poems he had written during his first stay in the United States and commented that they had an 'American ring'. But their concept of America differed immensely. Anderson argued that the American character and pattern of life came almost exclusively from the American soil. 'What difference does this or that European background really make? . . . Do we in America pay any attention to that? . . . The days of the melting pot are over. . . . They forget Europe. . . . America is the only reality for them.'

Jolas, on the other hand, knew well how deep the roots of America were buried in Europe. He could not limit his concern to either continent, but was seeking a way to build a bridge between Europe and America. More and more it seemed to him that he could do this best with an international literary magazine. *The Double Dealer*, published in New Orleans and edited by Lilian Marcus and Julius Friend, whom the Jolases knew well, had become moribund, and the Jolases discussed several times the possibility of taking it over. But Jolas felt that the primarily American audience of *The Double Dealer* would be too limiting for him to be able to organize the international conjunction that interested him. He also felt that New Orleans was too remote a starting point for such a venture. So he waited.

While writing for the *Chicago Tribune* Jolas had already pointed out that the atmosphere of Paris was an excellent climate for the kind of literary exchanges that little magazines thrived on. At that time Paris seemed the only vantage point from which they could hope to succeed.

That spring an incident occurred which convinced Jolas that he should leave New Orleans. As feature reporter it was his duty to cover the annual Shriners' convention. Aware of the delays that precede the bombastic speeches in which conventions culminate, he brought Gide's *Nourritures Terrestres*, in French, which like many French books of the day, was bound in yellow. As Jolas passed through the banquet hall, the cover caught the eye of one of the Shriners. 'What's that book?' he roared. 'It's foreign, isn't it? Well, we're Americans here. . . .' The Shriner represented just the sort of narrow-mindedness against which

Gide's book was written. That night Jolas announced to his wife that he was leaving New Orleans because he could not stand the provincial atmosphere any longer.

Back in Paris, Jolas reassumed his old position as city editor of the *Tribune*. But he began to work toward starting a magazine.

As he began to put his plans into practice his most immediate asset was his own personality. Physically he was a large man who gave the impression of strength and sensitivity that inspired confidence. He was erect, heavy-set, and broad-shouldered. His large face had angular features which gave an intensity to his expression. Kay Boyle said he had 'the fine head of a Roman senator and the wild gaze of a poet'.[2]

His European background won him easy access to the company of other authors. He enjoyed the leisurely lunches and dinners in Parisian restaurants and liked to sit afterward over a glass of wine. He needed both the alcohol and the male companionship afforded by these long sessions. But unlike the more frenzied Americans such as F. Scott Fitzgerald, Harry Crosby, and Robert McAlmon, who also sought fulfilment in Paris, he did not seek excitement and crowds, but intelligent conversation.

He was genial and loquacious among friends, but in discussions was often quiet, almost halting, until sure that his listeners were interested in one of his enthusiasms. Then he would talk spiritedly, sometimes almost stuttering in his eagerness to expound his beliefs. In moments of excitement, he would pound the table as he explained the urgency of accepting his viewpoint. There could be an erratic strain in his conversation. If a thought captured his attention, he might be silent for most of an hour while others around him talked. If the talk became too superficial or too aridly intellectual, or if a statement angered him, he might rush out abruptly to take a taxi home.

In private conversations he took the ideas and concerns of other people as seriously as he took his own. Kay Boyle said of him, 'He was one of the best listeners I have ever known. All his gifts were of unique proportions, but the ability to listen intelligently was a tremendous, an outsized gift.'[3] His contributors found him an agreeable editor with whom they could discuss their works easily.

These characteristics led to an amazing range of acquaintance among writers. In Strasbourg, where he used to bicycle from Forbach, he had met Kurt Schwitters and René Schickele who introduced him to other expressionists. In Paris he knew most of the members of the surrealist group and often spent the evening drinking and talking with Philippe Soupault or Robert Desnos or walking about the city with Paul Eluard. Through his work on the *Tribune* he knew most of the Americans who had come to Paris. He had also met many writers while in America and had corresponded with most of those he had met while making arrangements to translate their works for his *Anthologie de la Nouvelle Poésie Américaine*.

By temperament he fitted in more easily with the new romantics of Paris—the dadaists, surrealists, and the remnants of the symbolists— than with the tight-lipped writers like Ernest Hemingway, Robert McAlmon, and Morley Callaghan. Primarily self-educated since he had left the monastery at Montigny, he had oriented his reading toward idealist philosophy (Schopenhauer was a favourite), German romanticism, and psychology. This led to a tendency to talk in abstractions that further the cause of the literary resurgence. *The Dial*, which had been a hindrance, but Paris was undergoing a resurgence of the romantic attitude.

The revolution begun by the dadaists in Zurich had arrived in Paris and by the mid-twenties appeared on the verge of a great success. The surrealists had been publishing *La Révolution Surréaliste* since 1924. And their '*Bureau de recherches surréalistes*' in the Rue de Grenelle had been opened the same year. The newest works of James Joyce and Gertrude Stein gave indications that the anti-realism, irrationalism, and experimentation that had been sweeping Europe since the war was also going to find expression in English.

On both sides, among the realists and among those who were experimenting with a newer style, there was a feeling that English writing was undergoing a renewal in Paris and that a magazine was needed to further the cause of the literary resurgence. *The Dial*, which had been so helpful in promoting the imagist revolution, was by the mid-twenties busy trying to secure imagism as part of the established tradition. And as T. S. Eliot himself remarked, it seemed a little tired by 1927. *The Little Review*, which had encompassed almost all of the new movements that had appeared since 1914, had given up trying to stay abreast of new writing in 1926 and did not publish another issue until 1929 and only then to announce that it was ceasing publication

because there was too much chaos in the world to permit masterpieces
to be written.

Two magazines had brief successes in publishing new writing from
Paris. Ford Madox Ford's *transatlantic review* had appeared from
January 1924 to January 1925. Its format was basically conservative and
it stressed the works of Ford, Conrad, and imagists like Ezra Pound
and William Carlos Williams. But it also published more experimental
poems by E. E. Cummings, part of a new work by Joyce (placed by
Ford in a section headed 'Work in Progress', by which title Joyce's
novel was to be known until its appearance, in 1939, as *Finnegans Wake*)
and part of Stein's *The Making of Americans*. It had been a rallying
point for expatriate American authors and its loss was felt heavily. On
18 January, 1925, Jolas had devoted a large part of 'Rambles' to a discussion of the faults which led to the demise of the *transatlantic review*.
The chief of these, he felt, was 'an incurable drift' due to the lack of a
strong personality behind it. On 8 March, he noted that a group of
American authors in Paris was thinking of organizing a magazine to
take the place of the defunct *transatlantic review*. Nothing came of this
plan but that did not keep it from being a good one. Ernest Walsh and
his friend Ethel Moorhead did begin *This Quarter* which for a while
filled the need for an English language magazine in Paris. It placed its
emphasis upon younger writers and was more open to unorthodoxy
than the *transatlantic review*. By 1926, however, Walsh and Miss Moorhead were quarreling bitterly over the magazine and he was dying of
consumption. The magazine managed to survive his death in October
1926, but in a greatly altered form and it did not reappear until 1929.
In late 1926, it looked as if *This Quarter* would end with Walsh's
death.

To Jolas it seemed that he had been left to defend the cause alone and
he assumed the role of the champion of the new writing enthusiastically.
Some weeks after Walsh's death he telegraphed Kay Boyle in Monaco,
where she had been with Walsh in his last days, to say that he was
carrying on what Walsh had begun and asking her to contribute a
story to the first issue of his magazine to be called *transition*. In the
ensuing correspondence he wrote to her of the need for a new spirit in
literature so forcefully that she became certain of her own 'impatience
with at least nine-tenths of contemporary American writing'.[4] Later
she wrote about Jolas's enthusiasm, 'His belief in my work and in the

work of countless unknown others gave a new meaning not only to my life but to the international writing scene.'[5]

The questions involved in the new literature were more than matters of style for Jolas. They were deep philosophical beliefs, approaching religious concern. He was himself an intuitive man and had troubling psychological experiences. His dreams were particularly vivid and seemed portentous to him. At one time he had felt himself possessed and had actually had visions in which he had encountered the devil. These psychic experiences led him to seek new ways of expressing the unconscious with a fervour that made him unusually receptive to literary innovation in that direction. This led to extravagances in the style of his editorials and, on rare occasions, in his literary judgements, as for example in his regard for the work of George Pelorson. It also led to the perceptive appreciation of the newest developments in three linguistic cultures. Beneath the abstractions and rhetorical pronouncements that so unnerved his critics, Jolas displayed an uncommon ability to assimilate literary movements and to determine quickly what was essential in them.

Specific preparations for the first issue began in the late fall of 1926. The magazine would need the services of at least two people, and Jolas looked about for an editorial assistant. Elliot Paul, an intelligent and enthusiastic expatriate from Boston who had replaced him as editor of the literary page of the *Chicago Tribune*, appeared the logical choice for the position.

Paul's erratic love life involved him in intrigues and secrecy which ultimately made co-operation very difficult, but for a year he served as co-editor with Jolas. His mocking attitudes coloured the early issues significantly. He declared, for example, in one editorial that *transition* was founded solely for the editor's amusement (*t.* 8, p. 180). On another occasion he prefaced a derogatory article on Schoenberg with the biblical epigraph, 'Jesus Christ, the same yesterday, today, and forever' (*t.* 10, p. 142). By far the most virulent piece of anti-bourgeois criticism ever to appear in *transition*, 'Hands Off the Dike' (*t.* 5), was the work of Paul. His taste for American realism was also reflected in the inclusion of stories by authors like Virgil Geddes and W. C. Emory. His own experimental stories show the influence of Gertrude Stein's theories of literature as an abstract art. But strangely he had little appreciation for similar experimental efforts among the French, and frequently had to be convinced by Jolas of the value of writers who later turned out to be important literary figures.

In Paul, Jolas had his editorial assistant; now they needed an office. At first the dining-room table of the Jolases' Paris apartment at 7, rue Valentin-Haüy was sufficient for the daily editorial meeting, but when the work began to grow and to interfere with meals, Mrs Jolas insisted that the two editors find an office. They rented a room in the *Hotel de la Gare des Invalides*, 40, rue Fabert. Later Robert Sage described this office and its ambiance in an open letter to Jolas for *transition* 19/20.

> 40, rue Fabert is an historic address for me, as it must be for you and several others. I shall always remember that little fourth floor room with its single window looking out on the Esplanade des Invalides and the dim vision of Sacré-Coeur on the hill across the city. And I shall remember the just visible clock on the Gare des Invalides—sometimes a diabolic reminder of luncheon dates being missed, sometimes a convenient alibi for an apéritif at the corner bistro, the Métro, Chez Francis or Ferrari's. The walls of Room 16 should be saturated with arguments, jokes, discussions, worries, mockeries and those pleasant meandering conversations which at college we called pea-talks. I always preferred the talks en famille, but how many people managed to break through the inefficient consigne downstairs to tap hesitantly at the door of 'the business and editorial offices' of *transition*! Delightful people and impossible people, who always stayed on and on (totally disorganizing the unpleasant but necessary task of completing the business details) until they were rallied by the irresistible suggestion of, 'How about a little drink down on the corner?' (*t.* 19/20, pp. 370–1)

In room 16, among the plumbing which is the standard equipment of French hotel rooms, the first issue of the new magazine was put together.

Although work on this issue was progressing, still no name had been chosen. 'Bridge' and 'Continents' were suggested and seemed likely choices in view of the magazine's desired international orientation. However, Leonard and Virginia Woolf had recently published Edwin Muir's collection of essays entitled *Transition* at their Hogarth Press and it caught the attention of Jolas and Paul.

In his preface Muir stated, 'The things which it is most essential that the critic should deal with are the things of the present: the books which are being written, the books which might be written, the tendencies which have not still found a decisive direction.'[6] That was precisely the

kind of task which they hoped their new review could perform. Moreover, Muir saw the best of the new literature as a revolt against the spirit
of the age. He defined three kinds of literature: that which, like the
writings of Aldous Huxley, was 'fashionable' and reflected passively the
spirit of the age; that which, like the works of D. H. Lawrence, sought
to escape the spirit of the age by finding other societies; and that which,
like Joyce's books, was in conflict with the age. Paradoxically, the last
was the best reflection of the modern spirit. Muir found this only
natural because 'to a sincere or original spirit life must always be more
difficult than it is to the mediocre or the fashionable'.[7] In 'Rambles
Through Literary Paris' Jolas had already noted the tendency of young
French writers, above all the surrealists, to be at odds with contemporary
society and had expressed his sympathy with their attitude.

In another essay from the collection, 'Contemporary Poetry', Muir
pointed out that modern poetry is a minority voice in an age dominated by science, the city and the machine, and has in contrast to
nineteenth century poetry become 'stubborn, violent, and clever'.[8] The
facts of science were still only 'intellectually grasped' by the poets and
not yet part of a natural feeling toward the natural world. Thus the
scientific perspective remained foreign to poetry. Jolas hoped his magazine could help to overcome this estrangement. And finally, in his essay
'The Contemporary Novel', Muir had defined the main tendency of
the age as a desire to show the psychological complexities which lay
beneath abstractions such as 'love', which writers of the past had
largely been content to use without exploring very deeply. This unwillingness to accept the old values implied by old abstractions indicated that the age was one of a major transition between sets of values.
Jolas had been particularly interested in the attempts of Joyce and those
after him to penetrate the layer of consciousness on the surface to find
the complexity of thought below, and he too believed his contemporaries to be seeking a new set of values. Moreover, his title defined the
age while still suggesting the role of an intermediary between continents which the editors also envisaged for the magazine—so they
adopted it. Jolas insisted on a small 't' knowing from his newspaper
experience that it would create controversy among the critics.

In addition to using already established contacts with expressionists,
surrealists and American expatriates, Jolas and Paul also solicited manuscripts from all over Europe, including Central Europe, an area which

most of the reviews of the time completely neglected. A young Russian woman, Sofia Himmel, who lived in Paris had maintained contact with Russian literature and was able to suggest and translate for *transition* the works of the new Russian writers like Alexander Blok, Serge Essenin, Vladimir Lidin, Boris Pilniak, and others.

Paul had recently come under the spell of Gertrude Stein. He had been introduced to her through Bravig Imbs and was a frequent visitor to her Rue de Fleurus apartment. When Jolas had invited Paul to help him with *transition*, Paul had consulted Miss Stein and she had urged him to accept Jolas's offer with the idea that the new review would be a convenient outlet for her works. Accordingly he asked her for a contribution to the first issue. She chose 'An Elucidation', her explanation of her method of writing in her own style. While Paul was concentrating on Gertrude Stein, Jolas was interested in Joyce. He had met Joyce in 1924 at the testimonial dinner organized by Adrienne Monnier for Valéry Larbaud. When introduced to Joyce, he had asked point-blank if he could call on him for an interview (something Joyce never allowed). Fortunately, he had been warned by the negative gestures and reproving looks of Sylvia Beach in time to let the matter drop and avoid committing '*lèse-Dedalus*'. After that the encounter had been pleasant and Joyce had thanked Jolas for the article he had written about *Ulysses* for the *Chicago Tribune*. Later that night Miss Monnier told him that Joyce was writing a new book and that a chapter of it would appear in the first issue of her new review *Le Navire d'Argent*.

Two years later at the time the first issue of *transition* was being planned, the new work had not yet been published extensively in any English language review, but Jolas had read fragments in *Le Navire d'Argent* and *transatlantic review*. The thought occurred to him that since the work was not appearing regularly elsewhere, Joyce might consent to publish it in *transition*. He still did not know Joyce well enough to approach him directly and so decided to ask Sylvia Beach to talk to Joyce on the subject. Jolas and Paul called on her at Shakespeare and Company in December and she agreed to approach Joyce for them. A few days later Joyce sent a large manuscript of parts of 'Work in Progress' to the Rue Fabert office. On a Sunday afternoon in mid-December he invited Miss Beach, Miss Monnier, the Jolases and Elliot Paul to a reading of the work at his apartment in the Square Robiac. He read the opening pages to them, smiling occasionally. When he was

through, he turned to each of the guests and asked them individually
what they had thought of it. There was little to be said. The work was
a revolutionary personal solution to the problem of giving a new power
to words and thus not perfectly understandable at first, but it was
impressive as read by Joyce in his musical Irish voice. Jolas placed little
importance on the immediate intelligibility of literature and so accepted
the work more readily than many of Joyce's earlier supporters.

Arrangements were made for *transition* to begin publication with the
first part of the book, to republish fragments which had appeared in
transatlantic review, *Contact Collection of Contemporary Writers*, *Criterion*,
Le Navire d'Argent, and *This Quarter*, and to continue serially. Joyce
would receive the same twenty franc per page rate as all other contributors. These publishing arrangements were, however, left flexible to
suit Joyce. As it turned out the arrangements were perfectly satisfactory;
no serious misunderstanding of any kind ever developed between Joyce
and *transition*. Though neither party could have known it at the time,
Finnegans Wake had found the unusual circumstances for appearance
which the unique work demanded.

In the first three months of 1927 Jolas and Paul worked steadily at the
job of selecting texts and preparing them for printers. The task of
making translations was larger than might be expected. Almost half of
the twenty-three works which appeared in the first issue had never
been translated into English. The budget did not include funds for
translators and almost all of the work fell to either Jolas or Paul, the
bulk of it to Jolas. It was inevitable with a schedule of monthly publication that some of the translations should be less perfect than the work
of specialists made at a more leisurely pace. The remarkable range of
the magazine's coverage and the importance of getting new works
before the public precluded perfection. A good linguist, Jolas was
aware of this and regretted it but chose consciously to explore new
areas rather than to follow a more cautious policy. Later when *transition*
began to stress the sound of words and to publish works which used
personal neologisms, Jolas occasionally printed works, especially
poetry, in their original language.

By early February all the translations had been completed, the original texts carefully checked, and the complete manuscript for the first
issue was ready. The contents were impressive; in addition to the opening section of Joyce's 'Work in Progress' and Miss Stein's 'An Elucida-

tion' it contained among other things Hart Crane's 'O Carib Isle!' and a reproduction of Max Ernst's '*Mer et Oiseau*'. Charles Boni of Boni and Liveright was passing through Paris at that time and paid a call on the Jolases. When he saw the table of contents, he remarked, 'But this is worth a fortune!' and suggested that the material should be exploited more commercially. Jolas refused to respond. Wisely, he realized that any departure from the plan for a small, experimental review which paid all contributors at the same rate would be the end of the magazine as he conceived of it, and so he rejected from the first the idea of commercialization. The only advertisements to appear in *transition* were the not very lucrative announcements by publishers, friendly book-stores and other reviews. No more than 4,000 copies of any issue were ever printed and paid subscriptions never exceeded 1,000. Thus at no time did the magazine make money; there was often a deficit which the Jolases had to make up themselves with occasional help from friends.

Boni was not the only one to indicate approval of the idea of the new magazine. Pound heard of it before the first number appeared and wrote to Jolas saying that if he had realized earlier that *transition* was going to appear he would not have inaugurated *The Exile*.

It seemed from these reactions that all was going well and that the first issue would be able to appear in February, 1927, without trouble. There were, however, problems ahead. On the way to take the train for Mayenne where the magazine was being printed, Jolas and Paul stopped by the office and found a letter from Archibald MacLeish demanding that his poem 'Signature Anonyme' be withdrawn because in a preliminary announcement of the first issue it was not given the prominence which he felt it deserved. Jolas sent MacLeish a telegram expressing the editors' regrets and asking him to reconsider. He did and a telegram, again authorizing publication, awaited them in Mayenne. All seemed in order again. After three days of proofreading the magazine was passed for press.

Though a few advance copies were finished and sent to several con-tributors, the troubles with the first issue were not over. One of the pages of Miss Stein's piece, 'An Elucidation', had been printed in the wrong place. The piece, never so clear as the title suggested, was now even less so. Miss Stein was quite upset and sent a virulent letter demand-ing rectification. At first it seemed possible to print a correction, but technical difficulties proved insuperable. Miss Stein was propitiated instead by the promise of a special supplement to the first issue with the corrected text of her entire work. The supplement appeared with a contrite preface by Paul remarking how unfortunate the 'inadvertence in the printing establishment' had been and pointing out that 'An Elucidation' was 'particularly valuable' since in it 'Miss Stein hits upon the happy idea of explaining herself in her own terms'. To placate Miss Stein further, Paul closed on an almost hyperbolic note: 'To say that we regret an error is futile and inadequate. We deplore the fundamental mathematical law by which errors come about, and the human fallibility which is one of its elements.' The preface conciliated Miss Stein; the break which had impended was at least deferred.

Another impediment to placing the first issue on sale came from French law. This requires that the name of a *gérant*, a person legally responsible for the contents of a printed work, be visible on all French publications. When the printer asked who was to be the *gérant* for *transition*, Paul and Jolas said they would both assume the responsibility. Though he should have known better, the printer neglected to mention that according to the law only a French citizen can act as the responsible publisher of a work printed in France, and duly set their names in type as *gérants*. When the *préfet* of Mayenne inspected the first issue, he was baffled by the contents except for the words *gérant* and the names of Jolas and Paul. The fact that two foreigners had undertaken to be responsible for a review whose contents were beyond his grasp was more than the *préfet* could bear. He reported Jolas and Paul to the Parisian authorities and they were summoned to the Commissariat of their quarter. They were informed that they had committed a serious breach of French law and told that there could be no question of releasing the review at once. Hopes of a February appearance had to be abandoned. Paul and Jolas, meanwhile, were to 'hold themselves at the disposal' of the police until notified further. Fortunately, they were both companionable men and had become friends with the family who ran the *Hotel de la Gare des Invalides* in which their office was housed. The son-in-law of the proprietor was stationed at the Commissariat where they had been interrogated. A talk with him and a 100 franc *pourboire* cleared up the matter. No more was heard from the authorities. After a week's further delay to be sure the police had forgotten the charge, the first issue was finally placed on sale in Paris.

Meanwhile, the work of assembling the magazine and the contacts it involved began to occupy too much of Jolas's time. The Jolases, who now had a daughter, Betsy, realized that if they were to have the quiet necessary to live a normal family life, they would have to leave Paris. In late December, during the height of the work on the first issue, they heard of an old hunting lodge for rent in Colombey-Les-Deux-Eglises in the Haute-Marne near Chaumont. After an inspection visit the Jolases decided to rent 'La Boisserie', as the place was called. As a matter of economy and convenience for editorial work, it was agreed that Paul would come to live with the Jolases. Paul was too involved in love affairs in Paris for him to be content to remain for long periods in Colombey and that arrangement did not work out. He did, however, come down for editorial sessions; later on, Robert Sage, the Stuart Gilberts, and, on one occasion, the Harry Crosbys also came to Colombey, which served as the editorial headquarters for *transition* during its first two years of publication. When the Jolases left 'La Boisserie', it was sold to a young French army officer, Charles de Gaulle, and it has now become the most famous country house in France.

Despite the fact that most of the editorial work was done at Colombey, the magazine still needed a Paris office and the hotel room in the Rue Fabert was retained. Maeve Sage, Robert Sage's wife, was hired as secretary to handle correspondence and to meet the people who called at the office. She soon became an invaluable assistant.

Almost as soon as the first issue appeared, orders came in from all parts of the world, with New York, London, and Paris accounting for the largest numbers of sales. The magazine was also besieged with manuscripts from young writers. The bidet and lavabo in the hotel room which had at first been only bizarre embellishments were fitted out with planks to make tables for manuscripts. It was clear that *transition* had survived its birth and could look forward to continuing successfully, if not tranquilly.

Notes

1 Unless otherwise indicated, the information and quotations in this chapter are from Jolas's unpublished autobiography, 'Man from Babel', which he began in the 1930s and completed shortly before his death in 1952. The typescript copy is in the possession of Mrs Eugene Jolas in Paris.

2 Boyle and McAlmon, *Being Geniuses Together* (New York, 1968), p. 268.
3 *Ibid.*, p. 299.
4 *Ibid.*, p. 319.
5 *Ibid.*, p. 233.
6 Edwin Muir, *Transition* (London, 1926), p. vii.
7 *Ibid.*, p. 9.
8 *Ibid.*, p. 180.

II

SUBVERSION AND QUEST:
THE FIRST YEAR

So *transition* was launched and settled down into a relatively normal mode of publication. The introductory statement of the first issue makes clear the hopes of the editors that the magazine could combine the best of America with the best of Europe. 'The tangible link between the centuries is that of art. It joins distant continents into a mysterious unit, long before the inhabitants are aware of the universality of their impulses' (*t.* 1, p. 135). America had been less affected by art than other countries, but

> Lately, Americans have shown unmistakable signs of artistic awakening. . . . More important, still, a small group of intelligent readers has developed. As yet there is only a beginning but it gives a glorious promise.
>
> It is quite natural that the new interest in American literature should stimulate a curiosity about the literature of other lands. . . .
>
> *transition* wishes to offer American writers an opportunity to express themselves freely, to experiment, if they are so minded, and to avail themselves of a ready, alert and critical audience. To the writers of all other countries, *transition* extends an invitation to appear, side by side, in a language Americans can read and understand. (*t.* 1, pp. 136–7)

transition never departed from this programme announced in its first issue; in ten years of publication it continued to be a bridge between European and American literature, and at times, in fact, it seemed to be the only route between the two continents along which experimental

works could travel. This opening statement does not, however, antici-
pate completely *transition*'s development.

As Stuart Gilbert pointed out, the magazine was strongly revolutionary from the start.

> On the first page, I read an eyesplitting crash of thunder, the great fall of an
> offwall, entailing 'at such short notice the schute of Finnegan, erse solid
> man', and all but shared his schute. That initial fanfare was in a way symbolic
> of what was to follow, not only in the Irish author's contributions but
> throughout the magazine; the crash of ancient strongholds falling to a sound
> of trumpets and the *débâcle* of many a seeming solid firman. (*t.* 22, p. 138)

Jolas in a retrospective evaluation of the first five years of *transition*
characterized the first year as an 'Eclectic-Subversive Period' (*t.* 22, p.
146); in other words, although the 'Revolution of the Word' was not
yet announced, *transition* presented in this period many kinds of material
which showed little respect for established values and a desire to subvert
existing conventions.

In an early editorial statement, 'On the Quest', Jolas wrote of 'the
profound disquietude in which the sensitive man of our age lives. He
has trusted to pure reason too long. He lives in the obsession of despair.
Call it a new *mal du siècle*, if you wish, it is none the less a real thing that
goes deep into the consciousness of our epoch. The intellectualism
vaunted so long leaves him cold' (*t.* 9, p. 193). This *mal du siècle* gives
rise to 'a certain kind of barbarism which to some seems for the moment
the only solution . . .' (*t.* 9, p. 193). In their different ways, Pierre Drieu
La Rochelle's *The Young European*, Philippe Soupault's 'Hymn to
Liberty', André Breton's 'Introduction to the Discourse on the Dearth
of Reality', and Carl Sternheim's 'A Pair of Drawers', all of which
appeared in *transition* during the first year, are statements of fundamental
revolt against the conventional attitudes of society. Though they were
written earlier, Gide's *Les Nourritures Terrestres* (1897) and Lautréamont's *Les Chants de Maldoror* (1868–9) were also translated because
they exhibited a similar spirit and had exerted an influence on the
younger generation.

The Young European by Drieu La Rochelle was the most current and
emphatic statement of this new barbarism. An extract from the first
chapter appeared in the second number of *transition* prior to its appearance in novel form in French. And in the first year the editors devoted

two reviews to defining the attitudes that gave rise to the book. This one fragment of *The Young European* was the only publication of Drieu La Rochelle in *transition* and he played no large part in its programme. In that first year, however, his work served as a current example of the kind of dissatisfaction with the social order that was finding literary expression. A combination of fiction and autobiography, *The Young European* is the story of a completely rootless author, a man without nationality, racial heritage, or fixed residence. In his quest for significance he exhausts all that old Europe, America, and revolutionary Russia can offer. Nothing is beyond him. He steals and kills without remorse and sometimes without reason. At the end of the novel all he has left is the realization that nothing can relieve his sense of vanity. His only satisfaction is that he no longer feels the compulsion to seek ways to evade it.

Paul, in his essay, 'The New Nihilism', called the book 'A convincing statement of the contemporary artist's predicament. He has felt the persistent domination of the threadbare past and he has suffered from the emptiness of the present' (*t. 5, p. 151*). To him the book represented the first real impact of the war of 1914 on the novel. It showed an unparalleled nihilism. While rejecting the prevalent social order, Drieu La Rochelle also rejected the most fundamental moral beliefs of Western society. 'One man, alone, is concerned with a world which is contained within his own cravings and satisfactions. Never does it appear that he is aware of another's joy or pain' (*t. 2, p. 166*).

transition was not a nihilist magazine, but its policies grew out of the same intellectual and spiritual situation which gave rise to the nihilism of Drieu La Rochelle and others like him. Jolas knew personally the inadequacy of the traditional European schooling and customs which had been imposed upon him. He had also seen the disparity between the promise of wealth in America and the difficulties of the immigrant worker, and he had had more than enough contact with 'successful' Americans in his newspaper work to realize that wealth and position were no hedge against petty-mindedness and banality. He had not experienced Russian communism personally. But despite optimistic pronouncements by artists who had visited Russia, Jolas felt that communism would limit the artist's subject matter and his style. Many of his theoretical statements in *transition* try to define the alternatives others had chosen when faced with this situation.

Returning to traditional beliefs by new paths, as many were trying
to do, seemed too anachronistic and limiting even to be considered. In
the late twenties three important spokesmen offered this alternative, and
Jolas answered them directly. In 1928, when Jacques Maritain published
his book *Frontières de la Poésie*, Jolas declared himself 'in utter disagree-
ment with Jacques Maritain' for ignoring the 'diabolical principle'
embodied in the works of Lautréamont and allowing only 'dogmatic'
disquietude (i.e. a frank questioning which is always in search of the
God of Catholic theology). He concluded, 'We are not ripe for a
religious art. There are no saints among us. . . . We of this age have no
faith in anything, save in anguish and despair, save in being suspicious
of a humanity that has betrayed all our ideals and is becoming more
depressing everyday' (*t.* 7, p. 159).

When Eliot declared in 'Lancelot Andrewes' that he was a conservative in literature, a royalist in politics, and an Anglo-Catholic in religion,
Jolas again spoke out on the impossibility for the poet of a return to
religious orthodoxy. 'I cannot help feeling that Mr Eliot has committed
intellectual treason. His conversion may be sincere (though his royalism
is suspicious)—and I cannot sneer at mystic or transcendental hunger—
but, for a creative mind, complete absorption in a party or religious
institution is paralysis' (*t.* 15, p. 11).

When the 'new humanism' received a new burst of publicity in 1929
and 1930 from the anthology *Humanism and America*, edited by Norman
Foerster, and essays in *The Bookman* and *Criterion*, Jolas dismissed it
peremptorily. 'Of all the attempts to find a basic philosophic concept to
guide us out of the post-war confusion, it seems to me the most muddled
one so far has been the new humanism. . . . The application of moral
dogmas of this kind to literary expression is unacceptable' (*t.* 19/20,
p. 16).

As for the question of deciding between Russia and America, he felt
that neither offered an acceptable alternative to the old way of life.
Spender, Auden, the surrealists, and Americans like Malcom Cowley,
Matthew Josephson, Michael Gold, and V. F. Calverton hoped for a
socialist solution. A spirit of nationalistic American optimism marked
the poetry of Carl Sandburg and Vachel Lindsay. Jolas could not bring
himself to side with either of these groups. But still he did not share the
complete disillusionment with both Russia and America which led
Drieu La Rochelle and others like him to become fascists. For Jolas it

was not inconceivable that these two unacceptable alternatives might one day give way to others more acceptable.

America had potential to develop into a country where poetry could flourish, but its potential was being turned into a hindrance instead of an asset. Of America he wrote in 'On the Quest':

> The vertiginous pseudo-progress of industrialism has blinded us to the immense psychological importance of the machine. The latter which surely is the greatest single esthetic contribution of our age has enslaved the human spirit, instead of liberating it. . . . America, where the technical-mechanical development of our age reached its zenith, shows conclusively to what destructive ends the instrument of the machine can lead. . . . Noise has become the surrogate of beauty. (*t.* 9, p. 192)

Jolas also felt that in addition to the aesthetic potential of the machine, America offered hope in its great funds of primitivism in Indian, Negro, and pioneer art and myth. He applauded William Carlos Williams's return to that source in *In the American Grain* (*t.* 9, p. 195).

Jolas's attitude toward Russia was a similar mixture of hope and distrust. The spirit of the Russian revolution was attractive because it was 'aimed at the destruction of a thoroughly rotten structure, just as were the American and French revolutions' (*t.* 9, p. 175). But the developments in Russia did not seem to fulfill the promise. 'The proletarian ideology,' he wrote, 'makes Russian mass-life and expression the paramount ideal, and every functional element is rationalistic' (*t.* 15, p. 11).

Since none of the major paths the epoch seemed to offer was acceptable, Jolas felt that more of the old structures would have to be destroyed before a new way could be found, and as part of its programme *transition* undertook to define exactly the destructive attitudes which the situation demanded. Drieu La Rochelle had pictured the historical situation which gave rise to a new barbarism, but Lautréamont had preceded him and exerted greater influence among writers in arousing radical attitudes. It was his work, which Jolas cited in affirming what he called the 'diabolical principle'.

> In Lautréamont, who, with magnificent courage chose to hymn the satanic, we find the gnostic philosophy transmuted into pure poetry. In tremendous accents he glorifies the impulses which a stupid society fears, evokes the logic of pathological terror, and shocks the bourgeois morality to its foundation. . . .
> (*t.* 7, pp. 159–60)

At the conclusion of the essay, Jolas suggests that although this dark side of the imagination is necessary, it is not a sufficient end in itself. 'Like Blake . . . [Lautréamont] has given us again a belief in the duality and simultaneity of two forces. He lets us see into the occult beyond, where new and demoniac visions people our solitude' (*t.* 7, p. 160). The duality of which Jolas speaks here is a form of 'neo-romanticism' which he later defined in an essay entitled 'White Romanticism' written to accompany some translations of Novalis which he made after 1945. The essay does much to clarify *transition*'s place in a continuing tradition. In it he relates how in Paris during the early twenties he had studied Maeterlinck's works on the romantic epoch and read a great deal of Novalis as well as Henri Lichtenberger's study, *Novalis*. Through this reading, he realized that the French symbolists had much in common with the romantic writers. Many contemporary poets also seemed to him to be a part of the same tradition.

> From its very inception, in 1927, I conceived the review *transition* as a neo-romantic organism. Under an approximately collective ideology I tried to gather into it the leading pan-romantic writers—surrealist, dadaist, expressionist—who were striving to expand human consciousness. James Joyce, leaving behind him his naturalistic-expressionist period, which stretches from the *Portrait* to *Ulysses*, was entering upon a pan-romantic period with his *Work in Progress*, in which the night-world was to be explored once more by a poet of genius who, in addition, was able to invent the linguistic instrument that would permit him to give expression to these irrational concepts.[1]

Romanticism, for Jolas, was composed of a positive and a negative side. 'It is quite possible to distinguish between *black* and *white romanticism*. If, for instance, we call Achim von Arnim, with his cruel, fantastic stories, a *black romantic*, we may also assume that Novalis, who saw mystic or transcendental night as the romantic ambiance *par excellence*, professed a *white romanticism*.'[2] This white romanticism of Novalis does not ignore the darker aspects but seeks to combine them with positive forces. His philosophy of 'magic idealism' seeks to reconcile all such opposites in a higher unity.

The 'magical idealism' expounded by Novalis is a philosophy that might have special appeal not only to Jolas but to many modern thinkers. From the philosophical fragments one can deduce the outlines of a mysticism particularly compatible with modern intellectual developments. Novalis starts, like Kant and Fichte, with the mind thinking rationally about its own processes rather than with the ecstatic contemplation of the Deity as earlier mystic philosophers had done. Kant's problem of the bifurcation of the world into subject and object was Novalis's harmful illusion to be overcome by realizing that both subject and object (mind and world) are emanations of the 'creative imagination'[3] or 'Spirit'. All mental experiences, including visions, dreams, etc., are just as real as what we normally call reality. And in fact, what seem like unreal mental phenomena are the signs of the creative imagination in us.

The key to overcoming the apparent duality of the world lay in recognizing the self as the manifestation of the creative spirit in which all being was unified. '*Nach innen geht der geheimnisvolle Weg. In uns oder nirgends ist die Ewigkeit mit ihren Welten . . .*' (The secret road leads inward. If Eternity with all its worlds is not in us, then it is nowhere.) Man's innermost self is pure 'Spirit' connected with the external world only through the sense organs. While the 'Spirit' exists in perfect freedom in its own world, everything connected with the body appears to be ruled by necessity. The 'magical idealist' recognizes that necessity is an illusion and refuses to accept it. He seeks always to expand freedom so that the will of the 'Spirit' can be enacted without limitations. He may find freedom simply by turning inward and penetrating to the 'Spirit', through visions or meditation—that is what constitutes genius. Or by 'Magical Science'—which admits no limits, and works by intuition, and imagination—he can also learn ultimately to control nature so that it will be identical with his will. Throughout the fragments, the overriding idea is that man should cultivate any manifestations of his inner nature and try to bring the world into harmony with them. That is the programme of 'magical idealism'. Jolas felt a special affinity for Novalis and his programme because he had been able to present a daring transcendental vision and yet did not need to reject the positive spirit of Christianity.

The philosophical fragments mention but do not emphasize the dream. In Novalis's poetic works, however, the dream becomes the main source of indications that a unity which transcends our normal experience is possible. The dream is a central part of both *Hymns to the Night* and *Heinrich von Ofterdingen*, the works of Novalis which impressed Jolas most. In the romance, *Heinrich von Ofterdingen*, the process of 'magical idealism' is carried to perfection. 'The dream becomes life,

life becomes a dream', i.e. the young poet's vision of a blue flower in a
dream shapes his life by suggesting an ideal. The flower is, however, an
undefined ideal in the dream and gathers its specific connotations from
the poet's life. Thus an interior ideal and exterior cricumstances combine to give young Ofterdingen's life a transcendent quality.

Much of Novalis's thought is a continuation of the long tradition of
neo-platonic mysticism, but his particular branch of the tradition is
especially adapted to modern philosophy, the growing interest in the
nature of the self, and scientific advancement. It was thus a stock of
neo-platonism to which the great hopes of the machine age and the
findings of Freud, Jung, and other psychologists could be easily grafted.
Its major outlines, and above all its practical idealism and the emphasis
on the dream, are discernible behind almost every stage of *transition*'s
development. Jolas also adopted parts of Novalis's special vocabulary,
like the use of 'magic' to refer to events where the subjective element
of the mind is mixed with external reality. Phrases from Novalis
appear throughout Jolas's editorials.

Under the influence of Novalis, Jolas was never willing to allow
transition's programme to be simply a negative one. It included a frank
attack upon convention, but taken as a whole, it is remarkably positive.
The negative aspects of Lautréamont, the surrealists, and expressionists
all appeared because they represented one part of the romantic quest
upon which Jolas was embarked, not because their position coincided
exactly with that of *transition*.

Wyndham Lewis, however, perceived correctly that *transition* was
favourably disposed to revolutionary ideas and attacked this tendency
in his one-man review *The Enemy*. For Lewis, *transition* represented the
quintessence of all the forces that were undermining Europe. Though
his premise was partially correct, his methods of argument were dubi-
ous at best. Showing little regard for obvious differences, he deduced
that *transition* was the manifestation of a neo-romantic, Nietzschean
will-to-power and that the experimental writings which appeared in it
were deliberately obscure because obscurity gave *transition*'s writers and
editors a feeling of superiority over those who could not understand
these works. By equating *transition* with the surrealists and the surrealists
with the communists, Lewis concluded that *transition* was part of a
communist conspiracy. He was right in perceiving that *transition* was
neo-romantic and that it was in revolt against old ways of thought, but

he greatly oversimplified and overemphasized the political identity of the magazine.

Jolas and many of his contributors were concerned with the problem of reshaping the post-World War I world and 'discovering a new notion of man', but they chose to concentrate their attention on aesthetics rather than politics. In 'First Aid to the Enemy' they stated their position unequivocally. 'The editors of *transition* . . . are no more Communists than they are Fascists, for all forms of politics are outside the range of our interests . . . Contemporary society seems to us to be in an abysmally dark state and we are entertained intellectually, if not physically, with the idea of its destruction. But we do not share the illusion that reformation implies improvement. . . . Our interests are confined to literature and life' (*t.* 9, p. 175). In 'On the Quest' (*t.* 9), Jolas explains that 'Poetry in itself is a revolt. The mistake some of our contemporaries made is precisely that they failed to recognize that the poetic instinct has nothing whatever to do with the programmatic principles of politics' (*t.* 9, p. 196).

In 'Suggestions for a New Magic' the editors offered the first comprehensive statement of the kind of revolution they were leading. '*transition* will attempt to present the quintessence of the modern spirit in evolution. It may be interesting, therefore, to re-define some of the concepts that symbolize this spirit . . .' (*t.* 3, p. 178). As might be expected, a part of the programme was negative. 'We believe in the ideology of revolt against all diluted and synthetic poetry, against all artistic efforts that fail to subvert the existing concepts of beauty. Once and for all let it be stated that if there is any real choice to be made, we prefer to skyscraper spirituality, the immense lyricism and madness of illogic' (*t.* 3, p. 178). But this negative side is more a specific reaction against certain schools of English and continental literature than a general nihilism. American realism was the first type of literature singled out for criticism. The editors felt that it had reached a saturation point. 'We are no longer interested in the photography of events, in the mere silhouetting of facts, in the presentation of misery, in the anecdotic boredom of verse' (*t.* 3, p. 178). No names are mentioned; but probably the tendency of novelists like Upton Sinclair, Sinclair Lewis, J. T. Farrell, and poets like Edgar Lee Masters and Edward Arlington Robinson is being rejected.

The next group to receive reproach are the 'dilettantes', '*farceurs* whose sole claim to contemporary consideration is a facile sense of lilting rhythms', and 'epigones of Whitman' who have become 'hopelessly entangled in sentimentality, eclecticism, and "delicate perceptions" ' (*t.* 3, p. 178). A look at *Poetry* for the years 1925–7 will make much of this attack clear. Despite its great service in publishing such distinguished contributors as T. S. Eliot, Robert Frost, and Wallace Stevens, *Poetry* was quite eclectic and did contain much dilettantism. Harriet Monroe astounded Jolas by the casual attitude toward literature implied in her statement that a person about whom he inquired had 'dropped out of the poetry game'. Many of the works in *Poetry* were only superficially new. Carl Sandburg, Vachel Lindsay, and the followers of Amy Lowell were still quite prominent in the magazine in 1926 and 1927 and Miss Monroe continued to praise them highly while chastising Hart Crane for not writing more intelligibly. Jolas expressed dislike for the magazine and its editors by calling it 'Old Hat'. The attitudes evident in *Poetry* were widespread in other magazines, literary sections of newspapers, and volumes of verse.

In addition to the literature that was stuck in what Jolas considered anachronistic realism and Whitmanism, there was also a literature which struggled grotesquely to accommodate itself to the new manifestations of industrial society. The movement was by no means limited to F. T. Marinetti's futurists, but they represented this tendency at its most extreme, and Jolas seems to be dealing directly with the futurists in pointing out the third tendency which *transition* wished to oppose. In 1909 Marinetti had published the *Futurist Manifesto*, in which he had rejected everything that was of the past and did not partake of an active, aggressive, machine-fed frenzy. The manifesto had specifically attacked 'thoughtful immobility, ecstasy, and sleep' and had declared that the futurists would 'sing the great crowds tossed about by work, by pleasure, or revolt', and find their subjects in 'arsenals, railway stations, factories and airplanes'.[4]

Jolas shared some attitudes of futurism. Marinetti had declared that his aim was to free man from the intellect and to 'reawaken the divine intuition'.[5] In 'Words in Liberty', he wrote, 'Lyricism is the ability to make one's self drunk on life and on one's self.'[6] The poet, like the man who just experienced a shipwreck or an earthquake, speaks directly from his inner self without regard for syntax and conventions. This combination of interest in the intuitive part of man and the promised new freedom with language had for a while appealed to Jolas. But futurism proved a disappointment to him because it was not really directed inward so much as it appeared to be. For Marinetti, intuition turned out to be only a means of accommodating man to the machine, 'With the help of the intuition,' he wrote, 'we will conquer the enmity that separates our human flesh from the metal of motors.'[7]

The human element was to be eradicated from poetry entirely. 'One must destroy the "I" in poetry, that is get rid of all psychology.'[8] Matter and its properties are the correct subjects for the poet. Instead of ascribing human states to materials, poets should find out about their own cohesiveness, compressibility, solubility, and tensile strength.[9] But above all speed and the perfection of the machine were to be the subject matter of poetry. 'For the futurist poet,' he wrote, 'nothing could be more interesting than the movement of the keys of a mechanical piano.'[10]

The practical rules which Marinetti set up for poets in a 'Technical Manifesto of Futurist Literature' have the machine and the 'beauty of speed' in view rather than the expression of the intuitive part of the mind. Marinetti was too much centred in the present and too materially oriented for Jolas.

> We are not interested in literature that wilfully attempts to be of the age. Unless there be a perception of eternal values, there can be no new magic. . . . The poet may use the rhythm of his age . . . and thus tell us, with accelerated intensity, the Arabian Nights' adventures of his brain. [The *Futurist Manifesto* began with an allusion to Arabian Nights amid Persian carpets and hanging lamps.] But let him not forget that only the dream is essential. (*t.* 3, pp. 178–9)

He especially objected to Marinetti's attempt to replace the contemplative mood by an artificially active one. 'The rushing of new springs can be heard only in silence. To be sure, few of us can have Paul Valéry's ecstatic and fertile silence. This [however] is more of the spirit of poetry than the roar of machines. Out of it may come finally a vertical urge' (*t.* 3, p. 179).

In opposition to these movements Jolas called for a literature that reflected the 'chaotic age' by acknowledging the 'savagely intensified' subconscious as Rimbaud had done. In connection with this search for a literature which would be a lyrical expression of the subconscious, *transition* called for a new and radically different manner of expression.

We need new words, new abstractions, new hieroglyphics, new symbols, new myths. These values to be organically evolved and hostile to a mere metaphorical conception must seek freer association. Thus there may be produced that sublimation of the spirit which grows imminently out of the modern consciousness. By re-establishing the simplicity of the word, we may find again its old magnificence. Gertrude Stein, James Joyce, Hart Crane, Louis Aragon, André Breton, Leon-Paul Fargue, August Stramm and others are showing the way. (*t.* 3, p. 179)

Like many of Jolas's editorial statements 'Suggestions for a New Magic' is romantically extravagant. This should not obscure the fact that it is an important attempt to define theoretically what others were demonstrating with the creative works that appeared in the magazine. For these writers it was no longer adequate to describe existing reality or even to evoke the effects of inner visions or emotions; the visions and mental processes themselves must be depicted with all of the contradictions and unconventional means necessary to express them. They had found it necessary to dispense with 'normal' metaphors and associations and to use combinations arrived at less consciously. Their emphasis on the portrayal of an inner vision and the renewal of language formed the basis of most of the critical theory developed in *transition*.

In his essay 'The Revolution of Language and James Joyce' Jolas explained the need for linguistic change in more detail:

The word presents the metaphysical problem today. . . . The discoveries of the subconscious by medical pioneers as a new field for magical explorations and comprehensions should have made it apparent that the instrument of language in its archaic condition could no longer be used. Modern life with its changed mythos and transmuted concepts of beauty makes it imperative that words be given a new composition and relationship. (*t.* 11, pp. 109–10)

According to Jolas, Joyce had done most to meet the needs of expressing the unconscious by inventing a 'universal language' based upon the theories of Giambattista Vico. He was also a part of a literary tradition. In their separate ways a number of modern authors had been working to 'give language a more modern elasticity, to give words a more compressed meaning through disassociation from their accustomed connections, and to liberate the imagination with primitivistic conceptions of verbs and nouns. . . .' Léon-Paul Farque was 'creating astonishing neologisms' by transposing syllables from one word to another or splicing them onto new roots. The surrealists were exploiting a different association of words on planes of the spirit. Gertrude Stein was writing 'structurally spontaneous compositions in which words are grouped rhythmically' without regard for meaning. Earlier August Stramm, one of the first German expressionist poets, had developed a poetry of 'verbal deformations' by making nouns into verbs, adjectives and adverbs. As Jolas recognized, each of these writers had his individual approach to language, but they nevertheless formed a tradition of psychic exploration and linguistic experimentation which *transition* would foster throughout its existence (*t.* 11, pp. 110–11).

In the first year, Jolas had evolved the theoretical basis for a programme that presented English-language innovators along with the Europeans who worked in the tradition of linguistic experimentation. In the coming years he would develop and expand this programme into an unparalleled presentation of works that found new ways to give expression to the unconscious.

Notes

1 Eugene Jolas, 'Prolegomenon of White Romanticism and Mythos of Ascension', unpublished essay in the possession of Mrs Eugene Jolas, p. 6.
2 *Ibid.*, p. 3.
3 Novalis, *Fragmente*, ed. Ernst Kamnitzer (Dresden, 1929), p. 230.
4 F. T. Marinetti, 'Futurist Manifesto', in *The Modern Tradition*, ed. Richard Ellmann and Charles Feidelson (New York, 1965), p. 433.
5 F. T. Marinetti, 'Technical Manifesto of Futurist Literature', in Christa Baumgarth, *Geschichte des Futurismus* (Hamburg, 1966), p. 170.
6 Marinetti, 'Words in Liberty', in *Geschichte des Futurismus*, p. 173.
7 Marinetti, 'Technical Manifesto', in *Geschichte des Futurismus*, p. 169.
8 *Ibid.*, p. 168.
9 *Ibid.*, p. 168.
10 *Ibid.*, p. 169.

III

REVOLUTION AND SYNTHESIS:
THE GROWTH OF A THEORY

By the end of the first year it became clear that the arrangements between Paul and Jolas, though friendly, had not turned out in the way the Jolases had anticipated. Paul had been enthusiastic about *transition* and had worked with diligence and dedication, but he was too often unavailable when he was needed. With the twelfth issue Paul ceased to be a salaried associate editor and became an unsalaried contributing editor, in which capacity he continued until June, 1929.

Paul's position as associate editor was taken over by Robert Sage, also of the Paris edition of the *Chicago Tribune*. Sage had been in charge of the book reviews for *transition* since the third issue and had also helped with other editorial tasks. When he took Paul's place, he simply expanded his duties. He was a quiet, reliable man who shared most of Jolas's attitudes. His command of French was excellent and he showed more sympathy for the surrealists and other French writers than Paul had. His relationship with Jolas was harmonious throughout the years they worked together. He continued as associate editor until late 1929 when he was transferred from Paris to London as correspondent for the *New York Herald Tribune*, and he remained after that date as a contributing editor, though he was completely inactive, until the temporary suspension of *transition* in 1930.

Paul had been a full-time editor without other employment. Sage, however, retained his job with the *Chicago Tribune* and devoted only part time to *transition*. The editorial tasks involved in meeting a monthly deadline would have been too much for Jolas and one part-time assistant. So beginning in the summer of 1928 with the thirteenth issue, *transition* became a quarterly. It took the subtitle 'an international quarterly for creative experiment'.

transition had begun with great hopes for American literature. However, in the first year it had found most of its best contributors in Europe, with Joyce, the French surrealists, and the German expressionists dominating the magazine. Meanwhile there were some preliminary signs that the awakening in America that Jolas had written about in his first editorial was about to produce some positive results. Matthew Josephson and Malcolm Cowley, who had worked on *Broom* and *Secession*, two of the earliest expatriate magazines, felt that the literary centre was shifting back to America. Josephson, who was passing through Paris in early 1928 on his way back to the United States, called on Jolas and discussed his feeling that a burst of new literary activity was about to take place in America. His optimism convinced Jolas, who asked him to become a contributing editor so that *transition* could be kept abreast of the developments.

Jolas hoped that the return of Josephson and Cowley, who had been among the first to publish dadaists and surrealists in English, meant that America would soon be turning away from realism and imagism to a neo-romantic literature more like the kind he had been advocating in *transition*. The final monthly issue, March 1928, announced that while the new, quarterly *transition* would still consider itself 'a link between Europe and America' and would 'continue to publish translations of important European work, the emphasis in the future . . . [would be] placed on American contributions' (*t.* 12, p. 182). Number 13 was accordingly called 'the American Number'.

With the exception of a further installment of Joyce's 'Work in Progress' and an article by Elliot Paul on Picasso, the whole issue is devoted to America. Americans then living in Europe like Kay Boyle, Archibald MacLeish, William Carlos Williams, and Katherine Anne Porter (who had already appeared in *transition*) contributed material that dealt with American subject matter. A large number of pieces by previously unpublished Americans, both in Paris and at home, are included. None of them, however, was outstanding enough to merit editorial comment.

The only signs of the literary resurgence promised by Josephson

were not at all what Jolas expected. Bernard Smith, a New York critic
who often contributed to leftist periodicals, wrote an 'American Letter'
which announced, 'Politically America is dead. . . . America is beginning to decay. . . . But with decay comes movement'. The young men
of America are awakening from a state of impotence to 'destroy the
lies that bound [them] and banish the old men who tried to stunt
[their] growth with outworn ideals'. To help this spirit '*transition* must
look again to the west and forget Europe. The continent is well able to
take care of itself, but America needs help. . . . *transition* must show its
guts and lose interest in damp ineffectual dreams. *transition* must
nourish and water the incipient revolution' (*t.* 13, p. 247). In short,
transition was being asked to give up its interest in the unconscious and
the irrational in favour of a part in the social revolution.

A much less friendly form of the same argument came from Matthew
Josephson himself. Before he left Europe, Josephson had been asked by
Jolas to prepare a statement which would express the trend of literary
opinion in America. Jolas was familiar with the manifesto 'Aesthete
1925' which Josephson had prepared with the *Broom*, *Secession* group
(John Wheelwright, Slater Brown, Hart Crane, Allen Tate, and Kenneth Burke) in reply to Ernest Boyd's criticism of the younger generation as a warmed-over version of the aestheticism of the 1890s. That
manifesto had defended the cause of art against the claims of society,
and it is likely that Jolas expected that a similar attitude but with a more
recent perspective would prevail in the new manifesto. In preparing
'New York 1928', Josephson duplicated the procedure used by the 1925
group. He, Malcolm Cowley, Slater Brown, Kenneth Burke, and
Robert M. Coats locked themselves in a hotel room for a weekend and
wrote the document.

Though only occasionally clever and often clumsy, 'New York 1928'
is of some importance. The first part, an attack upon American adver-
tising and press-agentry in a series of mock advertisements, is of little
interest. But the second part, an attack upon America expatriates, indicated a new mood even among the young Americans who had themselves been an important part of the expatriate group. The attack
clearly separates the Americans who came home, took up the cause of
social justice, and became political activists from those who stayed in
Europe to follow what Cowley castigated three years later in *Exile's
Return* as the 'religion of art'.[1] Having come back, Josephson and Cow-

ley turned with the vehemence of reformed sinners upon those who had stayed. The manifesto began rather acridly with a series of incidental poems like the two following:

FRY TWO!
The vulgarity of these United States
Is something every Exile hates.
In Paris, though, they turn the table
And act as vulgar as they are able.

WE SEE THEM EVERY THREE YEARS
Exiles often return to the lands of their mother
With their hats in one hand and their palms in the other.

(*t.* 13, p. 87)

The tone of the central statement of the manifesto, Josephson's 'Open Letter to Mr Ezra Pound and the Other "Exiles" ' is, however, quite serious. Josephson takes issue with Pound and all who, like him, refuse to come home to America and take an active part in society. As Josephson said, he and the others had become concerned with 'the condition of existence'. They had experienced the 'new mass society' and realized that man is an 'economic animal'. No longer satisfied by a literature which had no social purpose, they wanted to 'apply what may have been discovered within tangible or living forms, rather than in those with which "life cannot co-exist".' The attack seemed directed at *transition* itself when it spoke of 'futurism prolonged' and dismissed 'the whole game of "making words play with each other" ' as 'a genteel, bourgeois sport' (*t.* 13, p. 100). Jolas was disappointed with the manifesto which he saw as an acquiescence (if not politically, at least artistically) in the status quo.

Still another call to turn his energies toward fomenting a social revolution in America had come to Jolas in a personal letter containing a copy of *America Arraigned*, a collection of poems on the subject of the Sacco-Vanzetti case. In responding Jolas answered Smith and Josephson, as well as the sender of the letter.

... I find the book utterly unimportant. ... You and a great many of your friends seem to feel that ... the poet's task is to use whatever force there is in him for the dissemination of subversive ideas. You demand that the American artist ... remain in America, participate actively in the fight. ...

Although I, too, demand the overthrow of the system into which a sinister fate has made me be born, I regard it as a waste of time for the poet to let himself be deviated from his most important business—that of creating.

Jolas saw the problem not so much as a matter of economic and social justice, but as a matter of the threat to the individual posed by a mass society. Even before he had asked Josephson to prepare a manifesto, he had circulated a questionnaire to European writers asking them to comment upon the influence of America on Europe. He published the answers in _transition_ 13 as an 'Inquiry Among European Writers into the Spirit of America'. It seemed to him that America and Russia both represented a similar tendency to adapt all of society to industrial production. As the epigraph to the 'Inquiry' noted, even Lenin on his death-bed had said to his friends, 'Americanize yourselves'.

Before posing direct questions to the European writers, Jolas had made a statement of his view of the situation. 'Next to Russia, the United States is today the most important problem among the nations of the world. The new conception of life and the accelerated rhythm of its pragmatic manifestations are slowly, but surely, being felt in the old world.' Some have found in America 'an impulsion towards a new culture and a new mode of living, while others denounce what they conceive to be a danger of intellectual mechanization that results from that spirit' (_t._ 13, p. 248).

The writers were then asked two questions: 'How, in your opinion, are the influences of the United States manifesting themselves upon Europe and in Europe?' and 'Are you for or against those influences?' (_t._ 13, p. 248). The questionnaire was answered by Georges Ribemont-Dessaignes, Benjamin Péret, Gottfried Benn, Marcel Brion, Tristan Tzara, Jules Romains, Ivan Goll, Theo Van Doesburg, Bernard Fay, Philippe Soupault, and Régis Michaud, among others. Their replies range from denunciation to wary approval. Benjamin Péret raged that the United States represented 'the most emphatic garbage, the ignoble sense of money, the indigence of ideas, the savage hypocrisy in morals, and altogether . . . a loathsome swinishness pushed to the point of paroxysm' (_t._ 13, p. 250). Ivan Goll admitted poignantly that the old Europe was 'going towards death' and pleaded with Americans to allow that death to be dignified and not to 'stamp about the silent parks of our dreams' or 'buy the saints of our cathedrals' (_t._ 13, p. 255). Marcel Brion stated affectionately, 'America has taught us to love whatever is young, and new' (*t.* 13, p. 252). In general the replies displayed a restrained respect for American efficiency and a deep distrust of American puritanism and materialism.

In a similar inquiry in the next issue American expatriates were asked to respond to four questions about why they lived in Europe. The questions reveal Jolas's own bias against what he felt was an over-emphasis on economics in America.

1. Why do you prefer to live outside America?
2. How do you envisage the spiritual future of America in the face of a dying Europe and in the face of a Russia that is adopting the American Economic vision?
3. What is your feeling about the revolutionary spirit of your age, as expressed, for instance, in such movements as communism, surrealism, anarchism?
4. What particular vision do you have of yourself in relation to twentieth century reality? (*t.* 14, p. 97)

Among the Americans who replied were Gertrude Stein, Robert McAlmon, George Antheil, Kay Boyle, Harry Crosby, Bernice Abbott, Hilaire Hyler, and Emily Holmes Coleman. Most respondents gave one long answer for all four questions. Several of the writers were surprised to be thought of as preferring life in Europe at all. Others had reasons as simple and practical as objection to prohibition, and others frankly admitted the charm of the old world as their reason for remaining. A large number of them, however, revealed an impatience with the American mentality. Gertrude Stein declared that 'America is now early Victorian very early Victorian, she is a rich and well nourished home but not a place to work. Your parent's home is never a place to work it is a nice place to be brought up in' (*t.* 14, p. 97). Robert McAlmon preferred Europe because 'there is less interference with private life here' (*t.* 14, p. 98). George Antheil was tired of 'explaining battles ... won years ago' (*t.* 14, p. 101). Harry Crosby chose Europe because (among thirteen other reasons) he preferred 'transitional orgasms to atlantic monthlies' (*t.* 14, p. 114).

Their reactions generally displayed the same distrust of the industrial society and political movements that Jolas expressed in asking the questions. Robert McAlmon, though unsympathetic with Jolas's terminology, said, 'I don't feel that my age has a revolutionary spirit, artistically, or politically,' and declared himself on the side of 'the

individual who does not look to a mass movement which lets him flow
in its current on to victory' (*t.* 14, p. 99). Kay Boyle complained that
America had 'no conviction which questions the value of inventions
that protect the flesh from everything except the importance of being
cared for. . . . Americans I would permit to serve me, to conduct me
rapidly and competently to wherever I was going, but not for one
moment to impose their achievements upon whatever is going on in
my heart' (*t.* 14, p. 103). George Antheil responded directly to the statement of the 'New York 1928' group. He thought Josephson's hopes for
a new millennium in which the artist's problems would be solved was
unrealistic. The number of symphony orchestras in New York had
decreased from three to one, backing for new operas and an audience
to appreciate them were still not available. There might be some hope
of improving these conditions, but until the economic situation for the
artists in America got better, he preferred to remain in Europe.

Josephson had meanwhile returned to Europe but he was still urging
artists to accommodate to the industrial society. His 'American Letter:
Some Contemporary Themes' was a response to the refusal of Jolas and
the other expatriates to heed his advice. This time he pleaded with
artists to change out of a sense of self-preservation. 'Economics—The
Machine—Mass Civilization—*Materialism*—all of these often reiterated
phrases, the banal catchwords, sum up the anxiety with which we
observe the present day, and await certain events. Of these events none
has fascinated me more than the apparently fated obliteration of the
artist' (*t.* 14, p. 59). The 'imperative needs' and 'the immense variety of
mindless diversions and convenience offered elsewhere' raised the
question of whether art could survive at all.

The only solution was for the artist to join the masses—'Although
participating in the spectacular mass-life, I observe clearly that these
men do not tend to become masses—in the sense of jelly. On the contrary, all the human sentiments are sharpened and exasperated by the
particular modern environment' (*t.* 14, p. 62). The artist will of necessity retain his identity through 'self-defense and opposition' (*t.* 14, p.
63). But he must also adapt his art to mass society to survive. 'The cur-
rents of aesthetic and verbal mysticism must run their course. . . .
America is plainly on the road to physical plenty, to achieved wealth.
(Europe has little choice as to following her economic course.) Until
this cycle is complete, the artist must cease to be a *pariah*, and essay

more ambitious rôles. Childish to think of "fighting the machine!" He must *compete*' (*t.* 14, pp. 63–4).

It had been evident since Josephson's first appearance in number thirteen that his position was incompatible with the programme Jolas had outlined for *transition*. Nevertheless he continued as a contributing editor until number fifteen. He wrote other pieces speaking of the 'industrial millennium' and regarding literature as primarily a political manifestation. In a review of Allen Tate's *Mr. Pope and Other Poems*, for example, Josephson suggested vaguely that 'economic conditions' were behind the lack of reception given to new American poets without ever specifying what condition he had in mind. With number sixteen his contributions ceased and his name was dropped from the masthead.

The immediate renunciation of social realism in America for which Jolas had hoped did not take place. Still, Jolas did not yet turn the emphasis of the magazine back to European authors. The bulk of material in numbers 14 and 15 is by American writers like Archibald MacLeish, Robert McAlmon, Malcolm Cowley, Hart Crane, and Katherine Anne Porter; contributions from elsewhere are lumped together under the title 'Other Countries'.

In 'Super-Occident', the lead article of number 15, Jolas expressed his hope that America would yet play a role in resisting collectivism. The essay displays Jolas's growing feeling that the social and economic crisis of 1929 was accompanied by a crisis in art, 'general disorder all along the line'. The situation was all the more deplorable because new forces were flourishing in many ways. In painting there was cubism and surrealism. Music was 'liberating itself of historicism' and was no longer considered 'a soothing-syrup'. In architecture men like Le Corbusier, Gropius, and Mallet-Stevens were envisioning 'a purer form of building' (*t.* 15, p. 14). Experimental photography also offered new possibilities. But while progress was being made in these areas, literature was ignoring the most exciting discovery of all, 'the reality of the *universal word*'—the realization that language was the key to the instinctive realm that was common to all men of all ages. 'Never,' he wrote, 'has a revolution been more imperative' (*t.* 15, p. 15).

By the next issue the focus of *transition* was no longer on America, but on the need for a general revolution in writing. There were statements enough in *transition* to launch several revolutions, but Jolas's essays, like newspaper editorials, often had their beginnings in topical events and the ideas were given varying emphasis or presented obliquely. In the course of the summer of 1928 Jolas and his wife had discussed these ideas and Jolas's attitudes toward them. Her mind, more concrete than his, found a need for clarification and crystallization. At her suggestion he had drawn up a statement. This personal manifesto subscribed to by fifteen other signers became 'The Revolution of the Word Proclamation'. It appeared on the first page of the double issue 16/17 of June 1929.

The manifesto did not, as many people have supposed, represent the desperate efforts of a Montparnasse revolutionary council. There was never a meeting of all the signers. Jolas discussed his manifesto individually with the writers he thought might be in accord with him. Those who were signed; those who weren't refused.

Most of those who signed were either directly involved with editing *transition* or else were newspapermen whom Jolas knew from working for the *Chicago Tribune*. Sage, Paul, and Gilbert were of course *transition* editors. Theo Rutra was a pseudonym of Jolas himself. Caresse and Harry Crosby had also helped in the editorial work of *transition*. Though not a member of the staff, Kay Boyle was a frequent visitor to the *transition* office and even used it as the mailing address for the magazine *Living Poetry* she edited briefly with Archibald Craig. She brought Laurence Vail, an American painter who also wrote novels, to *transition*. Whit Burnett, Leigh Hoffmann, Douglas Rigsby, and Harold J. Salemson were all newspaper reporters with varying degrees of literary aspiration. Hart Crane and A. L. Gillespie, a Philadelphia schoolteacher striving to become an accepted expatriate writer, were the only signers whose connection with the manifesto was primarily through their work. James Joyce and Gertrude Stein were not asked to sign—probably because Jolas knew that both were too independent. Jolas left no record of those who refused to sign the manifesto.

One of the revolutionaries made his own contribution before signing. Stuart Gilbert, always witty and sceptical, read the document and laughed, partly at its extremity and partly at the thought of the shock it would give to the bourgeoisie. He decided to make it a bit more shocking by adding aphorisms from Blake to accompany the statements; Jolas agreed to the additions and they became a part of the proclamation.

PROCLAMATION

TIRED OF THE SPECTACLE OF SHORT STORIES, NOVELS, POEMS AND PLAYS STILL UNDER THE HEGEMONY OF THE BANAL WORD, MONOTONOUS SYNTAX, STATIC PSYCHOLOGY, DESCRIPTIVE NATURALISM, AND DESIROUS OF CRYSTALLIZING A VIEWPOINT...

WE HEREBY DECLARE THAT :

1. THE REVOLUTION IN THE ENGLISH LANGUAGE IS AN ACCOMPLISHED FACT.

2. THE IMAGINATION IN SEARCH OF A FABULOUS WORLD IS AUTONOMOUS AND UNCONFINED.
(Prudence is a rich, ugly old maid courted by Incapacity... Blake)

3. PURE POETRY IS A LYRICAL ABSOLUTE THAT SEEKS AN A PRIORI REALITY WITHIN OURSELVES ALONE.
(Bring out number, weight and measure in a year of dearth... Blake)

4. NARRATIVE IS NOT MERE ANECDOTE, BUT THE PROJECTION OF A METAMORPHOSIS OF REALITY.
(Enough ! Or Too Much !... Blake)

5. THE EXPRESSION OF THESE CONCEPTS CAN BE ACHIEVED ONLY THROUGH THE RHYTHMIC " HALLUCINATION OF THE WORD ". (Rimbaud).

6. THE LITERARY CREATOR HAS THE RIGHT TO DISINTEGRATE THE PRIMAL MATTER OF WORDS IMPOSED ON HIM BY TEXT-BOOKS AND DICTIONARIES.
(The road of excess leads to the palace of Wisdom... Blake)

7. HE HAS THE RIGHT TO USE WORDS OF HIS OWN FASHIONING AND TO DISREGARD EXISTING GRAMMATICAL AND SYNTACTICAL LAWS.
(The tigers of wrath are wiser than the horses of instruction... Blake)

8. THE " LITANY OF WORDS " IS ADMITTED AS AN INDEPENDENT UNIT.

9. WE ARE NOT CONCERNED WITH THE PROPAGATION OF SOCIOLOGICAL IDEAS, EXCEPT TO EMANCIPATE THE CREATIVE ELEMENTS FROM THE PRESENT IDEOLOGY.

10. TIME IS A TYRANNY TO BE ABOLISHED.

11. THE WRITER EXPRESSES. HE DOES NOT COMMUNICATE

12. THE PLAIN READER BE DAMNED.
(Damn braces ! Bless relaxes !... Blake)

— *Signed* : KAY BOYLE, WHIT BURNETT, HART CRANE, CARESSE CROSBY, HARRY CROSBY, MARTHA FOLEY, STUART GILBERT, A. L. GILLESPIE, LEIGH HOFFMAN, EUGENE JOLAS, ELLIOT PAUL, DOUGLAS RIGBY, THEO RUTRA, ROBERT SAGE, HAROLD J. SALEMSON, LAURENCE VAIL.

'The Revolution of the Word Proclamation' as it appeared in *transition* 16/17, 1929

'The Miraculous Shepherd', a pencil drawing by a schizophrenic (Collection Hans Prinzhorn), which appeared in *transition* 24, 1936

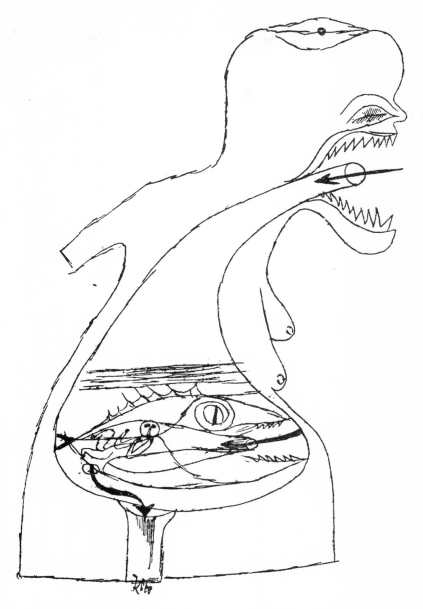

'Fish-Man; Man-Eater' by Paul Klee, which appeared in *transition*
19/20, 1930

Bob Brown

I accept transition's verdict
That words should be
Bro ken ᵘᵖ
‒ ‒ ‒ ‒ ‒ ~ ‒ ~
I only hope the slippery shiny
GLASS-SNAKE ONES
DONT
CRAWL AWL TOGETHER AGAIN

MERCURY, I'LL CONTINUE
DUSTING THE
ᴧᴧᴧ
MOUNTAIN TOPS FOR YOU AND
PEGASUS
ᴜᴜᴜ
WITH MY FEATHERED
ACHILLIAN HEELS

Poem drawing by Bob Brown, which appeared in *transition* 18, 1929

Eugene Jolas, 1948

Below is a self-advertisement assembled by the editors of transition *and printed in* transition *7, 1927. It is extracted from reviews of a previous number.*

HAS A PUNCH
  'I must admit that this sample leaves me wobbling.'

Brentano's *Book Chat.*

FEARLESS IN ITS ATTACKS
  'Onslaught and ravage upon the English language.'

Saturday Review of Literature.

POPULAR APPEAL
  'Hopelessly muddled and unintelligible.'

New York *Times.*

PROFUSELY ILLUSTRATED
  'The pictures look to the vulgar eye like the other crazy modernist stuff.'

New York *Sun.*

GOOD VALUE
  'Contains 182 pages.'

Samuel Dashiell, New York *Evening Post.*

CUT-OUTS FOR THE KIDDIES
  'Feeling it our duty to read both (Miss Stein's *Elucidation* as originally printed and corrected version), we did so, then we cut up the supplement and the magazine into little pieces, and pasted them in another order. This failed to make any sense either, so we next cut up the two versions again, pasted them on typewriter paper, and, standing at the foot of a tall stairway, threw them with all our might. We then collected them in the order in which they landed, but still the words, while they were all very nice words, didn't make any sense, so we gave up.'

Boston *Transcript.*

The first point proclaimed 'The revolution in the English language is an accomplished fact.' Joyce, Gertrude Stein, Jolas, and other of the magazine's contributors had demonstrated that there was a group of writers already employing English in radically new ways. Others might not approve of what they had done, but with such formidable examples as 'Work in Progress' before them, they could not deny that a revolution was taking place.

The manifesto goes on to establish the basis upon which the revolution was founded. 'The imagination in search of a fabulous world is autonomous and unconfined.' It does not depend upon what is outside it and is not subject to such limitations as verisimilitude, logic, proportion, harmony or any other criteria that might be imposed upon it.

In a later point Jolas further emphasized the independence of the mind by declaring, 'Time is a tyranny to be abolished'. He was probably referring to Freud's dictum that the time sense is a function of the ego, which is ruled by reason in order to accommodate reality, and not a characteristic of the unconscious. He had in 'Work in Progress' an example of literature which had evaded this tyranny. Joyce had depicted a dream state which takes place in 'universal' time where widely separated historical events were depicted as simultaneous. He may also have had reference to Bergson's theory that the self exists in a state of permanent duration and that only external events have temporal sequence. There was also another sense in which time could be overcome. Freud, Jung, Frazer, and others had shown that beneath the temporal surface of modern life, there was a stratum of primitive experience embedded in man which affects his thoughts and actions and thus gives them a timeless character.

The other points of the manifesto deal with the specific effects upon writing of recognizing the independence of the imagination. 'Poetry is a lyrical absolute which seeks an *a priori* reality within ourselves alone.' The essence of the poetic act is not in capturing moments in time, but in expressing intuition and visions that come from within. When the poet does choose to present the real world, he does so not merely to describe it, but to present it as it is changed by his own mind in the act of assimilating it. 'Narrative is not mere anecdote, but the projection of a metamorphosis of reality.'

The most revolutionary points of the manifesto are those that define the relationship of the writer to his medium. 'The expression of these concepts can be achieved only through the rhythmic "hallucination of the word".' In *Une Saison en Enfer* Rimbaud had written of how he had become intoxicated with words until he achieved a state of revelation. Jolas wanted a similar relationship to words, but he did not contend that the writer should necessarily lose control of his sense when writing. He meant only that he should be particularly attuned to the incantatory power of words and less concerned with the conscious problems of style and meaning.

The expression of the imagination could not be hampered by linguistic conventions. If the demands of the imagination dictated it, the writer could alter and invent language to suit his needs. 'The literary creator has the right to disintegrate the primal matter of words imposed on him by text-books and dictionaries. He has the right to use words of his own fashioning and to disregard existing grammatical and syntactical laws.' The implications of regarding language as 'primal matter' instead of as set units of information are great. It becomes raw material of sounds and rhythms to be experimented with and exploited in an infinite variety of ways. This gives rise to totally new forms. 'The "litany of words" is admitted as an independent unit.' Words can now be arranged in compositions which stress patterns and rhythms to evoke a response that is like the irrational mood of religion.

In expressing his imagination this way, the poet is to be as little constrained by the demands of his audience as he is by fidelity to external reality. 'The writer expresses, he does not communicate.' Least of all is he a propagandist trying to change the opinions of others by argumentation. 'We are not concerned with the propagation of sociological ideas, except to emancipate the creative elements from the present ideology.' Poets might band together to combat the influence of society on their lives, but they would not place their art in the service of political or social revolutions. The proclamation closes with a challenge that leaves no doubt about where the public stands in this programme. 'The plain reader be damned.'

Parallel with this crystallization of his aesthetic position, Jolas was developing a synthesis of concepts from depth psychology, cultural anthropology, linguistics and philosophy into a unified metaphysical position. The interest in the separate elements—the unconscious, primitive man, and language—which formed the basis of the synthesis had been present in *transition* from the first. It was Rimbaud's penetration to the dark realm of the instinctive that Jolas had praised in 'Suggestions for a New Magic', and he had praised the surrealists for grasping the importance of Freud's discoveries. A strong interest in primitive literature and art, though not loudly proclaimed, was evident in the first year of *transition*. The fourth issue promised an introduction to primitive art by Paul Eluard for the fifth issue. The essay never appeared but the issue did contain reproductions of Aztec sculpture. And curiously, Yvor Winters, whose criticism later displayed such an antipathy for all that *transition* came to represent, was an important contributor of material on American Indians. Other contributions like Maria Jolas's 'Black Thoughts' and Raymond Roussel's 'Impressions of Africa' also displayed an interest in primitive culture. The third element, the advocacy of a language that could express the inner reality, was a dominant feature of Jolas's programme and appeared in almost all that he wrote. The elements of the new programme had not been lacking during the first year; now, though, it seemed necessary to combine these interests and expand them in order to acquire a more unified perspective.

It was not enough to call for a new literature; it was also necessary to define a 'New Concept of Man'. 'Literature alone does not suffice. We also have to meditate about the motives and directions of our being. We must seek the new conditions of life around and within us, in order to avoid becoming aesthetes of a dying decade. We must plunge into philosophy and social science, while we form the things of our creative vision' (*t.* 15, p. 187).

The scientific findings which had changed the concept of man and had necessitated this new orientation were summarized by Jolas later.

> ... We have learned through the discoveries of Janet, Freud, Jung, Lévy-Bruhl etc., that there are hidden forces in the subconscious which are not only the residua of our own personal lives, but are remnants of those dark ages before history began. ... We have, within ourselves, direct contact with the primitive periods of humanity, as well as with the cosmic forces. Art according to these scientists, represents in its most characteristic specimens the wisdom of the ages.[2]

These findings were not new to Jolas; Janet, Freud, Jung, and Lévy-Bruhl had been a part of his reading for years. Why did he feel just at this time that it was necessary to turn to the scientists? Much of the impetus for the more direct inclusion of social science and discussions of its philosophical implications grew out of Jolas's association with Carl Einstein.

Einstein was a German art critic and author. He had been a part of the German expressionist movement before the war and had been associated with writers like Carl Sternheim and Ivan Goll in various little magazines like *Der Blutige Ernst*, which Einstein himself had edited, and *Die Weissen Blätter*, edited by Jolas's friend René Schickele. Einstein's novel *Bebuquin* (1912) had dealt with the search for the 'miracle' of 'the projection of the inner Eternity'[3]—a search which owed much to Novalis's concept of 'magic idealism' and was much like Jolas's own quest. In addition he was an early and perceptive critic of modern art as it had developed in Germany and his book, *Die Kunst des Zwanzigsten Jahrhunderts*, became a standard reference upon its appearance. Einstein perhaps influenced by Leo Frobenius had also become interested in African art. In a period when the art objects brought back from Africa were explained away as the crude work of undeveloped artists, Einstein had published, *Negerplastik* (1915), which in addition to providing excellent illustrations of African statuary, treated this art seriously as a highly developed form and pointed out its similarities to modern cubism. In 1925, he had also published a collection of African legends.[4]

Though a resident of Berlin at the time, Einstein made frequent trips to Paris in 1926 and 1927 while *transition* was getting started. As was almost inevitable for two men with so many friends in the same circles, be and Jolas met. Einstein's works impressed Jolas who published his poem, 'Design of a Landscape' in number 16/17 and a section of *Bebuquin* in number 19/20.

In the summer of 1928 Einstein moved to Paris. In the closing months of that year and in 1929, Jolas, Einstein, and Hans Arp met frequently at Einstein's apartment where they discussed the distressing rise of German nationalism and the possibility of combating it with 'a new expressionist ethos'. They condemned the 'jingoism of the German *littérateurs*' like Kurt Heynicke and Ernst Bertram but read and praised the work of Gottfried Benn, Georg Trakl, and the earlier expressionists.

During these months Einstein was concentrating on a new magazine, *Documents*, which he and Georges Bataille were publishing together. The magazine was to be devoted to articles on archaeology, art criticism, and ethnology in order to make primitive art more intelligible.

Naturally, Jolas, who had been from the very first interested in the prelogical elements of thought, was interested in material about societies whose way of thinking Lévy-Bruhl had characterized as prelogical. Jolas and Einstein discussed primitive art and its relation to *Documents* and *transition* in some detail. The first issue of *Documents* contained a contribution by Jolas to a symposium which collected contemporary evaluations of Picasso.

Jolas's discussions with Einstein also stimulated him to renew his interest in the German philosopher, Max Scheler. Scheler had attempted to adapt the phenomenological methods of Husserl to Catholicism. Instead of stopping at Husserl's 'phenomenological reduction' which allowed all phenomena (real, imaginary, etc.) an equal reality, he thought that the perceiving mind could find an absolute reality. The way to find this reality was to replace the old with a new structure. Modern man, dominated by positivistic thought and bourgeois society, had come to see all things under the aspect of 'Sein-für-das-Leben' (i.e. to ask unconsciously of everything what relation it has to biological needs and what practical gains it would lead to). To view the world this way prohibits the perception of the 'an sich', the absolute reality of things. If man would view the world more humbly and with love, he could perceive absolute reality. He would then transcend the psychological sphere of the personal, take part in the world of 'mit sein' (i.e. relate directly to objects and other men) and even have contact with the absolute. He would no longer be a partial being only fractionally in contact with all outside him: he would become a 'whole man', 'universal man'.[5]

This is clearly a call for a return to metaphysics, but as Scheler saw it, an important part of the way back to metaphysics was through a better understanding of man—metaphysics thus became 'meta-anthropology'.[6] He saw in the findings of Freud and the psychologists clues to the relation of man to the infinite. The absolute, he reasoned, must consist of two parts: an infinite spirit of reason (*Geist*) giving structure to the world and an irrational impulse (*Drang*) which was the origin of existence. Man lacks the infinite spirit of reason, but he has an irrational often demonic *Drang*, that is 'rich in imagination' and 'charged with infinite images'. This *Drang* is the eternal in man.[7] From it man may expect release from the mediocrities of this world.

Jolas was extremely responsive to the major concerns of Scheler. He too felt that man was facing a crisis brought about by materialism. And he felt that the way out of the crisis might be found through the discoveries of anthropology and psychology. Particularly he believed that the unconscious was 'eternal' and might afford transcendental knowledge. It seems likely, however, that Jolas's ideas were mostly formed by Novalis and other romantics before he read Scheler and that the German phenomenologist only provided confirmation of his beliefs. Scheler's main influence upon him was probably to lead him to give more emphasis in *transition* to the scientific and philosophical basis for his beliefs.

The attitudes that Jolas and Einstein shared, and which Scheler had discussed philosophically, were current in the expressionist circle in Berlin. Einstein had been a member of this group before leaving Germany and he often talked with Jolas about it. By the winter of 1929–30 Einstein had convinced Jolas to make a trip to Berlin to gather what he could of the last developments of the dying expressionist movement. While he was in Berlin, Jolas met again with Gottfried Benn who had called on him earlier in Paris. Benn's understanding of the unconscious was coloured by the fact that as a physician he was well aware of scientific discoveries and theories. Jolas's talks with Benn further confirmed an already strong feeling on the part of Jolas that *transition* should include scientific discussion related to his theories of the unconscious.

In 'Logos', his contribution to the 'Revolution of the Word' section of number 16/17, Jolas made the first of several attempts to relate the findings of psychologists to his neo-romantic revolution. Like Freud he saw the operation of the mind as an interplay between the unconscious which is the primitive will and consciousness which acts to restrain this will and make it accommodate to external reality through reason. 'We know,' Jolas wrote, 'that life in its psycno-physiological aspect is a syncretism of two hostile conditions' (*t.* 16/17, p. 27). On the one hand there are forces 'at work below the surface that deform and demolish the conscious recognitions we have of reality. Here life is fundamentally automatic. The rational impulse is without power.' In opposition there is 'the conscious state with its projection of the will through reason'. It 'tends to lead us away from the enormous forces which create spontaneous movement' (*t.* 16/17, p. 26).

Jolas goes on to explain that, 'Poetry . . . [is] the conflict between those two forces'. Through the poet's 'lyrical confessions transmitted in prismatic movement, we get the creative action towards a beyond' (*t.* 16/17, p. 27). Freud, in *The Interpretation of Dreams* had written that poetry like the dream, was a sublimated form of wish fulfilment. The unconscious desires of the poet are transformed through the processes of condensation and displacement to allow them to pass the censor and come into consciousness. Jolas's description of poetry as 'lyrical confessions transmitted in prismatic movement', though vague, appears to be a metaphorical reference to the way in which the unconscious is refracted and broken up (like light as it passes through a prism), in the act of becoming poetry.

Though obviously indebted to Freud, Jolas also differs markedly from him in the way that he conceives of the unconscious. He totally ignores the super-ego to which Freud ascribed a part of the action of the unconscious. On the other hand he attributes to the unconscious a transcendental character that Freud never assigned to it. Freud had said that the id, which responded to the inner, organic urges and not the outside world, was connected with external reality only through the ego and thus did not recognize the limitations of time and space. In this sense it responds to a 'reality' different from the outside world.

Jolas went much further. 'The tension towards the spontaneous and the organic is the tension towards a state of mind that is functionally an other-world reality.... The poet passes from the natural order of things into the supernatural' (*t.* 16/17, p. 27). In his *Introductory Lectures on Psychoanalysis*, Freud specifically denies that the unconscious is the source of 'supernatural' thoughts. 'It can easily be imagined, too, that certain practices of mystics may succeed in upsetting the normal relations between the different regions of the mind, so that, for example, the perceptual system becomes able to grasp relations in the deeper layers of the ego and in the id which would otherwise be inaccessible to it. Whether such a procedure can put one in possession of ultimate truths, from which all good will flow, may be safely doubted.'[8]

Jolas's interpretation of the unconscious is in many ways a romantic-idealist inversion of Freud's concept. After what is clearly a Freudian interpretation of the structure of the mind, Jolas refers to the conflict that gives rise to poetry in terms borrowed from Novalis. The poet is a 'magic idealist.... [He] brings together realities far removed from each other, that seem without any organic relationships, that are even tending to mutual destruction. But his imagination demolishes the tyranny of the world by eliminating its customary analogies and substituting new ones' (*t.* 16/17, p. 27). Jolas and Novalis are on the side of the unconscious; they see it as the source of great wisdom which must be freed. In Freudian terms they favour the 'pleasure principle' of the id over the 'reality principle' of the ego. Freud himself was on the other side. The object of psychoanalysis, as he saw it, was the expansion of the ego, 'to extend its organization so that it can take over new portions of the id. Where id was, there shall ego be.'[9]

In his article 'Notes on Reality' in *transition* 18, Jolas continued defining the relation of the unconscious to literature more specifically. He carefully distinguished his position from others like the surrealists and Eugene O'Neill who had also made use of psychology. He regarded the discoveries of the depth psychologists as a key to understanding the poetic process. 'In examining this region, the psychology of depth has facilitated the comprehension for the processes of creation. . . . We now have come near knowing the sources of inspiration' (*t.* 18, p. 17). The poetic process was a particular manifestation of sublimation. The unfulfilled desires which exhibit themselves most commonly in dreams and in neuroses also find expression in the poet's work. 'The absolute importance of the dream for the creative artist must now be assumed. . . . The dream is pure imagination. . . . At the limit of the creator's spirit there is always the pre-logical. Its expression is the prime factor in poetic operations. The creator is the carrier of all these images and associations, and the difference between him and the neuropath lies precisely in his capacity to get rid of his burden by means of his expressive power. The creator and the dreamer have identical roots' (*t.* 18, p. 18).

It is again apparent that Jolas's concept of the unconscious as the source of poetry is not like Freud's. He is much more like Jung. 'The subconscious is the immense basin into which flow all the inhibited components of our being. This is the primal psychic principle. But it was found by Dr Jung, a dissident of the Freudian school, that into the subconscious flow not only the unfulfilled elements of our lives, but that it contains also the collective mythos thus establishing connection with the social organism and even the cosmic forces' (*t.* 18, pp. 16–17). The unconscious is the embodiment of urges that are ideal as well as 'sexual' (in the broader use of the term). 'The projection of the will in Schopenhauer's sense—through sublimation—is the creator's solution of his problem' (*t.* 18, p. 17). The sublimation that Jolas speaks of is not only the expression of personal erotic desires in a form censored to be acceptable to the ego but also the expression of unconscious, metaphysical desires or intuitions by joining them with elements of objective reality.

Because he was convinced that poetry was the product of a conflict or 'synthesis' of unconscious and conscious forces, Jolas distinguishes his programme from that of the surrealists who overestimate the unconscious. 'The subconscious is not enough. We must organize. . . . It is blind fanaticism to deny the conscious will as a creative agent. . . . [The surrealists'] mistake lay in the fact that, after applying Freudian and Dadaist discoveries, they did not transcend them' (*t.* 18, p. 19).

He also attacked those at the other extreme who had not given a broad enough interpretation of the unconscious.

> It is understood that I do not consider the childish applications of Freudian theories which certain English and American writers have indulged in as of the slightest importance. They failed to understand the elementary magic of the pre-logical. With typical pragmatic insensitiveness they have 'psychologized', celebrating a narrow pan-sexualism as a new 'philosophy of life', and using the text-book information they had gained to engage in their little literary game. The most obvious case is that of Eugene O'Neill, who, in his *Strange Interlude*, and his other *biedermeier* dramas, has not recognized the subconscious as a new well of inspiration, but has worked rather from the exterior, never going beyond the all too simple task of artificially constructing his protagonists around the more familiar 'complexes'. (*t.* 18, p. 18)

Jolas understood Freud better than many of his contemporaries and behind all of the interest in the unconscious the shadow of Freud may be perceived. But Freud was a sceptic who rejected metaphysics and Jolas was an idealist. His own ideas were much closer to those of Jung, and the Zurich psychoanalyst played a much more important role in the formation of his theories than Freud.

Jolas met Jung in May 1930 when he and his wife went to Zurich to help Joyce with the second section of 'Work in Progress' while he was recovering from an eye operation performed by Dr Alfred Vogt. A childhood friend of Mrs Jolas, Dr Cary Baynes, was working with Jung at the time. At their request she arranged a meeting with him at her home. Jolas found Jung congenial and interesting and saw none of the gratuitous hostility Joyce thought he detected in Jung's proposed preface for the German edition of *Ulysses*.[10] They met again at Jung's home where they discussed Tanguy (whose work they both admired), Jolas's dreams, and the possibility of Jung's contributing to *transition*. When he left Zurich, Jolas took with him a copy of Jung's essay 'Psychologie und Dichtung'. Jolas's translation, published in number 19/20, was the first appearance in English of Jung's essay on the nature of literary creation.

The essay divides literature into two groups: 'psychological' works and 'visionary' works. Psychological works are those like *Faust I* in which the author manipulates his characters according to his conscious theories of psychological motivations. Since for the most part the material does not come from the subconscious, the psychologists can at most criticize or approve the author's theories of motivations. It is in 'visionary' works like *Faust II* that the unconscious presents the 'primal vision' of the poet. To the Freudian this 'primal vision' is a manifestation of deeply buried personal experience and explained as the manifestation of 'dream work'—a pathological attempt to hide the origins of experience. Jung rejects this explanation and suggests instead that the substance of 'visionary' literature is not a secondary, altered form of personal experience but a primary experience of 'psychic reality'—a manifestation of the racial unconscious. It is a type of experience shared by prophets and seers as well as poets. Since this primal experience is 'word and imageless' and paradoxical, the poet needs 'a refractory and contradictory form of expression' (*t.* 19/20, p. 36). The myth, the hymn, and the grotesque are frequent forms in which this vision is expressed. But in literature the collective unconscious does not remain unalloyed with contemporary material. 'Wherever the collective unconscious forces its way into experience and weds itself to the collective consciousness, there occurs a creative act. . . . The work emerging from this is, in the deepest sense of the word, a message to the contemporaries' (*t.* 19/20, p. 38). The poet is thus not to be explained as a man concerned with his own personal problems. He is rather 'the *collective man*, the carrier and former of the unconsciously active soul of mankind' (*t.* 19/20, p. 41).

There was little in this statement to which Jolas could not subscribe. Not only did it provide at least the possibility of a metaphysical perspective, it established the poet as a seer and in explaining that the poet's means of communication must be 'refractory and contradictory', it

sanctioned the linguistic experimentation which Jolas felt was so important. If Jung's statement was inadequate for him in any respect, it was
only in stopping short of accommodating these findings to similar discoveries derived from other areas of the social sciences, philosophy, and
the romantics' exploration of the mind. That, however, did not present
a large problem, since he was working out a complete synthesis of his
own.

He was not able to present these ideas without delay, however. The
Chicago Tribune and the *New York Herald* had merged foreign editions
and Robert Sage had been sent to London by the new paper leaving
Jolas without an assistant. Stuart Gilbert had become an assistant editor
with number 16/17 and took over some of the work of answering
critics, reading manuscripts, making translations, and helping with
proofreading, but still the burden of the work fell to Jolas. The expense
of making up the constant deficit of each issue was placing a heavy load
on Jolas's family finances. Moreover, Joyce's eyes had worsened and he
had asked to be relieved of his commitment to publish segments of
'Work in Progress'. Joyce had missed issues before, but this time it
seemed doubtful that he would be able to continue at all. In the face of
these problems the double issue 19/20 was planned as the last.

Robert Sage wrote a long letter summarizing the work of *transition*
and lamenting its end. Philippe Soupault recalled its importance to
French poetry. 'At a time when we stood in France before the collapse
of all poetic values, when those most qualified to consider poetry had
become discouraged, and when, for reasons that seem to me superfluous
to enumerate here, those same persons turned their attention in other
directions, *transition* represented the only living force, the only review
which did not despair of poetry, and thus authorized the poets to continue their work' (*t.* 19/20, p. 376). He added that by providing 'an
entente between action and poetry' in such programmes as 'The Revolution of the Word', *transition* kept poetry from being completely given
up for action and thereby became 'a geometric link' in the development of poetry (*t.* 19/20, p. 376). Ultimately, Soupault was philosophical about the matter. 'We should . . . feel less regret at the disappearance
of a review which has reached its goal. It can die in peace, the direction
has been suggested, the impulse has been given' (*t.* 19/20, p. 376).

Notes

1 Malcolm Cowley, *Exile's Return* (New York, 1951), p. 286.

2 Eugene Jolas, 'transition: An Epilogue', *American Mercury*, XXIII (1931), p. 190.

3 Carl Einstein, *Gesammelte Werke*, ed. Ernst Nef (Wiesbaden, 1962), p. 13.

4 *Afrikanische Legenden*, ed. Carl Einstein (Berlin, 1925).

5 Max Scheler, *Vom Ewigen im Menschen*, in *Gesammelte Werke*, Band V (Berne, 1954), p. 90.

6 Max Scheler, *Philosophische Weltanschauung* (Berne, 1954), quoted in Maurice Dupuy, *La Philosophie de Max Scheler* (Paris, 1959), II, p. 682.

7 *Ibid.*, p. 691.

8 Sigmund Freud, *New Introductory Lectures on Psychoanalysis*, in *The Modern Tradition*, ed. Richard Ellmann and Charles Feidelson, Jr. (New York, 1933), p. 112.

9 Freud, *The Ego and the Id*, in *Complete Works*, ed. James Strachey (London, 1961), XIX, pp. 24–5.

10 In the preface Jung had said that the book could be read as easily backwards as forwards and had characterized it as an example of the schizophrenic mind. As Richard Ellmann reported in *James Joyce* (p. 641) Joyce asked his German editor, Daniel Brody, 'Why is Jung so rude to me? He doesn't even know me. People want to put me out of the church to which I don't belong. I have nothing to do with psychoanalysis.' Jung's preface was never used with *Ulysses*. A revised version was later printed in *Nimbus*, volume II (June–August 1953), pp. 7–20.

IV

VERTICALISM

transition seemed at the time to have reached its end, and Jolas even wrote an article entitled 'transition: An Epilogue' for the *American Mercury*.[1] No issues appeared between June 1930 and March 1932. In late 1931, however, an unexpected opportunity to resume publication presented itself. With little advance warning, Mr Carlus Verhulst, representing The Servire Press of The Hague, called on Jolas one day saying that his firm wanted to publish a revived *transition*. The Dutch press styled itself 'printers to moderns, specialists in editions deluxe, all art printing' (*t*. 21, p. 326). They believed that a profit could be made in presenting new works from many countries in translation, and they were familiar with Jolas's ability to find new works. The new series would be under Jolas's sole direction as the old one had been, but the Servire Press would underwrite the venture for a stake in the profit. Jolas, who wanted to resuscitate *transition* but lacked the funds, accepted the offer.

When *transition* appeared again in March 1932, the subtitle 'An International Workshop for Orphic Creation' replaced the previous 'An International Quarterly for Creative Experiment'. This title reflects a new emphasis on poetry as an approach to revelation. *transition* had ceased publication just when Jolas had been able to formulate his view of poetry as an expression of 'universal man'. In the two years of dormancy he had been able to draw together a small book, *The Language of Night*,[2] to document his position and clarify his ideas.

The book is a compact and direct statement of the background of twentieth century romanticism. In addition to presenting the philosophical basis of the search for a renewed metaphysical perspective of Scheler and the findings of Janet, Freud, Jung, and Lévy-Bruhl which had already been presented in *transition*, the book traces the interest in visionary literature from Heraclitus to the twentieth century. Though Jolas does not label it as such, *The Language of Night* develops a theory of history which sees the life of man as a series of confrontations between rationalism and mystic irrationalism. For him 'The Eleusinian mysteries epitomized a state of mind that was the antithesis of the "serenity" and formality of classical Hellas.'[3] In turn, the resistance to hyper-rationalism in the West had been taken up by the early Christian gnostics, mystics like Eckhart, Jan van Ruysbroeck, and St John of the Cross. The romantic period represented a 'fanatic opposition to the rationalism of the *Aufklärung*'[4] and led to an unprecedented exploration of the irrational. In the twentieth century a new romanticism opposed scientific positivism. It is of course different from its predecessor, but it has fundamental similarities. 'The romantics' fundamental belief that the forces of life are irrational ones before they become creative entities . . . establishes our method of thinking in a link with theirs. . . . But our age demands a different realization. . . . We hope to create a sense of the miraculous that is not a looking-backward into the middle-ages, but a use of more modern elements of development.'[5] The book traces in detail the linguistic innovations of twentieth century French, German, and English authors.

With the documentation of a tradition behind him, Jolas asserts that poets must now rediscover the sense of the vertical, that which Scheler had called the eternal in man, and give to language 'a mediumistic function' and a 'mode of liturgy'.[6]

The Language of Night in effect defined a crisis in the metaphysical concept of man. The irrational and metaphysical side of man seemed to be threatened as never before. In number 21 Jolas restated his conviction that such a crisis existed and inaugurated an inquest into the problem to establish to what extent others felt the crisis.

The inquest, using a phrase borrowed from Scheler, was called 'Metanthropological Crisis'. It asked what the fate of individuals under collective regimes would be and what would happen to metaphysics in an age of science. Neither H. L. Mencken, defending America, nor

David A. Siqueiros, representing the communist view, sees the collective life as a threat to the individual. Mencken even denied the power of the collectivist forces. 'I do not believe that this is a collectivist epoch. It seems to me that the effort to set up collectivism in Russia is bound to fail, and that little will be heard of it by 1950, save historically. Such a man as Stalin is really not a collectivist. At heart he is quite as much an individualist as J. Pierpont Morgan' (*t.* 21, p. 128). Siqueiros felt the collective movement of communism was a panacea to individual problems. 'If Communism did not really open wide the gates to the production of a superior beauty such as has never been imagined by men poisoned by the class-struggle, Communism would simply be a retrograde movement, and not, as it is in reality, an immense step forward in the march of human civilization. Communism will create the material and moral conditions which art needs for its real evolution' (*t.* 21, p. 135).

Dr Richard Huelsenbeck, one of the founders of dadaism in Zurich in 1916, made a 'plea for the partyless'. '. . . there exists no acceptable truth, neither in these party programmes, nor in the world views back of them. . . . The state we long for is not yet visible, and perhaps not realisable at all. Thus we are forced to return for consolation to ourselves and the atmosphere created by us' (*t.* 21, pp. 121–5). Gottfried Benn, C. G. Jung, and Leo Frobenius also belonged to the partyless[7] who could not be satisfied by collective political programmes. Their statements all pointed out the encroachment of the outward, hyper-rational life of modern man upon the inner, a-logical, and eternal portion of man. Martin Buber, Camille Schuwer, Georges Ribemont-Dessaignes, Stuart Gilbert also express dismay at increasing materialism. Buber's statement depicts most briefly and directly the feeling of urgency which the partyless shared. 'Your question is very difficult. I envisage the evolution of individualism, in a collectivistic regime, as revolutionary; and the evolution of metaphysics as partaking of the mood of catacombs' (*t.* 21, p. 112).

In selecting respondents for his inquiry, Jolas had consciously picked authors like Jung, Benn, and Frobenius that he knew would explain the loss of metaphysical awareness as a loss of 'primal faculties'. Number 21 also contained an article by Benn entitled 'The Structure of the Personality (Outline of a geology of the "I")' which discussed the decline of the visionary faculties in man. It is the most thorough

discussion of scientific discoveries and theories concerning the development of the unconscious ever printed by *transition*. Along with Jolas's
own 'The Primal Personality', which appeared in number 22, it was
one of the chief documents of *transition*'s development. Much of the
article covers the same ground as earlier ones by Jolas like 'Logos' and
'Literature and the New Man' in giving the background of the discovery of the irrational by psychologists, but it also contains elements
which the depth psychologists had largely ignored and which were to
grow in importance in *transition*'s programme.

The basis of the essay is an examination of the evolution of the
human brain. The brain is like a geological formation, a stratification
of elements of former eras built up one upon another. It is composed
of many 'functional systems', each of which was at one time 'formed
in an isolated way' and characterized by 'its own determined evolu-
tionary stage'. The most recent development of man has been the
growth and domination of 'the big brain' specialized in the conscious,
rational activity of intelligence. But at an earlier stage man had a 'pre-
logical mentality' seated in a 'parietal organ', the 'pineal eye which
conferred nature-intuition, the magical feeling, telepathy and telekine-
sis' (*t*. 21, p. 2–4). The inevitable plan of nature is 'unconceivable mutation'. It is quite possible, according to Benn, that the future development of man will 'relegate the big brain . . . to its runes . . . revivify all
the [pre-logical] rudiments' (*t*. 21, p. 2–5) or produce completely new
powers. The essay seemed to Jolas to offer a scientific explanation and
justification for his belief in man's visionary capacity. The 'pineal eye'
became for him a dominating symbol of this capacity. In his own
essay, 'The Primal Personality' in the next issue he discusses the theory
of the 'third eye' and cites in support of his belief the works of Ludwig
Klages, Lévy-Bruhl, Edgar Decqué, and Franz von Baader (*t*. 22, p. 81).

A great deal that had been groping and provisional in earlier issues
had been stated more clearly in *The Language of Night* and in Benn's
article. A new manifesto was now possible. For number 21, Jolas devised
a statement declaring 'Poetry is Vertical'. The manifesto is largely
Jolas's own, but it is possible that Carl Einstein and Hans Arp also
made suggestions and contributions. The names of the other signers
were solicitied individually as in the case of the 'Revolution of the
Word'.

Poetry is Vertical

[1] In a world ruled by the hypnosis of positivism, we proclaim the autonomy
of the poetic vision, the hegemony of the inner life over the outer life.

[2] We reject the postulate that the creative personality is a mere factor in
the pragmatic conception of progress, and that its function is the delineation
of a vitalistic world.

[3] We are against the renewal of the classical ideal, because it inevitably
leads to a decorative reactionary conformity, to a factitious sense of harmony,
to the sterilisation of the living imagination.

[4] We believe that the orphic forces should be guarded from deterioration,
no matter what social system ultimately is triumphant.

[5] Esthetic will is not the first law. It is in the immediacy of the ecstatic
revelation, in the a-logical movement of the psyche, in the organic rhythm
of the vision that the creative act occurs.

[6] The reality of depth can be conquered by a voluntary mediumistic con-
juration, by a stupor which proceeds from the irrational to a world beyond
a world.

[7] The transcendental 'I' with its multiple stratifications reaching back
millions of years is related to the entire history of mankind, past and present,
and is brought to the surface with the hallucinatory irruption of images in
the dream, the daydream, the mystic-gnostic trance, and even the psychiatric
condition.

[8] The final distintegration of the 'I' in the creative act is made possible by
the use of a language which is a mantic instrument, and which does not
hesitate to adopt a revolutionary attitude toward word and syntax, going
even so far as to invent a hermetic language, if necessary.

[9] Poetry builds a nexus between the 'I' and the 'you' by leading the emotions of the sunken, telluric depths upward toward the illumination of a
collective reality and a totalistic universe.

[10] The synthesis of a true collectivism is made possible by a community of
spirits who aim at the construction of a new mythological reality.

Hans Arp, Samuel Beckett,
Carl Einstein, Eugene Jolas,
Thomas McGreevy, Georges
Pelorson, Theo Rutra, James
J. Sweeney, Ronald Symond
(*t.* 21, pp. 148–9)[8]

Points 1, 2, and 8 are reiterations of principles announced in the
'Revolution of the Word'. Number 3 had also been latent in the earlier
manifesto, but now for the first time classicism is singled out as an evil.

The new emphasis in the programme is the suggestion in points 4, 5, 6, 7, and 9 that the poet's function is genuinely orphic, depending upon the use of a primal faculty which the poet exercises like a medium through dreams, trances, and even psychopathic derangement. Points 9 and 10 in seeing the function of poetry as relating the personal consciousness to the metaphysical totality of the universe and establishing a sense of community are also new. The manifesto defines an importance for the poetic vision even greater than that which *transition* had claimed for it earlier. In 'Suggestions for a New Magic' Jolas had declared, 'perhaps we are seeking God. Perhaps not. It matters little one way or the other. What really matters is that we are on the quest' (*t.* 3, p. 179). It was clear now that *transition* was seeking God—if not an orthodox God, at least the God of theological existentialists like Martin Buber.

Terms like 'story' and 'prose' seemed inadequate descriptions of works which presented the orphic vision that verticalism demanded, so as part of the verticalist programme Jolas invented new terms to describe them. The 'anamyth' he defined as 'a fantastic narrative that reflects preconscious relationships' (*t.* 21, p. 324) and the 'psychograph' as 'a prose text that expresses hallucinations and phantoms' (*t.* 21, p. 324). The terms did not become widespread, but they are not so gratuitous as the critics who ridiculed them suggested. The old terms like fairy tale, vision, prose poem, or surrealist text under which such writings had been lumped in the past had inaccurate connotations, and Jolas's new terminology was a serious attempt to replace them.

No other issue appeared until February 1933; almost a year after Jolas published the verticalist manifesto. An even longer period elapsed before the third issue of the new series appeared in July, 1935. Despite the long interval between issues, numbers 22 and 23 continue development along lines evident in 21. In number 22 the term vertical was changed to vertigral. Vertical, though clearly in opposition to the horizontal plane of normal life, encompasses both the direction of descent and ascent. Jolas believed a combination of negative and positive forces was necessary for an adequate view of life but, still true to Novalis, he also thought that the final resolution of forces should be in upward movement towards religious experience. Only through eternal quest could the positive movement be assured. The grail was the symbol of quest; by taking the German word *Graal* and dropping one 'a' he could include this concept in his key term. The new word also had overtones of 'integral' and thus also suggested the universality which Jolas was seeking.

The 22nd issue included a large section of experimental poetry by Hans Arp, Hugo Ball, Jolas, and others. Another section was devoted to the 'Laboratory of the Mystic Logos' and contained articles discussing language. Carola Giedion-Welcker's contribution, '*Die Funktion der Sprache in der heutigen Dichtung*', is a perceptive and well-informed attempt to trace the growth of the attitudes toward language which *transition* had championed from Rimbaud through Joyce. It covers very nearly the same material as Jolas's own *The Language of Night*, but more briefly. It is one of the best introductions available to the linguistic revolution in twentieth-century poetry.

In Number 23, Jolas included a section called 'Three Romantic-mystic Texts', containing Franz von Baader's 'From: Extasis as Metastasis', Franz Werfel's 'From a Discourse on the Religious Experience', and Hugo Ball's 'Gnostic Magic', as well as a section of 'Primitive Documents' containing a French astronomical legend about the origin of the stars by Gustavo Barroso, two Cuban voodoo prayers translated by Alejo Carpentier, a Yoruba folktale about the origin of day and night from Leo Frobenius, seven-year old Betsy Jolas's fantasy about a conversation among the letters of the alphabet, and F. M. Huebner's essay 'Possession', a description of psychic conditions which demand exorcism.

Still pursuing the question of the accommodation of language to the needs of the deeper levels of the mind, Jolas also published in the issue an inquest on the 'Mutation of Language'. Two questions were posed: Do you believe that, in the present world crisis, the Revolution of Language is necessary in order to hasten the re-integration of human personality? and: do you envisage this possibility through a readaptation of existing words, or do you favour a revolutionary creation of new words? Twenty-nine writers and linguists responded; among them were Gottfried Benn, Marcel Brion, Henry Seidel Canby, Norman Foerster, Ivan Goll, H. L. Mencken, C. K. Ogden, P. D. Ouspensky, Philippe Soupault, and Jean Wahl.

The responses indicate the widespread feeling between the two wars that language had become a dulled instrument incapable of dealing adequately with newly developed concepts of man. Thirteen of the respondents answered the first question completely in the affirmative, indicating their sympathy with the kind of revolution in language which *transition* had been fostering.[9] One expressed sympathy for the revolution but thought it was perhaps too extreme.[10] Four thought a revolution was in order, but favoured an approach closer to that of Ogden, Richards, and the other logical positivists—i.e. a conscious attempt to redefine existing terms so as to avoid the confusion raised by the ambiguous denotations of words and by their emotional connotations.[11] Four sidestepped the question of desirability of a revolution on the grounds that conscious efforts by small groups to change language are impossible.[12] Only three thought that a linguistic revolution was either unnecessary or undesirable, and these three were committed to that position by previous alliances: Malcolm Cowley and Gorham Munson opposed linguistic revolution on the basis of economic determinism, saying that economic factors alone were responsible for the current confusion and that only a change in them could bring relief, while Norman Foerster, the new humanist, rejected the revolution on the grounds that it was not inadequate means of expression but a departure from old ideas, 'the wisdom of the ages', which led to confusion.

The feeling that language needed changing was widespread, but the correspondents were less sure that the solution to the problem lay in the introduction of new words as Jolas had suggested. Only eleven agreed that a general attempt to introduce new words was desirable.[13] Three opposed introducing new words among the general population but thought that it was desirable for poets to do so.[14] Thirteen opposed the introduction of new words fearing either that the results would be unintelligible or that an artificial jargon would arise.[15] The experts saw many problems in carrying through a revolution in language on a large scale. Both Ogden and Mencken, who were experienced in the problems of linguistics, felt that it was impossible to change language through a conscious programme. Jean Wahl, the linguistic philosopher, felt that the subconscious did not invent new words but merely worked through combinations of old ones. Despite the sincere interest of those who favoured the revolution, the experts felt that it could at best offer personal solutions to the problem of expression. Their conclusions seem to have been borne out by time, but the fact that the revolution did not reach the entire population does not keep it from being an important element of modern poetry.

By the fall of 1935 Jolas was beginning to think of a return to newspaper work. The rise of fascism in Europe was distasteful to him.
America, despite all its manifest faults catalogued in *transition*, still held
a mythical fascination for him. He decided to try once again to realize
his dream of taking part in the development of America which seemed
to him younger, more hopeful, and more alterable than Europe. He
left Paris for New York where he took a position with the French news
service, Havas.

With Jolas in America, a reorganization of *transition* was necessary.
James Johnson Sweeney, who had been a part of the Einstein *cénacle*,
a contributor to number 21, and a signer of the 'Poetry is Vertical'
manifesto, was also now back in New York. Maria Jolas had remained
in Europe with her bilingual school at Neuilly, so the Sweeney apartment served as a kind of second home for Jolas while he was away from
his family. There the two men discussed art and literature and the
future of *transition*. When Jolas proposed that Sweeney become associate editor, he agreed to take the position beginning with number 24.
He continued actively in that capacity until Jolas returned to Paris in
1937 to prepare number 27 alone.

In 1936 after the publication of number 24, the Servire Press went
bankrupt. Jolas and Sweeney were now faced with the problem of
either discontinuing the magazine or finding new financial support.
They decided to continue, with the understanding that the expenses
that remained unpaid after subscriptions and sales would be shared.

With two editors the magazine could maintain for a while a more
regular schedule of appearances than it had had since its resumption in
March 1932. Three issues appeared in America at quarterly intervals:
one in June 1936, another that autumn, and a 'winter' issue in May of
1937. The three New York numbers are neater, more attractive and
more professional than any of the previous issues. Their organization is
more consistent and regular departments, as in less experimental magazines, were established. In addition to sections of poetry and prose, each
number has sections for 'The Eye' (containing art reproductions and
criticism), 'The Ear' (containing fragments of unpublished musical
scores), 'The Cinema', 'Architecture', and 'Interracial Documents'
(containing primitive art and literature).

The watchword was still 'Vertigral'; the poetry was still linguistically
experimental; prose works were called 'paramyths'; and the presentation

of twentieth century mysticism and primitive arts continued. But despite the continuity of interests, the tone was altered. The subtitle 'An Orphic Workshop' was dropped for the more conservative 'A Quarterly Review'. Under Sweeney's influence the tendency to encompass all the arts, which was always a part of *transition*, became more pronounced; the word remained important, but it no longer held its paramount position unchallenged. To many it must have seemed that the institutional air of the Museum of Modern Art had overcome the Parisian fervor of the early issues.

Though more proper and less exciting than in earlier days, *transition* continued to publish excellent material. Joyce did not contribute to numbers 24 or 25, but in these issues parts I and II of Kafka's 'Metamorphosis' were published. Number 26 contained both a section of 'Work in Progress' and the third instalment of 'Metamorphosis'. Several works by Dylan Thomas, then an obscure young Welsh poet, also appeared in these issues.

In the summer of 1936 Maria Jolas came to America with their two daughters, Tina and Betsy. Her reports of the impending political crisis in Europe alarmed Jolas. He decided to return to Paris, liquidate his activities there, and come back to America. By September Jolas and his family were back in Paris and the American period of *transition* had come to an end. Jolas prepared the tenth anniversary issue alone in Paris during the winter of 1938 amidst the 'slightly hysterical world's fair gaiety' which masked a frightened silence in the face of almost certain war.

As Jolas listened to the speeches of Hitler broadcast by German radio stations, he was saddened by the frenzy which was animating Germany. He came to feel, as he wrote in his autobiography, 'that the poet had not the right to remain entirely aloof'. He also realized that the rapid and inevitable movement of political events would make the tenth anniversary issue of *transition* the last. He thought of the final issue as an attempt to gather together the artistic and literary forces not yet enslaved by totalitarianism. It was a defiant gesture against the Nazis, who had condemned German expressionism, dadaism, and Joyce, and had publicly burned a copy of *transition* in Munich during one of their infamous campaigns against 'decadent' literature. In particular, Jolas sought to bring together for a last time in *transition* all the romanticist tendencies of the epoch.

The earlier romantics were represented by Albert Beguin's essay, 'The Night Side of Life', part of his famous study of German Romanticism, and by Hoelderlin's poem 'The Titans'. Dadaism was represented by an essay of Gabrielle Buffet-Picabia on 'Arthur Cravan and American Dada' and two poems by Hans Arp, one of the original dadaists. The last instalment of Kafka's 'Metamorphosis' and portions of his famous letter to his father were the examples of German expressionism. From the surrealist camp the issue included the opening letter to André Breton's *Mad Love*. Philippe Soupault's poem 'Manhattan' represented the young Frenchmen who had been part of surrealism at first but had later moved away from it. Even elements which had not formed an important part of the new romanticism as expressed earlier, but were related to it, such as a fragment of Barzun's *'l' Universel Poème'* (which had influenced the dadaists) and a portion of Henry Miller's 'The Cosmological Eye', a call for a return to primitive visceral knowledge, were included. And of course, Joyce, whose 'Work in Progress' was also a kind of new romanticism, appeared too in this issue which tried to sum up all that *transition* had stood for in its decade of existence.

'Work in Progress' was nearing completion, and much copy in the form of heavily corrected *transition* proof had been sent to Faber and Faber. Joyce was worried about the book's reception and told Jolas, 'This book of mine must appear before the war breaks out or no one will read it'.[16] Perhaps to spur himself on, perhaps to place more of his work before the public, Joyce wanted another portion to appear in *transition* and gave Jolas the manuscript of 'The Russian General' section. This was Joyce's last serial publication, his last contribution to one of the 'little magazines' which had been so important in his career. The first complete edition of *Finnegans Wake* (Faber and Faber) appeared in February, 1939, almost simultaneously with the much delayed last issue of *transition*.

transition had held on for nearly a decade after the first wave of expatriates had left Europe to return to America to write their memoirs, but the war was too great an obstacle even for *transition*. This time Jolas was correct in thinking he had prepared his last issue. By allowing *transition* to come to an end, Jolas was in a way upholding one of the basic principles of the magazine. At the very first he and Paul had emphasized their dissociation from politics. Jolas now felt that he must adopt a more active political attitude. He might have turned *transition* into a political magazine. One can imagine how readily Jolas, who was by 1940 a member of the rapidly growing colony of anti-Nazi European artists and writers in and around New York, might have changed the direction of *transition* and produced a rather creditable vehicle for intellectual anti-Nazi propaganda. Instead, he remained true to the belief that poetry is demeaned when the poet is called upon to produce propaganda. The circumstances called for direct action, and Jolas could contribute directly to the war effort, but as a journalist, not as a poet or literary editor.

In 1941 he joined the United States Office of War Information and remained in government services until 1950. His assignments took him to London, then to France with the Normandy invasion, and finally to Germany where he remained for four years after the fighting was over to help the Germans establish a renovated press and to wean the German newspapers away from a subjective, propagandistic style of news reporting.

Between the publication of the last issue of *transition* and his enlistment Jolas published one more volume which was in a way an outgrowth of the magazine. Verticalism was Jolas's answer to psychological, religious, and linguistic problems which had held his attention since childhood; it was not likely that he could simply abandon it. After returning to New York he continued to find examples of 'verticalist' poetry and art, much of it previously untranslated material from German and French. The materials deserved to be published but since it was only a matter of time until he entered service there was no question of starting a magazine. Instead he arranged with his friend Frances Steloff to publish *Vertical: A Yearbook for Romantic Mystical Ascenscions* under the imprint of the Gotham Book Mart press. The book was a worthy successor to *transition*, it included drawings by Alexander Calder and André Masson, poetry by Paul Claudel, Charles Péguy, Guillaume Apollinaire and Richard Eberhard.

The yearbook was the last volume edited by Jolas. Although he was a member of the editorial board of *Transition Forty-Eight*, this post-war magazine was edited by the French critic, Georges Duthuit. Duthuit, a friend of Jolas who had been interested in verticalism and a contributor to the *Vertical Yearbook*, wished to introduce the new French literature to English-speaking readers as Jolas had done earlier. Paper, like almost every other commodity, was scarce and rationed. Publications already established before the war had priority and there was hardly enough to meet those needs. Publishing supplies to start a new magazine were unobtainable. When Jolas heard of Duthuit's plight, he generously allowed him to use the name *transition* and accepted the title of advisory editor to satisfy the authorities that the new magazine, *Transition Forty-eight*, had continuity with the pre-war version. The continuity was hardly more than nominal, although Maria Jolas did make a number of translations for it. The magazine was instrumental in introducing the works of René Char, Jean-Paul Sartre, and other Frenchmen (occasionally in unsigned translations by Samuel Beckett). However, it lacked the audacious enthusiasm which marked Jolas's magazine. Jolas himself was in Germany during the years in which the new *Transition* was formed, so he never took an active part in editing it.

Even after Jolas returned to Paris there was no question of reviving the old *transition*. The basic conflict between a mechanistic, positivistic society and the claims of the unconscious and the imagination which had been the uniting concern of *transition*'s contributors remained, but the war had made irreconcilable differences among those who had formerly felt themselves a part of the same cause. At one extreme Jung, Benn, Drieu La Rochelle, and others had fallen in step with the Nazis in various ways. At the other extreme Carl Einstein had committed suicide after escaping a German extermination camp. Paul Léon, the close friend of Joyce and Jolas, had died during deportation. Joyce died in 1941. Bitterness, shame, and death precluded any hope of again forming the old alliances.

Germany was in too great a disorder to provide new literature. The new writing in France concerned itself with some of the same kind of interest in the difference between internal and external reality and in a search for new ways to use language, but it distrusted the unconscious and insisted that the artist must be *engagé*. To have continued in the old tradition of presenting the best of Europe to America would have required a departure from the principle that the imagination must be freed from the constraints of social involvement. *transition* was too closely identified with an attitude peculiar to the years between the wars to have fitted easily into the post-war period.

Jolas spent the last two years of his life in Paris working on his translations of Novalis and writing his autobiography. After a long illness he died from acute nephritis on 26 May, 1952.

Notes

1 Jolas, 'transition: An Epilogue', *American Mercury*, XXIII, pp. 185–8.
2 Eugene Jolas, *The Language of Night* (The Hague, 1932).
3 *Ibid.*, p. 43.
4 *Ibid.*, p. 45.
5 *Ibid.*, p. 46.
6 *Ibid.*, p. 56.
7 Benn and Jung later were indulgent towards the Nazis, but did not show political leanings until the war began.
8 See below, pp. 141 ff.
9 Benn, Bosquet, Brion, Goll, Pelorson, Petitjean, Rao, Schuwer, Soupault, Untermeyer, Vail, Warren, and Wahl.
10 Edmond Vandercammen.
11 Canby, Ogden, Orage, and Lamour.
12 Mencken, de Miomandre, Mounier, and Sanford.
13 Bosquet, Brion, Canby, Pelorson, Petitjean, Rao, Rutra, Soupault, Untermeyer, Vail, and Wahl.
14 Benn, Ogden, and Munson.
15 Cowley, Foerster, Lamour, Mencken, de Miomandre, Mounier, Orage, Quint, Sanford, Vandercammen, Wahl, Durtain, and Ouspensky.
16 Jolas, 'Man from Babel', p. 257.

Part 2

EUROPEAN COUNTERPARTS

V

SURREALISM

Most of the material which appeared in *transition* was related directly to the theories which Jolas advanced there. It was an American exile magazine only in that its programme was to bring the best of the new literature of Europe together with the best American and English writing. Many of its contributors happened to be in Paris, but the proximity of these writers was seldom the determining factor in the selection of material. Manuscripts came from Americans in Paris and at home. Jolas found many among them which he could use but much of the material he solicited or uncovered himself through direct contacts in other European cities. Some of it, like the contributions of Carl Jung and Alfred Doeblin, he went personally to obtain. Some of it he translated from the works of writers of the past like Novalis, Jean Paul, and Friedrich Hoelderlin.

In part, Jolas considered *transition* a 'documentary organ' dedicated to presenting what he referred to later as 'pan-romanticism'.[1] Not only was it to publish the authors directly involved in its own revolutionary programme, but also to present similar movements which had preceded it and were contemporary with it. It was in this respect that works of the surrealists, dadaists, and German expressionists appeared.

The most obvious documentary service for *transition* to perform at the time of its inception in Paris was to provide American readers with translations and discussions of surrealism. The movement which had gathered momentum through the presence in Paris of Tristan Tzara and other former members of international dadaist circles had been underway since about 1921 when André Breton and Philippe Soupault wrote *Champs Magnétiques*. It was defined in a manifesto by André Breton in 1924. By 1927, it was clearly the most vital and influential literary force in France.

transition was not the first American magazine to publish the surrealists or even to advocate their cause. In 1921, Margaret Anderson had published Louis Aragon, Francis Picabia and Philippe Soupault in *The Little Review*. Between 1924 and 1926, she continued to publish selections from their works. Alfred Kreymborg's *Broom* and Gorham Munson's *Secession* had also published pieces by the surrealists. Still, none of the magazines had been sufficiently in touch with the movement to make an effective presentation of it.

Samuel Putnam, writing in *Contempo* in 1931, expressed the opinion that the earlier attempts to bring the whole tradition of dadaist and surrealist revolt to America had been feeble and misleading and that only *transition* had published a large enough amount of material with enough understanding to convince readers to take the movement seriously. Commenting on a quarrel among the editors of *Broom* and *Secession* as to who had introduced the European literary revolutions to America, Putnam discounted the claims of both magazines as attempts to take undue credit. 'And now comes the question: WHO BROUGHT DADA TO AMERICA? This, to me, has been the most amusing aspect of the recent sufficiently amusing Cowley-Munson-Secessionist imbroglio. The whole episode impresses me as being a confession of impotence on the part of the Secessionists. The answer is, NO ONE BROUGHT DADA TO AMERICA! No one, certainly, before Eugene Jolas, although Margaret Anderson may have made something of an attempt. And what Jolas and the old *transition* brought was not Dada but a version of *Surrealism*'.[2] Roger Shattuck in his introduction to *The History of Surrealism* by Maurice Nadeau also pointed out *transition*'s importance in introducing surrealism. 'Eugene Jolas's *Transition*,' he wrote, 'was long associated as closely with surrealism as with Joyce's work in progress.'[3]

transition's success where others had failed came from Jolas's personal contacts which gave him access to surrealist material that perhaps no other editor could have got. Paul Eluard was particularly helpful; he gave his own poems willingly, authorized Jolas's translations of them, and arranged for other members of the surrealist group to provide

material for *transition*. Marcel Noll was another valuable contact. In his
position as director of the *Galerie surréaliste* he provided Jolas with
photographs of important paintings by surrealists.[4]

Even André Breton, who usually tried to prohibit members of the
group from publishing in reviews other than *La Révolution surréaliste*,
came to trust Jolas. In 1928 he authorized an official *transition* anthology
of English translations of surrealist texts and gave *carte blanche* to make
publishing arrangements in America. The book would have been the
first extensive publication of surrealist material in the United States,
but at least six major publishing houses to whom Maria Jolas presented
the project showed no interest whatsoever. Their representatives, if
they had heard of surrealism at all, seemed to think that it was only a
minor radical effusion in France that would come to nothing.

Jolas's personal attitude toward surrealism was a mixture of sympathy
for the movement and hesitation to ally himself totally with it. In 1924,
he had experimented with automatic writing under the influence of
surrealist friends. Even after he returned to Paris to begin *transition*, he
came home one day after a discussion with some members of the group
and told his wife, 'I almost signed up today,' meaning that he nearly
took the formidable step of joining the group officially and thus
subjecting himself to Breton's regulations.

Two things dissuaded Jolas from becoming a surrealist—their doctri-
naire insistence that literature derive exclusively from the unconscious,
and the rigid organization of the movement under the almost tyrannical
leadership of Breton. In defining his own theoretical position, Jolas
stated explicitly his belief that some conscious activity must be allowed
even in dealing with material which comes originally from the unconscious. As for the rigidity of the movement, Jolas had occasion to
observe first hand the bitterness it caused and be thankful that he was
not embroiled in the quarrels to which it led. At one of his own parties
he had tactfully arranged for Philippe Soupault, who had been expelled
from the movement that day, to slip out quietly to avoid meeting Paul
Eluard. However, even after *transition* was begun Jolas, Elliot Paul, and
Robert Sage did meet occasionally to experiment with joint attempts
at automatic writing—though with nothing like the dogmatic application of theory that dominated Breton's group.

The list of contributors that resulted from Jolas's close association
with surrealists is impressive. In the twenty-seven issues of *transition*

Jolas published over sixty pieces by surrealists including works by André Breton, Louis Aragon, Philippe Soupault, Robert Desnos, Paul Eluard, Julien Gracq, and other lesser known members of the group. André Breton's 'Introduction to the Discourse on the Dearth of Reality' (*t.* 5, p. 129), the opening chapter of his autobiographical novel *Nadja* (*t.* 12, p. 28), and Georges Ribemont-Dessaignes' 'Confiteor' (*t.* 9, p. 41 and *t.* 10, p. 14) appeared in *transition* even before their publication as books in French. Works by Benjamin Péret, René Crevel, Julien Gracq, Tristan Tzara, and Michel Leiris appeared only weeks or months after their appearance in French surrealist magazines. During 1927, when the surrealists could not agree enough among themselves to publish more than one issue of their official organ, *La Révolution surréaliste*, there was probably more surrealist material published in *transition* than in any other magazine.

The surrealists even used *transition* to publish one of their more 'infamous' manifestos. Charlie Chaplin's young wife had sued him for divorce and accused him publicly of asking her to commit what she called 'unnatural acts'. To the surrealists no acts of love were 'unnatural', but the laws which bound a man to be faithful to a woman he no longer loved were. To defend Chaplin, the surrealists prepared a statement entitled 'Hands Off Love'. It concentrates on the justification of fellatio, but also manages to advocate abortion, child desertion, and a *ménage à trois* involving Chaplin, his wife, and another young girl. 'Hands Off Love' appeared in *transition* 6 with the signatures of Paul and Jolas added to those of the official members of Breton's group whose names Parisians had come to expect at the bottom of provocative manifestos.

transition's achievement with regard to surrealism, however, lay less in serving the surrealists or in being the first to publish their material than it did in providing a wide-ranging selection of surrealist works that allowed English readers to see all aspects of the movement in perspective. Among the contributions by surrealists are important illustrations of surrealist theory, some unorthodox but interesting criticism, and several very fine poems.

The first and overriding tenet of surrealism was, of course, the predominance of the unconscious in the act of creation. The automatic texts upon which so much of surrealism was based were represented by Michel Leiris 'From the Heart to the Absolute' (*t.* 16/17, p. 277), and several selections from Paul Eluard's 'The Human Pyramid' (*t.* 2, p. 112). In his 'Introduction to the Discourse on the Dearth of Reality' André Breton concluded an automatic text with a defense of the method. He compares the mental explorations of the surrealists to the journeys of geographical explorers and complains of the attitudes that will allow the second as interesting and valuable while denying the first. '. . . a certain practical necessity prevents us from ascribing to poetic testimony an equal value to that given for instance, to the testimony of an explorer. Human fetichism, which needs must try on the white helmet, or caress the fur bonnet, listens with an entirely different ear to the recital of our expeditions. It must believe thoroughly that it really has *happened*' (*t.* 5, p. 141). Man has to date been 'riveted . . . to this vulgar universe' of external reality by words used over and over in the same combinations (*t.* 5, p. 140). Against this Breton offers the alternative, 'I believe it is not too late to recoil from this deception, inherent in the words we have thus far used so badly. What is to prevent me from throwing disorder into this order of words, murderously to attack this obvious aspect of things? Language can and should be torn from this servitude. No more descriptions from nature, no more sociological studies. Silence, so that I may pass where no one has ever passed. Silence! After you, my beautiful language!' (*t.* 5, pp. 140–1).

In the opening chapter of *Nadja* in *transition* 12 Breton presented an introduction to another of the great concerns of surrealism, 'objective chance'. His book was to be autobiographical, but not in the usual way. In it he was going to relate 'the most characteristic episodes of my life, *in the way I can conceive it outside of its organic plan*, and in the very degree in which it is subject to chance, to the smallest as well as the biggest chance, when for the moment, it escapes my influence, introduces me into an almost forbidden world, which is that of sudden rapprochements, petrifying coincidences . . .' (*t.* 12, p. 34). He goes on to relate how a number of the most significant events of his life have been announced or have come about as the result of chance events. 'I hope,' he says, 'that the presentation of a dozen similar observations and the one about to follow [the account of an amazing series of coincidences which brought Breton and a young woman named Nadja together] will be such as to speed a few men into the street, after having made them conscious, if not of the void, at least of the grave insufficiency of every so-called rigorous calculation about themselves, of every action

that demands a consistent application, and that might have been premeditated' (*t.* 12, p. 49). From the importance of chance in his own life
Breton draws the conclusion that the meaning of life will not be made
clear by working toward premeditated goals. 'There is no use in being
alive, if one has to work. The event through which everybody has the
right to expect the revelation of the meaning of his own life, this event
that perhaps I have not yet found, but on the road to which I am
engaged in the quest of myself, *is not at the price of work*' (*t.* 12, p. 50).
The unexpected combinations of events with which Breton concerns
himself here are just as important a part of surrealism as the unexpected
combinations of words and images explained in the 'Discourse on the
Dearth of Reality'.

Passionate, irrational love was a third major element of surrealism.
Breton presented this great surrealist value in the section from his 'Mad
Love' published in *transition* 27. The excerpt is the famous letter written
to his eight-month-old daughter intended for her to read when she is
sixteen. She has, the letter says, come into being because of her father's
dedication to love as opposed to family. And for her he says, 'My wish
is that you may be loved to the point of madness' (*t.* 27, p. 47).

In the course of 'Mad Love' Breton spoke of the Spanish civil war
and his rejection of temptations to become engaged in the collective
struggle for the betterment of mankind. This was one pole of surrealist
thought. There was also an opposite view. Since surrealism was a revolution against the fundamental attitudes of bourgeois society and was
roughly contemporary with the Marxist revolution in Russia, there was
always the question of its joining forces with communism. Louis
Aragon who had visited Russia in 1930 and written a long pro-Marxist
poem, 'Red Front', felt that the two movements should merge. He saw
surrealism as the artistic wing of the world-wide social revolution. In
his remarks at a discussion held in 1936 at the *Maison de la Culture* in
Paris and reprinted in *transition* 25, Aragon attacks the way in which art,
even the art of the surrealists, has become a commercial commodity
for the benefit of capitalists. 'Your pictures,' he told the audience,
'became the cards in this baccarat of the period of prosperity . . . and
when the black and uncertain days of the depression arrived, your
patrons discarded you, as stableowners might worn-out horses' (*t.* 25,
p. 121). He makes allusion to Hitler, saying '. . . the real enemy . . .
takes down yesterday's works of art from the walls of the museums,

sells them at public auction and burns them with books in the market-place. Learn to recognize your true allies . . . "My friends, your realm is of this world" ' (*t.* 25, p. 122). Jolas's personal sympathy was not with Aragon. His own programme insisted that the kingdom of the poets was not political. But Aragon represented an important element of surrealism and as such his ideas were presented in *transition*.

Apart from the works of Breton and Aragon, the two leading spokes-men for the opposed tendencies of surrealism, there were a number of articles of criticism and theory by other surrealists which helped *transition* readers to understand the movement. The two great forerunners of surrealism, Rimbaud and Lautréamont, were discussed in articles by Roger Vailland and Léon-Pierre Quint. Vailland's essay compares Rimbaud's struggle to free himself from the world of tradesmen, judges, and generals to the current surrealist revolt. According to Vail-land, Rimbaud's one failure in his 'war on man' was that he had under-taken his descent into the hell of his own mind too consciously and wilfully; he made of it a search for his self.

Rimbaud had thus been defeated. But that is not to say that his opponents had won. Vailland renews Rimbaud's challenge to the world, 'I am a beast you say, "gone nigger". But I—I may be saved. *You* are whitewashed niggers, one and all: madmen, brutes, Shylocks. You, Mr Tradesman, are a nigger; you, too, my lord the Judge; you, too, General. . . .' In closing Vailland adds his own warning to these people and brings the challenge up to date by including a reference to Paul Claudel who, when he was French Ambassador to Japan, had attacked the surrealists as '*pédérastique*' in a famous interview. 'Do you hear that, tradesman, judge, general? Do you hear that, ambassador? Rimbaud was beaten. A point for you. But the battle is not over. "Other artisans of horror will arise and advance from the horizon where their pioneer has fallen" ' (*t.* 18, p. 71). The surrealists would take up where Rimbaud left off, but they would not commit his mis-take of making their assault on the rationally oriented world a personal search for the self.

Another of the forerunners of surrealism had been Lautréamont's hero, Maldoror, who waged war not only against man but against God. 'Man in revolt against his creator—this is the subject of the *Chants de Maldoror*' explains Quint in the first sentence of his essay 'Lautréamont and the *Chants de Maldoror*'. Lautréamont's greatest effect comes in 'horrible or grotesque portraits of an anthropomorphic god. . . .' It is in these depictions, in which the foul barrenness of colour is reinforced by the comic, that such writers as Ribemont-Dessaignes or Blaise Cendrars have found one of their sources of inspiration (*t.* 16/17, p. 293).

Some of the most interesting surrealist ideas are presented in essays on non-literary topics—Roger Vitrac on the paintings of G. L. Roux, Robert Desnos on the work of Man Ray, and Antonin Artaud on movies. Vitrac's essay on Roux is an impressionistic appreciation of how the painting of Gaston-Louis Roux 'opens up a gap'. 'I say it smashes repose, it shakes repose, it shakes the pyramid and mounts to the theatre. . . . Roux takes account of that which is *beyond measure* by throwing his peasants, his criminals, his were-wolves, with their arms and tools, and their new gestures, into the rotting world of the last bourgeois enchanters' (*t.* 16/17, pp. 289–90). In connection with the article *transition* published photographs of two paintings by Roux: 'Combat d'Oiseaux' and 'Le Loup-Garou'.

Robert Desnos discussed all aspects of Man Ray's work: painting, sculpture, and photography. The article is illustrated by Man Ray's picture of Desnos supine with closed eyes. In the same issue eight photographic studies by Ray of abstract scenes are included. As a painter Ray is more interested in the 'spirit' than anything else, Desnos says. 'He arrives between two shocks of an earth-quake, stops creation on the peak of a plunge, immediately before the return to the normal position. He catches faces at that fugitive moment between two expressions. Life is not present in his pictures and still there is nothing dead about them. There is a pause, a stop, only: Man Ray is the painter of the syncope' (*t.* 15, p. 265). As a sculptor, Man Ray takes on new materials 'to realize, in space, constructions that are independent of their resistance to human forces'. His major achievement is as a photographer. There he 'derives neither from artistic deformation, nor from the servile reproduction of "nature". Your planes and humps will reveal to you a person you do not know, and whom you have never dared glimpse in your dreams. A new "you" will spring from the delicate hands of the chemist in the red glow of the laboratory' (*t.* 15, p. 265).

Desnos's article is itself surrealistic in that it tries to convey the impact of Man Ray's work through sentences that are subjective almost to the point of uncontrolled lyricism. He says, for example, 'An attentive

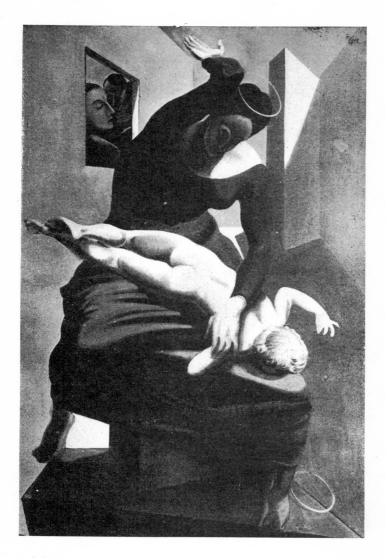

'The Virgin Corrects the Child Jesus Before Three Witnesses' by
Max Ernst, which appeared in *transition* 9, 1927; it shows, as
witnesses in the window, Paul Eluard, Max Ernst, and André
Breton.

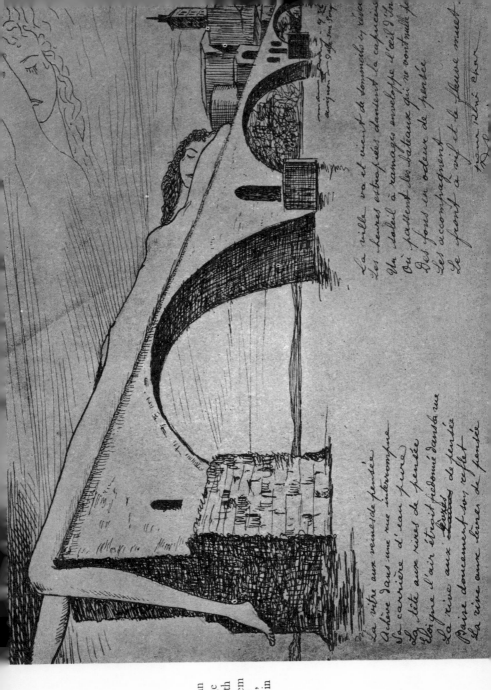

Drawing by Man Ray, 'The Bridge of Avignon', with Paul Eluard's poem 'Le Pont Brisé', which appeared in *transition 26*, 1937

chloroform will communicate to you the metaphysical anguish without which there is no dignity on earth. If you are able to abandon terrestrial conceptions, you will penetrate into a world having neither longitude nor latitude, into a bit of that infinite which, open to a few, is the most moving excuse that the modern epoch could give for its productive aptitude' (*t.* 15, pp. 265–6). This is possible, Desnos feels, only because Man Ray does not calculate or predict the results of his manipulation of the film.

In writing, painting, film, in criticism itself as in every aspect of art and life the surrealists' aim was to make the subjective element predominate, unhampered by a concern for reason and objective representation. It was thus natural that from a purely literary point of view, independent of theory and controversy, the best results of the movement were in the shorter lyric forms. *transition* published a number of the most appealing works of this type.

Robert Desnos's poem 'I have Dreamed so Much About You', which Jolas translated for the first issue of *transition*, describes the power of a purely mental image to dominate a life even when the physical person with whom it is supposed to be associated does not exist. This poem has become a permanent part of French culture by being engraved on the Monument at the tip of the Ile de France to those in France exterminated by the Nazis with the aid of French collaborators during the Second World War. Desnos was one of the victims. The importance of the phantoms in our lives is expressed simply but movingly.

I've dreamed so much about you
that you lose your reality

. . . .

I've dreamed so much about you that it is doubtless too
    late for me to wake. I sleep standing up, with my
    body exposed to all the appearances of life and love;
    and you, the only one who counts for me today, I
    could more easily touch the brow and lips of any stranger

Than your lips and brow.

. . . .

. . . nothing remains for me

but to be a phantom among phantoms and a hundred-
 fold more shadowy than the shadow that walks and
 lightly will walk on the sun-dial of your life.

(t. 1, p. 104)

Eluard's untitled piece in *transition* 5, evokes the 'essence of night'.

She is here—but only at midnight when all the white birds again have closed
their wings upon the ignorance of darkness, when the sister of myriads of
pearls has hidden both her hands in her dead hair, when the conqueror is
ready to sob, weary of his devotion to curiosity. . . . (t. 5, p. 109)

The best known single poem of the surrealist group to appear in
transition is Breton's 'Tournesol' or 'Sun-flower', an 'automatic' poem
he had written in 1923 which turned out to be the prophetic announcement of his meeting with the famous Nadja almost ten years later. The
poet meets an unknown woman totally by chance in Les Halles, formerly the great central market of Paris, and the results are extraordinary:

 The Japanese lanterns slowly took fire in the chestnut trees
 The lady without shadow knelt on the Pont-au-Change

 . . . .

 The promises of the nights were kept at last

 . . . .

 A farm prospered in the middle of Paris
 And its windows gave onto the Milky Way

The poet realizes that he is something more than he was before the
experience.

 I am not the plaything of sensorial powers
 And yet the cricket that sang in the hair of the ashes
 One evening near the Etienne Marcel statue
 Threw me a glance of understanding
 André Breton is passing it said

(t. 27, p. 378)

Few of the other works of surrealism that appeared in *transition* were as valuable either for their literary appeal or for the insight they gave into the theory and background of the movement as the pieces already discussed. They did, however, give readers examples of the work of a large number of surrealists in a wide variety of genres. There are extracts from Marcel Noll's notebooks, an extract from Tristan Tzara's surrealist 'epic', 'The Approximate Man', a scenario of Antonin Artaud, surrealist narratives somewhere between automatic texts and conventional stories by Georges Ribemont-Dessaignes and Philippe Soupault, poems by Pierre Unik, Jacques Baron, and Pierre Reverdy, and pictures by Francis Picabia, Max Ernst, André Masson, Georgio de Chirico, and Yves Tanguy. With the exception of Salvador Dali, there was something in *transition* by almost every important surrealist.

For all the sympathy he had for the movement and all the thoroughness with which he presented it, Jolas was never content to have *transition* considered a surrealist magazine in any way. In the earlier stages, he merely pointed out the differences between his attitudes and those of the surrealists, as he did in 'First Aid for the Enemy'. But after the attempt to revolutionize language began to occupy more of his thoughts, the connection with surrealism became irksome to Jolas and he declared ' "The Revolution of the Word" owes nothing to the surrealists' (*t*. 22, p. 125). These remarks were never directed at the surrealists themselves, but at the critics who refused to recognize the difference between *transition* and surrealism. Jolas remained on good terms with the group and their works appear randomly throughout the entire ten years of *transition*. For a non-surrealist publication *transition* probably did more over a longer period to make the movement understandable to England and America than any other magazine.

Notes

1 Eugene Jolas, 'Pan Romanticism in the Atomic Age', *Transition Workshop*, ed. Eugene Jolas (New York, 1949), p. 393.
2 Samuel Putnam, 'If Dada Comes to America', *Contempo*, II (July 25, 1932), p. 5.
3 Maurice Nadeau, *The History of Surrealism* (New York, 1965), p. 30.
4 Max Ernst, Yves Tanguy, Georgio de Chirico, André Masson, Man Ray, Francis Picabia, Joan Miró.

VI

EXPRESSIONISM

In Germany the anti-rationalist spirit was embodied in the expressionist movement. Presenting this movement to Americans who knew very little of it was another of the documentary services of *transition*. Expressionism had no clear starting point; the authors associated with it had published works in the style later called expressionist as early as 1902, but for convenience historians of German literature date the beginning in 1910 with the activity of a group of writers and painters centred around the Berlin review *Der Sturm*. In this periodical, edited by Herwarth Walden, the works of Wassilij Kandinsky, Paul Klee, Oskar Kokoschka, and other important German artists were reproduced along with the poetry of Else Lasker-Schüler, August Stramm, and Georg Heym. The novelist and short story writer Gottfried Benn, the satirist Kurt Tucholsky, and the dramatist Carl Sternheim were also friendly with the *Sturm* circle.

There was never any manifesto or common statement. In so far as there was any unity to the movement at all, it consisted of a rather general sympathy of writers and painters from both the older and younger generations for each other's efforts to depart from the traditional adherence to 'common sense' and fidelity to external reality. In addition to *Der Sturm* a number of periodicals like *Die Aktion*, edited by Franz Pfemferts and *Die Weissen Blätter*, edited in Strasbourg by René Schickele and the publishing houses of Kurt Wolff and Rowohlt, became centres for expressionist writing. In Berlin, Hamburg, Strasbourg, Prague, Munich, and other German cities there were loosely knit groups called expressionist. The writing produced by the members of these groups varied widely. Authors as different in attitude and technique as Ernst Toller, the strident social and political critic, and Franz Werfel, the romantic mystic, considered themselves part of the movement. By 1927 the expressionist magazines were all defunct and the movement had largely dispersed. Few of the writers had changed their style but they no longer banded together as they had just before and just after the war.

Partly because of its lack of an organized centre, expressionism was more appealing to Jolas than surrealism. The movement also had aspects which surrealism lacked. While the surrealists had taken very few steps to introduce new words, certain expressionists like August Stramm and Wassilij Kandinsky had been the first to change old words and invent new ones. Others like Franz Werfel were also more receptive to religious beliefs that tended toward orthodox mysticism than were the surrealists. Jolas saw these expressionists as the forerunners of his 'Revolution of the Word' and 'Verticalism'.

To some parts of expressionism Jolas was not receptive. In his selection of writers to appear in *transition* the militant social critics like playwrights Georg Kaiser and Ernst Toller are noticeably absent. Particularly in the verticalist stage of *transition*, Jolas much preferred the opposed expressionist tendency to avoid temporal concerns in search of religious experience. In *transition* 23, for example, he praised Franz Werfel because he 'declared himself against the naturalistic rationalism of many of his contemporaries' and 'had the courage, in the city of Freud, to make a frontal attack on the psychoanalytical credo', and to 'come out in favour of a new belief in a transcendental view of the world' (*t.* 23, p. 85).

To find expressionist material with which he was in sympathy, Jolas relied at first upon his contacts with René Schickele and Carl Einstein. After his trip to Berlin in 1929 to visit some of the few remaining active expressionists, he established direct contact with Alfred Doeblin, Gottfried Benn, and the artist George Grosz. Later in New York he met Max Brod, Kafka's literary executor and close friend.

Through these contacts the readers of *transition* were presented with remarkably wide coverage of the non-political element of expressionism. The authors ranged from the very earliest expressionists like

August Stramm to Franz Kafka who had been published in Germany only after the fervour of the movement died down in the middle twenties. Geographically, the selection was equally wide-ranging including the works of members of the expressionist groups in almost every German city where expressionism flourished.

The numerous literary genres in which the expressionists worked were also represented. Some of the most characteristic poems of the movement appeared in *transition*. Else Lasker-Schüler's 'Farewell' exemplifies the deep feelings of betrayal and disillusionment with the world felt by many expressionists. To her the poet is like a deserted girl whose lover has promised her much hope, but ultimately leaves her.

Farewell

But you never came with the evening—
I sat in my mantle of stars. . . .

I painted your sky blackberry
With my heart's blood—

But you never came with the evening—
. . . I stood in golden shoes.

(*t.* 5, p. 122)

Though the poem is about the poetess, and exploits the traditional material of the woman betrayed by her lover, it is not a direct imitation of life. It is rather a series of images united through their somber emotional overtones.

The poems of Georg Trakl and René Schickele which appear in *transition* exhibit a similar attitude of weariness and a similar method of expression. These poets, like Hoelderlin whom they regarded as their immediate forerunner, show a movement in German poetry away from the understandable dramatic situation to the poem in which images are used directly for their emotional reference and not as a description or as metaphors with connections that can be explained and ordered rationally.

While much of the early impact of expressionism came through lyric poetry, the major achievement of the movement was in other genres, so most of *transition*'s attention to the movement was focused on them. The size of the magazine and its policy of including a large number of contributors in each issue would not allow for more than one expressionist play. As it was, Carl Sternheim's 'A Pair of Drawers' (*Die Hose*) had to be serialized throughout four issues. Only its attack upon what Jolas called the philistine burghers' 'conspiracy against the visionary and magical things of life' (*t.* 6, p. 178) justified the extraordinary amount of space devoted to it.

The most important achievement of *transition* with respect to expressionism was in presenting works of prose fiction. Gottfried Benn, Alfred Doeblin, Kasimir Edschmid, and Franz Kafka were almost entirely unknown to Americans when they first appeared in *transition*. Now they are ranked among the best German writers of the century and Kafka has been recognized as one of the great innovators of world literature.

Some expressionist fiction was simply fantasy, like Carl Einstein's 'Bebuquin' published in number 16/17 in which a feather hat in a barroom talks and moves about. Most of the stories of the expressionists were, however, more than just fantasy. Freud's discussion of the unconscious had played a large part in stimulating expressionist fiction and frequently the visions and distortions of reality that appear in the stories are indications of unconscious motivations.

'The Humiliating Room' by Kasimir Edschmid, for example, presents the unconscious of a 'real' character in a realistically defined context through a series of fantasies which he constructs about a series of pictures. He reveals himself as a man torn between the extremes of sadism and masochism. The point of the story is not that these extremes are unacceptable horrors beneath a placid surface, but that in 'daily life' these tendencies must exist in 'disunion . . . never to be grasped with one grip, complete to fulfill our lives. . . .' They are like 'the sensation of an express train racing through a small twilit station—and the experience of a store showing billowing silks, one early spring day, on a shopping street in Strasbourg . . .' (*t.* 14, p. 253). There is no explanation of how the man might have moved beyond daily life to find unity and fulfillment. These separate images, however, suggest what the mental experience of such a fulfillment would be: the union of the masculine train with the yielding of the billowing feminine silk.

The kind of story represented by Edschmid was not a large part of *transition*'s programme. The foremost exponents of a similar use of sexual repression in America were Sherwood Anderson and Eugene O'Neill. Jolas felt that their explorations of the unconscious were too clinical. It should be noted, however, that Edschmid's story, despite its preoccupations with sexual guilt advocates a solution that cannot be found in the real world at all but only in the set of images (the train and the silk) which exist in the imagination. In that sense the story calls into play the 'fabulous' unconscious which creates new worlds and new experiences as well as the Freudian unconscious which merely transmutes reality into symbols.

Gottfried Benn was a writer much more to Jolas's taste. He knew and admired Benn's stories and poems from reading them in expressionist magazines as early as 1912. He had solicited the first of Benn's work for *transition* by mail. Later Benn called upon Jolas in Paris and in 1929 when Jolas went to Berlin the two men became more closely acquainted. As Jolas's use of Benn's 'The Structure of the I' in his own essays indicates, they had a very similar concept of the unconscious. Benn's stories were almost perfect examples of the kind of interplay between the conscious and unconscious that Jolas wanted.

Four poems by Benn had been translated into English by Babette Deutsch and Avram Yarmolinsky for their anthology, *Contemporary German Poetry* in 1923. Other than that he had received no attention in America. *transition* was the first to translate his stories and theoretical pieces and it was also the first American periodical to contain a discussion praising his work.

In an essay entitled 'Gottfried Benn' Jolas introduced him to *transition* readers. 'Benn's cosmos was that of a man wounded by life. As a physician who for years had been active in hospitals, his consciousness of the pathology of existence did not produce in him any sense of metaphysical solutions, but, on the contrary, the feeling for a cerebral escape' (*t.* 5, p. 147). To find this mental escape and to dramatize his need of it, Benn wrote a series of semi-autobiographical short stories about a young doctor named Rönne. In these stories which he grouped under the title '*Gehirne*' (Brains), mental processes are recreated with great detail and accuracy. As Jolas put it, 'he began to dissect his own mind, as if it were an anatomical segment, and ended with a psychic nowhere. Life is an aimless idea to Dr Werff Rönne' (*t.* 5, p. 147). About Benn's style he explains, 'his images are sharp and explosive. They startle the reader, because his imagination projects deformations and disassociations in a manner to which a life of superficial reading has not accustomed us' (*t.* 5, p. 148).

transition published three stories by Benn, all of which have a similar form. They are meditations that begin with normal cognizance of the external world; soon the world is rejected as unpleasant or inadequate; then by a partly controlled and partly involuntary process, the meditations begin to change from concern with the external world to concern with memories. After memories come distortions of events. This voluntary escape by the relatively normal manipulation and reconstitution of elements of reality initiates the flow of highly imaginative thoughts from within. At times the minds of Benn's characters also cast up memories of real events that come from the distant past and belong to some deeper, racial unconscious. As Rönne says, 'I live on this island and think cinnamon forests.' 'Within me reality and dream merge with one another,' he had said in an earlier story.

Dr Rönne is a completely disillusioned man who can sum up his wife's death with no more passion than the remark 'the child wept a few tears' (*t.* 5, p. 33). He only narrowly misses being a posturing schoolboy nihilist. When juxtaposed with the admitted escapism of his dreams of southern isles, this nihilism appears particularly overdone and Rönne's personality seems simplistic. Because Benn has not faced these problems, the reader remains neither hostile nor approving of Rönne and yet not caught in any tension between these attitudes either. The stories thus lack the power of *Ulysses* or even of Dujardin's *Les Lauriers sont coupés* with which their method invites comparison.

Even with this serious flaw, the workings of Dr Rönne's mind are presented with an impressive fidelity to detail that helps to generate interest. This detailed mental realism was almost unknown in German prose before Benn, and when one realizes that the stories first appeared prior to the serial publication of *Ulysses*, Benn's achievement becomes more impressive. The development of the 'stream of consciousness' or interior monologue techniques is most frequently talked of in terms of Joyce, Dorothy Richardson, and Edouard Dujardin. Benn, too, deserves a place in these discussions.

In the early years of *transition* Benn was a frequent contributor whose theory of the unconscious was probably closer to Jolas's than any other that appeared in the magazine. When Hitler took over Germany in 1933 and Benn chose the path of 'innerer emmigration' his relations with Jolas cooled rapidly. Nothing by him appeared after 1934 and he is conspicuously absent from *transition* 27, Jolas's anti-Nazi issue. After the war when Jolas was working to establish a new press in Germany, Benn tried to re-establish contact with him by sending his greetings through a third party. Jolas did not respond and there the association, so close except for political issues, ended.

Much in the same tradition as Benn was Alfred Doeblin author of *Berlin Alexanderplatz*. Jolas translated Doeblin's book in 1929 and included a chapter of it in *transition*. The importance of the work for Jolas lay in the fact that it was the first full length novel in German to use the technique of the interior monologue extensively. Though Doeblin claimed not to have been influenced by Joyce, the book also has other parallels with *Ulysses* besides technique and may have appealed to Jolas for that reason. Its hero, like Leopold Bloom, is a contemplative man from the working class who lives in a large industrial city. The book places the outer movement of the city in juxtaposition to the inner movement of the hero's mind. The chapter in *transition*, for example, shows young Franz Biberkopf moving through Berlin to his job at a slaughterhouse, and the thoughts he has along the way when stimulated by what he sees and hears. This was the only chapter of *Berlin Alexanderplatz* to appear in *transition*. Doeblin never played any large part in shaping Jolas's attitudes, but like Edschmid he was representative of a stage in the assimilation of 'inner reality' to German literature and thus was represented in *transition*.

The situation with Franz Kafka was different, his works were much more than representative and received more than passing attention in *transition*. They became one of the main attractions of the magazine. Jolas began to publish them just as they were receiving their first widespread public attention in Germany. As a member of a small expressionist group in Prague, Kafka had received enthusiastic praise from his friends as early as 1913, but he had published only a few stories in journals like *Die Weissen Blätter* and in Kurt Wolff's 'Der jüngste Tag'. He did not become widely recognized until after his death in 1924. He had requested his friend Max Brod to burn the manuscripts still unpublished at the time of his death, but Brod had thought them too good to destroy. Their appearance in rapid succession—*Der Prozess* (*The Trial*) in 1925, *Das Schloss* (*The Castle*) in 1926, and *Amerika* (*America*) in 1927—impressed the public and finally won him fame.

It was Carl Einstein who, on one of his visits to 'La Boisserie' in 1927, brought Kafka to the attention of Jolas. Through him Jolas arranged

'The Little Agitator' by Georg Grosz, which appeared in *transition* 19/20, 1930.

Sketches by Franz Kafka, Courtesy Max Brod.

Sketches by Franz Kafka, which appeared in *transition* 27, 1938.

with Max Brod to publish an example of Kafka's work. Brod had first published Kafka's story '*Das Urteil*' in his yearbook *Arkadia* in 1913; he regarded it as one of the most important works for understanding Kafka. Probably at his suggestion Jolas began by translating it as 'The Sentence' for *transition* 11, February, 1928. This was the first time that any of Kafka's works appeared in English. In his note on the contributors to that issue, Jolas commented on the state of Kafka's reputation. 'Franz Kafka, who died several years ago before reaching the age of thirty, was a native of Prague. Most of his work was published posthumously in Germany, where it is only now beginning to be appreciated' (*t.* 11, p. 151). Unlike Benn and Sternheim, Kafka received no special essay introducing him to *transition* readers. But Jolas was aware from the first of his importance and he received prominent billing in the magazine. In his review of the first year of *transition* Jolas included Kafka among the small group of German writers whose work he considered 'indisputable and magnificent' (*t.* 12, p. 144). 'The Sentence' was among the stories he chose to reprint in *Transition Stories*. Robert Sage wrote in 19/20 that the introduction of Kafka was among the most important achievements of *transition* and in number 22 his work was placed prominently in the list of first publications.

As new Kafka material was published in Germany, *transition* was consistently ahead of other journals in presenting it to America. In England Edwin Muir had taken up the cause of Kafka and has often been given credit along with Max Brod for introducing him to readers of English. In translating the longer novels and complete books and in writing articles about Kafka, Muir's claim may precede Jolas's, but in preparing the way for stories like Kafka's and in presenting the most significant and at the same time most typical of Kafka's short material, Jolas was several years ahead of Muir. Muir did not, for example, publish any translation of Kafka until 1930, two years after 'The Sentence' appeared in *transition*. His translation of *The Great Wall of China* in 1931 came a year after *transition* had published three of the most typical stories of that collection. His edition of 'The Metamorphosis' was not published until 1937 while Jolas began serializing the story in 1936. 'The Housefather's Care' ('Die Sorge des Hausvaters'), which Jolas published in 1938, was not published elsewhere in English until 1946 and Muir's translation did not come out until 1948.

'The Sentence' is a key story in the development of Kafka's great theme of reaction against authority. It was thus an excellent introduction for the other works. The story contains the essence of almost all that Kafka was to produce later. Written in one evening during the period when he was torn between the desire to remain in artistic isolation and the urge to marry his fiancée, Felicia Bauer, and to become a business success, the story dramatizes the conflicts of Kafka's own mind. George Bendemann, a young salesman, finally decides after months of secrecy to write a letter to his isolated friend in Russia to tell him that he is engaged. When his father is told of the decision, he becomes angry and sentences his own son to death by drowning. This sentence is carried out when George commits suicide by jumping from a bridge. Beneath this series of events a whole conflicting network of suppressed guilts and fused identities is concealed. George and his friend seem to be the aggressive and retiring elements of one personality. But the father also has intimate knowledge of the friend and seems unaccountably allied with him. The guilt George feels toward the father is revealed in the arbitrariness of the father's sudden death sentence and George's resulting suicide. It is all a classical Freudian pattern of conflicting urges to overcome the father and to flee from him. Kafka himself admitted that he thought of Freud while writing the story. But the story is more than a conventional piece of realism merely using Freudian motivation to explain the characters. We are not yet in the world of trials, castles, and men changing to insects, but we are already in a mental world with inexplicable connections and events in which the deepest urges and guilt are brought to light without the analysis and commentary of the 'psychological' novel.

For Kafka, the story was an important beginning in a new mode of expression. He wrote in his journal, 'The terrible stress and joy as the story developed itself before me, as I came toward the water. Several times during the night I carried my own weight on my back. How everything can be said, how for all even the most unusual thoughts, a great fire had been prepared in which they disappear and rise up. . . . It is only in this way that one can write, only in such a continuity like this with such a complete opening up of the body and soul.'[1]

By letting the events and characters of the story be determined by his own irrational and contradictory thoughts he could express the guilt, resentment, and bafflement that were in his mind. It was a method that Kafka was to use to greater advantage as he wrote more. He had for the first time found the way to deal with the great conflict between his father and himself that was at the heart of almost everything he wrote.

The importance of this conflict in his work was made clear to *transition* readers by Max Brod in a section of his biography of Kafka published in number 27. There Brod presented to the public for the first time passages of the now famous letter which Kafka wrote to his father in November 1919 to explain his relations with him. Brod, who was living with Kafka at the time the letter was written, describes the obsession with his father that led Kafka to write it. 'Dominating all his youthful impressions, there was the important figure of his father—its importance exaggerated, of course, by Franz's own notion of this supreme importance' (*t.* 27, p. 303). The attitude which Kafka supposed his father had toward him was revealed in fictional statements which Kafka has him make in the letter. He calls his son a 'vermin, which not only pricks, but also sucks the blood for its preservation. . . . You are not fit for life,' he tells him, 'but in order to make it comfortable for yourself, without care and without self-reproach, you prove that I have taken all your fitness for life and have put it into my pockets.' This imagined attitude of his father, Brod, says, is 'an explanation through which Franz Kafka's story, "Metamorphosis" as well as the story, "The Sentence" become understandable in their genesis' (*t.* 27, p. 306).

Brod rejects the idea that there is nothing more in the stories than the projection of Kafka's own Oedipal complex. There is a great deal of that, but the stories he says are also 'something more'. The father figure has become for Kafka a central image in which many other things are also included. He quotes Kafka as saying that all his words are an 'Attempt at flight from the father' (*t.* 27, p. 312).

Even before the explanation by Brod in the last issue, readers of *transition* would have been able to detect the elaboration in 'The Married Couple' (*t.* 21, p. 58) of a theme much like that of 'The Sentence'. Kafka's most impressive working out of this theme was 'The Metamorphosis' which appeared serially in *transitions* 25, 26, and 27. There the elements of inadequacy and retirement from society, alienation from the family, and guilt at challenging the family authority are all united in Gregor Samsa's condition of becoming an insect. The method which he had found when he wrote 'The Sentence' is still being exploited, but in this story it has been pushed a great deal farther than in the earlier ones. Gregor Samsa's change is presented without any mechanism such as a dream that invites the reader to suspend disbelief. The story claims for the strange events a reality absolutely equal with any account that one might read in the newspaper. In this respect it was another important step in establishing the kind of literature free from naturalism that Jolas advocated. It avoided any problem of fidelity to ordinary events, but did not become merely the depiction of abstract thought processes and never degenerated into a rational analysis of irrational emotions.

Even in the stories that deal primarily with a family situation, Kafka's works describe unexplained events with wider implications. In his longer works these implications overshadow the personal conflicts. The two stories from *Beim Bau der Chinesischen Mauer* which Jolas translated along with 'The Married Couple' for *transition* 21 emphasized this aspect of his work. They deal with a larger, inexplicable accountability. In them the whole order of the universe seems to call the characters to judgement for ostensibly minor acts. 'An Everyday Confusion' gives readers an abstract in miniature of the kind of causal connections at work in *The Castle* and *The Trial*.

The one page story tells of a salesman, A, who travels to another city to meet with a customer, B, but misses him and returns home. At home he finds that B has been waiting there for him all day. Hurrying upstairs to see him, A breaks his leg. While he is lying there, B, who now knows that A has arrived, leaves. At the end of the story we find out that A had passed B on his way out of his house that morning but had been in too great a hurry to notice him. Adding to the confusion, is the fact that the most elementary relationships of time and space are not constant. On one occasion it takes ten minutes to travel between towns, the next time ten hours, the next only a second.

There is a kind of irrational justification in all of this, in that A who earlier overlooked B is overlooked by B in the end, but still a strong element of malignant chance remains in the story. Why should the paths of the two men cross so futilely? Why should a journey take so long at one time and at another be so short? Why should A fall down mounting the stairs and why would the patience of B give out just at that moment? It all suggests that we live in a world either so perverse or so absolutely just that our normal perceptions of it cannot begin to make it intelligible.

'A Knock at the Farm Gate' in the same issue is a similar exploration of consequences disproportionate to their causes. Two other very short pieces by Kafka published in *transition* also have implications more metaphysical than psychological. A piece in *transition* 23 entitled simply 'Fragment' is a legend of Prometheus. After centuries of suffering everybody tires of hearing his story, his wound dries up, and he is forgotten. The implication is that even great suffering, no matter how noble its origin or how bravely it is borne, does not necessarily have importance in the universe. It may well be that the pangs that result from revolt against authority are without any significance at all to anyone except the sufferer. 'The Housefather's Care' in *transition* 27 tells the fear of an old man that the 'Odradek', a unique living machine without origin or function, will remain in the world after he is gone to raise questions for his children just as it has done for him. Both stories create the impression of a world of ominous futility and anguish.

These works by Kafka gave *transition* readers a more than adequate introduction to the scope and variety of his work long before it became popular in America. This 'discovery' was possible only because Jolas had a programme of fostering all kinds of modern romanticism and had kept in contact with the expressionist movement at a time when most people regarded it as dead. He continued introducing Kafka to America by publishing additional sections of Max Brod's biographical material in the *Vertical Yearbook* and by making the first English translation of 'In the Penal Colony' for *Partisan Review* in 1941.[2]

Though it was much more closely allied in the mind of the public with surrealism than with expressionism, *transition* was closer in the outlook and tone to the more eclectic expressionist magazines of Germany than to the programmatic surrealist publications of France. The literature of the expressionist movement published in *transition* has found wider acceptance in English speaking countries than the works of the surrealists. The inclusion of the expressionists must be regarded as one of *transition*'s most enduring accomplishments.

Notes

1 Walter H. Sokel, *Franz Kafka Tragik und Ironie* (Munich, 1964), p. 44.
2 Franz Kafka, 'In the Penal Colony', *Partisan Review*, trans. Eugene Jolas, VIII (March–April 1941), p. 98. The same translation appeared in *Horizon* (March 1942), p. 158.

VII

DADAISM

While Jolas presented surrealism and expressionism primarily as movements related to *transition* but different from it, he was quite willing to consider his theories an extension of dadaism. In the same issue that he made the difference between surrealism and *transition* clear in an editorial, he acknowledged the influence of dadaism and called it 'One of the most important literary movements of our times' (*t.* 22, p. 10).

To understand Jolas's attraction to dadaism, it is necessary to dispel some of the common misconceptions about it. Behind all of their humorous destructiveness the founders of the movement in Zurich in 1916 had an almost religious purpose. This aspect of the movement was emphasized by Dr Richard Huelsenbeck in *Die Geburt des Dada* (*The Birth of Dada*), the official account of the movement written in 1956 by the living founders of dadaism. There Dr Huelsenbeck wrote an imaginary conversation with Hugo Ball, the originator of dadaism who had died in 1936. Reminiscing about his dead friend, Huelsenbeck hears him say,

> As I understood it . . . dadaism was something from which mankind was to profit . . . I would like to ask you . . . not to emphasize the prankish, comical, the circus-like side of dada, but rather what you in your works have called the existential. What we all wanted . . . was not dadaism. Dadaism was only a byproduct of a great piety. . . . Read your own 'Fantastic Prayers' and you will see that the deeper meaning of our activity was suffering. Only through

the suffering from our times and from ourselves was it possible for us to go beyond the borders of our selves. . . . I myself have never done anything in my whole life but believe in God, all the while I have been fighting with the devil. Dadaism was for me no more or less than a hellish mass through which I had to pass in order to come to God.[1]

Of the other founders Hans Arp and Huelsenbeck both shared Ball's attitude to a large extent, while Tristan Tzara generally refused to talk rationally about the aims of dadaism and tried to disrupt any serious conversation about the group.

By the time Jolas began to publish material about the movement, it had fragmented and dispersed. Some of the force had been absorbed by surrealism through Tzara, and to a much lesser extent Arp, but the other members of the group had gone their separate ways. What remained of dadaism as it was first practised in Zurich were public memories of wildly destructive and irrational attitudes and a host of conflicting claims from the members of the group themselves about the purposes and origins of the movement. The public image of dadaism did very little to indicate that it was a positive or important force. Through his talks with Huelsenbeck and Arp and later through reading Hugo Ball's diary, *Die Flucht aus der Zeit*, Jolas understood the deep spiritual revolt that motivated the dadaists. He was in strong sympathy with this attitude and set about to help make the public picture of dadaism more accurate and to show its relevance long after it was thought to be dead.

In *transition* 25 Jolas published a special section called 'Dada: 1916–1936'. Under the title 'Dada Lives' Dr Huelsenbeck gave his account of the founding of the movement. Ball, he explained, had begun the movement of 1916 by starting the Cabaret Voltaire as a stage from which the public could be assaulted with irrational readings to the beat of kettle drums. Soon the group had grown to include Hans Arp, Tristan Tzara, Marcel Janco, Dr Huelsenbeck himself and at times other poets and artists who came and went. The group was held together by their opposition to established art and literature. 'All of us were enemies of the old rationalistic bourgeois art which we regarded as symptomatic of a culture about to crumble with the war' (*t*. 25, p. 77). One day while looking through a dictionary for a possible slogan, Ball's finger had pointed to the word 'dada'—'a children's word meaning hobby-horse'. Huelsenbeck had seen the word and exclaimed, 'It's just

made for our purpose. The child's first sound expresses the primitive-
ness, the beginning at zero, the new in our art' (*t.* 25, p. 78).

Huelsenbeck goes on to distinguish his concept of dadaism from that
of Tristan Tzara who in Paris in the early twenties appropriated for
himself the role of spokesman for the movement.

> Tzara did not invent dadaism, nor did he really understand it. Under Tzara
> in Paris Dada was deformed for the private use of a few persons so that its
> action was almost a snobbish one. What Dada really is, and what it still
> means today, can be gauged from the hatred nurtured against it by people
> who would like to turn the history of the world backward. . . . The eternal
> value of Dada can be deduced from the fact that in Germany an exhibition
> of 'Dadaistic Works of Shame and Filth' was organized officially [by the
> Nazis] in order to frighten off the constructive burghers. (*t.* 25, pp. 79–80)

The rest of the section was comprised of Jolas's translations of passages from Ball's *Die Flucht aus der Zeit.* The entries which Jolas chose
show the serious motivations of dada even more than Huelsenbeck's
essay had. On 3 March, 1916, at the very inception Ball had written,
'What we are celebrating is at once a buffoonery and a requiem mass...'
(*t.* 25, p. 73). On 12 June he wrote, 'what we call Dada is a harlequinade'
made of nothingness in which all higher questions are involved . . .'
(*t.* 25, p. 73).

The means by which Ball and the others sought to stimulate the
irrational were important to Jolas, for they were precursors in an attitude almost exactly like his own. On 18 June, 1916 Ball had written in
his diary,

> We have developed the plasticity of the word to a point which can hardly
> be surpassed. . . . We have charged the word with forces and energies which
> made it possible for us to rediscover the evangelical concept of the 'word'
> (logos) as a magical complex of images. . . . (*t.* 25, p. 74)

A separate section of number 25 with the title 'Sound Poems' was
devoted to the portion of the diary in which Ball told how he had
invented ' "Verse Without Words" . . . in which the balancing of the
vowels is gauged and distributed only according to the value of the
initial line' (*t.* 25, p. 159). Two poems by Ball which illustrate his
attempt to work with sound alone to create a contact with the inner
mind had already been published in *transition* 21 before his diary was

available for translation. The first stanza of 'clouds' is indicative of the
rest of Ball's poetry.

> elomen elomen lefitalominal
> wolminuscaio
> baumbala bunga
> acycam glastala feirofim flinsi
> elominuscula pluplubasch
>
> (*t.* 21, p. 304)

The whole poem is a kind of incantation deliberately intended to
disturb the mind's concentration upon conventional meaning. It was a
reaction against the rationalism of the bourgeoisie meant to baffle and
annoy the uninitiated, but also it was a first step toward a metaphysical
experience. On the occasion of his first public reading of these poems,
Ball had spontaneously assumed the role of a priest and begun to chant
in the rhythms of the mass.

Further emphasis was given to Ball's attempts to find religious experience through irrational poetry in number 22 when Jolas reprinted a
chant in 'the ecstatic and hymnic language of gnosis which was used
during the mystic rites' from Ball's book *Das Byzantinishes Christen-
tum* (*t.* 22, p. 83). In number 23 a discussion by Ball of the religious use
of magic rites of incantation appeared. Magic, Ball wrote, is 'the only
worship worthy of divinity. Without the use of magic which builds
the bridge with God man cannot be saved. If he wants to escape error,
decline, extinction, he must strive to become a particle of the Godhead'
(*t.* 23, p. 87).

While presenting the revaluation of the Zurich branch of dadaism
and reviving briefly the works of Ball, *transition* also published the work
of the German branch of the movement. Kurt Schwitters, who had
gone to Zurich in the early stages of dada and brought the teachings of
the group to Berlin, had founded a personal branch of the movement.
While looking at a huge billboard for the *Kommerz Bank*, he had been
struck by the syllable '*merz*'. Like 'dada' it could be used as an ironic
piece of nonsense to satirize the meaninglessness of bourgeois concerns.
At the same time it could also show the interest inherent in the most
commonplace and unpretentious materials. From this idea Schwitters
developed the '*Merzbild*', the collage of found objects frequently using

bits of signs or newspapers with syllables on them. He describes them as 'consisting of mutually incompatible parts, blended into the world of art, with the aid of glue, mud, paper, rags, engine parts, oil paint, lace, etc.'[2] He applied similar principles to poetry and called the results *merz* poems. Thus, under another name, Schwitters continued the tradition of dadaism in his own works and in his *merz* gallery and *merz* press.

Schwitters' main emphasis was upon the potential of materials while the earlier dadaists had emphasized the attack upon rationality and a quest for metaphysical experience. Ultimately, Schwitters too had a larger concern, but his first concern was with the problems of the artist. As he explained, 'all values exist only by virtue of their relation to one another and . . . all limitation imposed upon a material is petty. Out of this recognition I created *Merz* at first as the sum of a single branch of art, *merz* painting, *merz* poetry . . . my final ambition is the unification of art and non-art to result in a universal philosophy of life.'[3]

Even though Schwitters placed more positive value on creating aesthetic works and less upon achieving certain states of mind than the earlier dadaists, he also was trying to write poetry which would call up the irrational. From 1921 when he first heard Raoul Hausmanns' phonetic poem 'fmsbw', Schwitters worked on a long poem '*Sonnatta in Urlauten*' (primordial sonata) which used only sounds and no words.

transition presented selections of all of the several kinds of poetry which Schwitters wrote. 'priimiitittiii' exemplified the primarily visual arrangement of letters, 'Ann Blossom Has Wheels', the first *merz* poem, showed his technique of literary collage of found phrases, and 'Lanke Tr. Gl.' illustrated the technique of the 'primordial sonata'. Reproductions of his painting and sculptures also were published in *transition* and in number 24 a description of the strange, dadaistic *Merzhaus* that he had constructed. He also provided an original woodblock for the cover of number 18.

Schwitters, Ball, and Huelsenbeck were not intimately associated with *transition*; Hans Arp, both an original founder of dadaism and a signer of the 'Poetry is Vertical' manifesto, was a more direct link between the magazine and dadaism. He became a frequent contributor to the magazine in 1930 after he and Jolas began to meet with Carl Einstein to discuss ways to counter the spirit of Nazism.

A reproduction of one of his paintings had appeared in *transition* 6. In number 7 his poem 'The Light-Shunning Paradise' had been published. Both gave primary importance to the medium in which he was working and the forms suggested by it. 'The Light-Shunning Paradise' deals with the alphabet itself.

> we wrap the a the e the i the o in water
> turned on a lathe
> and only the u we leave unwrapped
> we know the feminine a b c by heart
> anna bertha clara e t c (*t.* 7, p. 130).

Later works, in this same spirit, began with number 21. His cover for that issue, his signature on the 'Poetry is Vertical' manifesto and the publication of selections from his diary signalled the new alliance. Arp's wife, Sophie Taeuber-Arp, designed the cover for the next issue. In *transition* 23 Carola Giedion-Welcker discussed 'New Roads in Modern Sculpture' with special reference to pictures of Arp's work. In number 24 Arp's sculpture 'Human Concretion' was used as the illustration for James Johnson Sweeney's essay 'Seeing and Representation' a discussion of abstract art. Number 26 contained Arp's poem 'The Skeleton of the Day', and number 27 had two of his French poems, '*Porte—Nuage*' and '*L'Age l'Eclair la Main et la Feuille*'.

In the sections of Arp's diary which Jolas translated for *transition* 21 Arp provided a defense of non-objective art which is central to the aesthetics of *transition*.

> man is a beautiful dream. man lives in the sagalike country of utopia where the thing-in-itself tap-dances with the categorical imperative. today's representative of man is only a tiny button on a giant senseless machine. nothing in man is any longer substantial. the safe-deposit vault replaces the may night. how sweetly and plaintively the nightingale sings down there while man is studying the stock-market. (*t.* 21, p. 190)

Despite this perversion, man still thinks of himself as a great important being.

> man thinks he is related to life. gladly this big-mouthed frog calls himself a son of light. but light dwells magnificently in the sky and chases man far from its path. only as a murderer is man creative. he covers with blood and

mud everything within his reach. only the physically unfit among men compose poems pluck the lyre or swing the paintbrush.

Man's corrupted nature in turn affects his art.

in art too man loves a void. it is impossible for him to comprehend as art anything other than a landscape prepared with vinegar and oil or a lady's shanks cast in marble or bronze. every living transformation of art is as objectionable to him as the eternal transformation of life. straight lines and pure colours particularly excite his fury. man does not want to look at the origin of things.

It is this resistance to seeing what is beyond man's puny nature that leads people to misunderstand modern art and misname it.

man calls abstract that which is concrete. . . . i understand that he should call a cubist picture abstract because parts have been abstracted from the object which served as a pretext for the picture. but a picture or plastic for which no object was pretexted i find as concrete and as perceptible as a leaf or stone. (*t.* 21, p. 191)

Part of the problem as Arp saw it was that art has been considered as an imitation for nature for too long. 'i love nature but not its substitute. illusionistic art is a substitute for nature' (*t.* 21, p. 191).

Arp's rejection of contemporary society and its desire for what he called 'illusionistic art' in favor of a deepseated psychological force connected to eternal nature was in general the same feeling which Jolas was trying to harness in the verticalist movement. Verticalism was more obviously serious than dadaism and more positive, but as the close alliance with Arp indicates, the philosophical foundation and many of the methods advocated by Jolas were very much in the same tradition as dadaism. The poetic technique which grew out of this attitude has not led to great poetry. The incantory verse of Ball, Arp, Schwitters, and Jolas is almost completely unread today. Nevertheless the experiments with this kind of verse and the parallel between them and non-representational sculpture and painting is an important part of the literary atmosphere of the 1920s and 1930s. The discussion of theory and the presentation of the tradition in *transition* helps to make the efforts of these and other writers more understandable. Nowhere else is this tradition so well displayed as in *transition*.

Notes

1 Hans Arp, Richard Huelsenbeck, and Tristan Tzara, *Die Geburt des Dada* (Zurich, 1957), p. 14.

2 *Dada Monographie einer Bewegung*, ed. Willy Verkauf (St Gallen, 1958), p. 113.

3 *Ibid.*, p. 109.

Part 3

THE
FIGURES OF THE CAUSE

VIII

transition's REVOLUTIONARIES

English and American authors had no strong tradition of participation in movements with leaders, official organs, programmes and manifestos. Even if there had been such a tradition, there was not enough agreement among Jolas's major contributors to have brought them together as active exponents of a single movement based upon his manifestos. In attempting to accommodate the large literary trends of Europe and the practice of writers he admired to his own opinions, Jolas wrote statements too closely tailored to his own needs to be widely accepted by other writers. And as he later admitted, his pronouncements were frequently 'resounding' and 'prolix.'[1] Jolas did find signers for his manifestos, and some followers, but the contributors to *transition* who have made the greatest impact remained, in spite of important similarities, almost totally independent of each other. There was only a general area of agreement more evident in their practice than in public pronouncements.

Among the signers of the manifestos who wrote in English, remarkably few produced literature connected with the programme of the magazine. Many of them (Ronald Symond, Harold Salemson, Leigh Hoffman, and Douglas Rigsby) were not primarily authors at all but editors or newspaper reporters who signed only to show sympathy. *transition*'s associate editors, Robert Sage, Stuart Gilbert, and James Johnson Sweeney, did make at least one contribution of creative material each but they were primarily critics and their contributions were also only incidental excursions into fiction and poetry.

Kay Boyle was one of *transition's* most frequent contributors and one of its most faithful defenders, but the pieces she published in *transition* did not reflect the tenets of the manifestos. Her stories deal with realistic subject matter in normal syntax and a normal vocabulary.

Kay Boyle's husband, Laurence Vail, wrote three stories which did depart from realism. One of them, 'Gaspar Loot', did celebrate the 'HINSURRECTION' of the word (*t*. 21, p. 318). Vail was primarily a painter, though, and his writing amounted to only a minor contribution.

Whit Burnett, the founder of *Story* magazine in 1931, contributed five stories dealing freely with dreams and other unusual phenomena and employing neologisms. His surrealist scenario, 'Home Edition', in which the parts are played by sections of a daily newspaper was a direct outgrowth of Jolas's theories. His wife Martha Foley also wrote a brief piece in the new style. But neither of them can be considered important to *transition*; their interest was ultimately in the more traditional short story and not in revolutionizing English. Their editorial policy at *Story* was to accommodate all short fiction whatever its style, and particularly to provide a place for the kind of material that did not interest *transition*.

The Irish Catholic poet, Thomas McGreevy, was seriously committed to the search for metaphysics through literature when he signed the 'Poetry is Vertical' manifesto. His own contribution, 'Treason of Saint Laurence O'Toole' (*t*. 21, p. 178), displays a wish to dispense with reality and go directly to an inner vision. McGreevy soon discovered, though, that Jolas's programme was too unorthodox to be compatible with his devout Catholicism and he did not make further contributions.

The most active adherent of the programme was, of course, Jolas himself. He published more than fifty pieces of his own fiction and poetry in *transition*. His works range widely in form and content, reflecting his always evolving critical theories. At first his contributions were relatively conventional. In *transition* 3 and 4 he published a series of poems from two larger, autobiographical groups called 'Nocturnes' and 'Frontier'. These poems mix real scenes from his childhood in Lorraine with fantasy in highly romantic terms, but they do not yet depart entirely from external description. Even at this early stage there were already some stanzas in which words were linked in syntactically

correct but semantically unusual combinations that characterize surrealistic writing:

> and words drift in illuminated by a singing hand
> that holds a fever in the strings of a broken
> darkness (*t*. 3, p. 123)

In 'Monologue' in number 6 Jolas gave up the background of a
realistic situation to describe the purely mental events. He did not
remain with this purely free associative style, but also experimented
with more structured visionary works which often took the form of
mental quests for elusive female figures who hold the key to wisdom
or contentment as in 'Construction of the Enigma' (*t*. 15, p. 56) or
'Walk Through Cosmopolis' (*t*. 8, p. 133).

Meanwhile, beginning in number 6 Jolas had begun to publish his
attempts at writing in an 'Ur-Language' that was not a limited cultural
inheritance but his own direct expression of the unconscious.

> Oor forests hear thine voice it winks
> Ravines fog gleamen and the eyes
> When night comes dooze and nabel sinks
> Trowm quills unheard and lize. (*t*. 8, p. 145)

A number of the words like 'dooze' are Jolas's own concoctions, but
'nabel' is obviously a modification of the German word '*Nebel*' ('fog')
and 'Trowm' unites English 'down' and 'town' with German '*Traum*'
(dream) while 'lize' joins English 'lies' and German '*leise*' (quietly).

In 'Intrialogue' in *transition* 22 Jolas introduced completely trilingual
poetry in which he allowed his thoughts to be expressed in whichever
of his three main languages seemed most natural to the thought.

> Chrismata?
> Our ducts are full of heartling hour,
>   denn unheimlich ist die Asphaltnacht
>   ohne Birken
> La nuit est devenue un masque-cuir. (*t*. 22, p. 21)

Even though he had reverted to a poetry that used only words from
conventional languages, Jolas did not give up his search for a language
of the mind, as is evident from 'Incantation' which goes even farther

toward dispensing with conventional meaning than his early experiments of this type.

> lilla mo málilla istoon tl lássa
> minna thone néenuna glústamilóo
> miélavo gróla atlántu ganásta
> il fait chaud dans la neigeade de ta nuit
> (*t.* 25, p. 13)

None of the modes which Jolas tried in the magazine was entirely successful in attracting widespread recognition. Although Jolas's command of English was essentially that of a native speaker, his use of it is sometimes coloured by his complex linguistic background in ways that make it difficult for readers with only the heritage of the English language and its relatively restrained literary tradition to accept. For example, he frequently links two words together to form a new one with suggestions of both as in 'starspace'. While the principle works well in German to give a more complex meaning, it can appear laboured in English or lead to unnatural sentence rhythms. Words like 'dark', 'doom', 'dream', 'cry', 'night', 'despair', 'gloom', and 'hunger'—common in Jolas's poetry—might arouse little notice in French or German poetry, but they appear highly dramatic and emotional in an English context. These difficulties are heightened by the fact that in his search for a means to express the unconscious Jolas moved rapidly from mode to mode.

Apart from the approval of his friends and limited support from other little magazine editors like Charles Henri Ford and Ernest Walsh, Jolas's poetry has largely been ignored in English. Nor has he found a place among the national poets of France or Germany, though he has been the subject of critical articles and radio broadcasts in those languages. The circumstances of his trilingualism have left Americans, French, and Germans uncertain as to the national category he belongs in. This lack of a clearly defined place in a national tradition and his use in much of his work of all three of his languages left Jolas a poet without countrymen for an audience. His trilingual background, which made for such brilliant editing, almost precluded his finding acceptance as a poet. Jolas belonged to the small but growing number of multi-national and multi-lingual artists in the twentieth century whose circumstances have forced them to exist outside the cultural mainstream of their native lands. This tradition was defined by Carola Giedion-Welcker in her German-French anthology, *Les Poètes à l'écart, Anthologie der Beseitigen* where Jolas is represented along with Hans Arp, August Stramm, Kurt Schwitters, Pablo Picasso, and others. The fact that Jolas has found limited recognition as a poet is of less significance than the fact that, as an editor, he was able to recognize, assemble, and provide introductions to many of the best works of literature of the century. His major achievement was as an editor.

Another of the signers of the manifesto, Lincoln Gillespie, attracted attention at the time far greater than warranted by the circumstances of his relationship to the magazine. A young high-school mathematics teacher from Philadelphia, Gillespie had come to Paris to lead the expatriate life. He frequented the famous cafés of Montparnesse like Café du Dôme and La Coupole where he assailed all comers with his strange theories of writing. For opponents of *transition* he became a symbol of the worst that the literary revolutionaries in Paris could offer.

He wanted desperately to be a writer as current and innovative as any and deliberately created his style from a combination of Gertrude Stein's and Joyce's techniques, though the greatest influence was from Joyce. When he thought he had perfected his new style, he went to the *transition* office where he talked with Elliot Paul who looked at his work and accepted it for publication. Paul's acceptance of Gillespie's work was more an act of bravado than a serious assessment of its lasting literary worth and his pieces were generally considered a joke. Gillespie, however, took himself seriously. Samuel Putnam reports that on the evening the issue in which he was first published appeared Gillespie parted from his wife because she was no longer his intellectual equal now that he had made *transition*.[2] The story which Putnam tells is apparently true. It has been used by ill-wishers as evidence that *transition* was the work of a set so fanatically devoted to literary innovation that they lost sight of all other values. The incident does, of course, say a great deal about the values of Gillespie, but it would be a mistake to assume that the values of Gillespie were those of *transition* simply because he appeared there.

Gillespie was not the complete fool that Putnam's anecdote makes him seem. His method of writing, though peculiar, is not unintelligible. Gillespie explained it in 'Textighter Eye-Ploy or Hothouse Bromidick?'

The question raised by the title is whether writing should continue to be the old 'hothouse bromides' or new kinds of texts which employ the eye more. Gillespie contends that if grammar is ignored, redundant words left out, and new compound words invented, writing can be a better means of communication.

> I assert-venture that there are 1–5 nick-Ideate particles, Image-PeerFlints grammarwise unpresentable, even ungetatable—wriggle-or-dent-IN Sculp-Fillers of each centrosomicant MindMonent, the which would, given steNeoALLOW-Utterance, come through, to teemly convoke *vraies idéographes d'intéret*—ideographs knit with byProduct-Addits not only FORMstressive, also Context-so. (*t.* 12, p. 174)

That is, if writing could contain indications of what the mind had gone through in the process of forming an utterance, it could convey both the form and context of ideas better. When, for example, Gillespie writes of 'SteNogriphs' one can see that he is combining the ideas of writing that is short, rapid, new, allows a special grip on the material it expresses, has elements of graphic presentation and is in some way connected with Gertrude Stein's writing. (The connection is with her earlier works like *Three Lives* where she was more concerned with representing consciousness exactly than with the later, more abstract works in *transition*.)

The basic assumption of Gillespie that language could be changed to express thought more exactly was correct. There is no doubt that one gets a more detailed idea of Gillespie's thoughts through this kind of writing than if he had written in conventional style. He has not, however, faced the question of the relationship of this writing to the reader. Even though the method involves the reader in the author's mental processes more than conventional prose, it also inhibits his own subliminal responses to the material by determining the direction they shall take more than normal prose does. To try to control the response of the reader in this way is not in itself wrong; the validity of the technique depends upon the quality of the mind in control. Gillespie's works fail not because of the method, which was in part the method of *Finnegans Wake*, but because the mental processes they depict are not particularly interesting.

The failings of Gillespie are not simply madness nor are they the failings of *transition*. His works move in the direction toward which *transition* encouraged experimentation, but they are not the best examples of that experimentation and they were never hailed as such in *transition*. Only the sensationalism that surrounded Gillespie made him appear so important to *transition's* critics.

Harry Crosby was another enthusiastic supporter whose personal life attracted so much public attention that for its more sensation-loving critics he became a convenient symbol of *transition*. Crosby, an American, an heir to part of the J. P. Morgan fortune, had come to Paris with his wife Caresse to escape becoming a Boston banker. As he grew away from his Boston background, he came more and more to search for intense experience in literature as well as in life. They set up The Black Sun Press where they published deluxe editions of their own works along with some of the century's best authors.

Under the influence of surrealism and his readings in Egyptian mythology, Crosby developed a private mystique of sun worship. For him the sun represented the source of all life to which everything must ultimately return. Passionate experience, dreams, sexual orgasm, and death were man's means of access to this great power. The point of life was to live and dream at a fever pitch and to die at the height of passion. The result was a strangely positive personal cult of suicide which he expounded in several lyrical prose pieces like 'Hail Death' in *transition* 14. In 'Hail Death' Crosby urged:

> [Die] at the right time, when your entire life, when your soul and your body, your spirit and your senses are concentrated, are reduced to a pin-point, the ultimate gold point, the point of finality, irrevocable as the sun, sun-point, then is the time . . . enter upon coition with the sombre Slave-Girl of Death . . . in order to be reborn. . . . (*t.* 14, p. 169)

He saw himself and others like him as different from the generation of 'hollow men' defined by Eliot.

> . . . for the Seekers after Fire and the Seers and the Prophets (hail to you O men of transition!) and the Worshipers of the Sun, life ends not with a whimper, but with a Bang. . . . (*t.* 14, p. 170)

Crosby expressed his solidarity with *transition* in practical ways as well as in his writing. In the spring of 1928 he sent Jolas a cheque for $100 'to send to the poet who in your judgement has written the best poem in the first twelve numbers of *transition*. But for God's sake, don't make a prize out of it. Instead of going to some fathead organization,

I should like this small amount to go to someone who will spend it on cocktails and books rather than on church sociables and lemonade. If you accept this, please forget it as quick as possible' (*t.* 19/20, p. 228). Jolas did not give the award to one person, but paid 'a few writers who needed the money' whom he had previously been unable to pay. The next spring when Jolas needed outside financial help to continue with *transition*, he turned to Crosby, who again responded generously (*t.* 19/20, p. 229).

From then until his death a year later Crosby became a close supporter of *transition*, signing the 'Revolution of the Word Manifesto' and writing an essay 'The New Word' (*t.* 16/17, p. 30) and a 'Short Introduction to Words' (*t.* 18, p. 206), in its defence. He also contributed accounts of dreams and a photograph of some sculpture he had made (*t.* 18, p. 252). Out of his connection with *transition* also came a number of books by *transition*'s contributors published in the Black Sun Press. They include a collection of Kay Boyle's *Short Stories*, Joyce's *Tales Told of Shem and Shaun*, Crane's *The Bridge*, and Jolas's *Secession in Astropolis*.

More than anything else Crosby is remembered for his death. On 11 December 1929, in New York he acted out his sun-worship by commiting suicide with a married woman whom he called 'The Fire Princess'. The event was front page news. It was taken as further proof that the dissolute life of the Parisian expatriates led to no good. Since he had been associated with *transition*, the magazine also absorbed some of the scandal. The immediate comments were reinforced three years later in 1934 when Malcolm Cowley in *Exile's Return* depicted Crosby's involvement with 'The Revolution of the Word' as the determining factor in his death. In his diary, Crosby had written, 'The first of October is the day I should like to die on, only not this year. But I must remember what Jolas said, "that time is a tyranny to be abolished."'[3]

Cowley took this as evidence that Jolas's teaching filled Crosby's mind in the last months of his life and finally led him to his death. The suicide, however, came four months after 'The Revolution of the Word' proclamation was signed and it took place on the other side of the Atlantic from Jolas. The interpretation of the statement calling time a tyranny was, moreover, a product of Crosby's own preoccupation, and not of any interpretation Jolas had given to it. Nevertheless, Cowley generalized, a bit sanctimoniously, 'His death, which had seemed an act of isolated and crazy violence, began to symbolize the decay from within and the suicide of the whole order with which he had been identified.'[4]

The reaction in *transition* to Crosby's death was not at all like Cowley's. A memorial section including tributes by Kay Boyle, Stuart Gilbert, Hart Crane, Philippe Soupault, Archibald MacLeish and selections from 'Sleeping Together', a collection of dreams by Crosby in poetic prose, appeared in 19/20. Miss Boyle, Stuart Gilbert, and MacLeish all emphasize the intensity and courage of Crosby's life; Crane emphasizes the access to vision in death, while Soupault's short note tries to find the cause of the suicide in a willingness to be a 'victim without protest' (*t.* 19/20, p. 232). Jolas speaks mostly of Crosby's generous spirit. None of them appears attracted to his cult of suicide. They see his death as a personal tragedy, not as a symptom of 'decay' in which they all shared. *transition* itself was to continue for eight more years during which it would publish some of the most important material ever to appear in it.

Criticis like Putnam and Cowley who have judged *transition* solely by its manifestos and their more vocal adherents have consistently misunderstood the nature and importance of the literary revolution which was accomplished by the magazine. The real revolutionaries in *transition* were not the young men who wrote the experimental pieces full of neologisms called for in the manifestos, but Joyce, Gertrude Stein, Samuel Beckett, Hart Crane and Dylan Thomas—major writers who achieved in English new freedoms like those the surrealists and expressionists had won in French and German. Without ever attacking Pound, Eliot, imagism or the practitioners of the modern psychological novel, these writers replaced some of the most basic principles of the modern movement by writing works based on a new set of assumptions about subject matter, form and the medium of expression.

By 1927 most moderns were smug in the assumption that they had done away with the literature of the exterior. Joyce in his early works, Virginia Woolf, Sherwood Anderson, Eugene O'Neill, William Faulkner, D. H. Lawrence, Katherine Anne Porter and many less important figures had all penetrated the surface to show the minds of their characters in greater detail than ever before in literature. Few of them, however, were in any way concerned about how much their works were still determined by the necessity to represent the external world

realistically. For every set of mental phenomena in their works there is
a character presented in a more or less naturalistic environment. The
end of the mental presentation is to explain the character's actions in
that world. Character of any sort is almost entirely absent from Miss
Stein's later works. *Finnegans Wake*, Beckett's stories (and later his
plays), Dylan Thomas's prose, all present internal material directly for
its own sake, with little attention to the external stimuli which might
determine it and usually without any explanation of its relation to the
exterior world at all. In the terms used by Jung in his essay 'Psychology
and Poetry', the writers are 'visionary' as distinct from the 'psychological' writers who want to 'depict human destinies'.

   In matters of form the *transition* writers also broke away from fidelity
to external models. One of the great discoveries of Ezra Pound's 'men
of 1912' was the use of myth as a principle of structure. As T. S. Eliot
announced in *The Dial*, 'In using myth, in manipulating a continuous
parallel between contemporaniety and antiquity, Mr. Joyce is pursuing
a method which others must pursue after him. . . . It is simply a way of
controlling, of giving shape and significance to the immense panorama
of futility and anarchy which is contemporary history. . . . Instead of
narrative method we may now use the mythical method.'[5] The discovery had become a convention. Not only *Ulysses*, *The Waste Land*,
Pound's *Cantos*, Crane's 'For the Marriage of Faustus and Helen', but
also large numbers of lesser works like MacLeish's 'The Pot of Earth'
had employed this mythical method.

   By the time they were writing for *transition* both Joyce and Crane
had left that method and Beckett, Miss Stein, and Dylan Thomas never
adopted it. In different ways the major *transition* writers all sought
inductively for the order within the material itself. Instead of imposing
pre-existing forms they discovered new forms inherent in the organization of the author's mind or experience (or in the case of Miss Stein in
the formal qualities of the language itself). These intensely personal and
yet recognizable new forms, like those of Kafka, are the new myths
Jolas called for.

   Finally, the *transition* revolution restored the word to a position of
respectability that it had relinquished to the image. In reaction to nine-
teenth-century abstraction and didacticism, the modernist movement
had turned for models to Pound's imagism and Hemingway's terse,
realistic fiction. Like Pound's Mauberly, these writers 'observe the

elegance of Circe's hair / Rather than the mottoes on sundials.' That is, they rejected platitudinous generalizations in favour of the particular details which might suggest much but said nothing discursively. On the surface this attitude would seem to be a rejection of generalizations of all types. In fact, the early moderns do not turn away from formulated restatements but only from the mode of their presentation. They are willing enough to sum up truth, but not just in words. The single compact image as a summary is common to the works of Pound, Eliot, Yeats, William Carlos Williams, and Wallace Stevens. It is almost equally characteristic of the novelists of the first quarter of the century. One may think of Henry James's *Golden Bowl*, Mrs Gould's painting in *Nostromo*, or of the shooting star which crosses the constellation Leo in *Ulysses* and Virginia Woolf's lighthouse. For the most part the *transition* writers avoid this kind of generalization entirely. Miss Stein deliberately excluded any sensory imagery in her later works. Both Crane and Thomas were urged by friends to create unifying images to make their poetry more easily intelligible, and both rejected the suggestions.[6] *Finnegans Wake* is so far from the method that Harry Levin somewhat exaggeratedly claims that it chiefly 'lacks visual imagery.'[7] When they do wish to 'present an emotional complex in an instant of time' (as the imagists defined the function of the image) their devices are more likely to be verbal—a pun or word used so as to play on its fullest etymological suggestiveness.

The stylistic preference for the image was based in part at least upon an assumption about how the mind operates. For the imagists and their followers, the imagination is essentially visual and non-verbal. The image is the 'primary pigment' of the imagination. Words are a secondary and thus an inferior mode of perception. As Pound put it, 'the image is itself speech. The image is the word beyond the formulated language.'[8] In using the image they are no longer dealing in mere artifice of expression but in the primary matter of the mind. The result is that the image, as the form of direct revelation, becomes an object of veneration while the word is seen as debased. As Eliot was to say in *Four Quartets* language is 'shabby equipment always deteriorating'. Words lack the stillness, perfection and unity of a Chinese jar (the image of the image).

In *Finnegans Wake*, Beckett's poems and stories, Thomas's 'Altar wise by owl light' sonnets, and Crane's *The Bridge* the tendency is in the opposite direction. The word, or at least utterance, replaces the image as the primary form of consciousness and the 'Logos' becomes the object of veneration. The *transition* writers show no hostility to language at all. Their attack upon linguistic convention is an effort to make language approximate states of consciousness as it had not done before, but not an effort to reduce language to the sensual data of an image. As a result verbal elaboration, word play, and experimentation replace the understatement and hardening of diction that had prevailed for over twenty years.

In presenting material completely free of the conventional concerns for character and representation, in deriving forms and creating myths from the interior rather than imposing pre-existing forms from without, and in restoring the word to its position of eminence, the writers of *transition* were united. They are the forefront of an important second wave of the modern movement in English. Their appearance in *transition* does constitute a successful literary revolution, but none of these authors was the kind to relinquish much independence to a common cause. Each is different from the others in theory and in practice and each had his own peculiar relationship to the magazine, which must be examined separately if we are to understand 'the revolution of the word' as the important change in attitudes it was and not as a short-lived extravagant call for experimentation.

Notes

1 *Transition Workshop*, ed. Eugene Jolas (New York, 1949), p. 15.
2 Putnam, *Paris was Our Mistress*, pp. 224–25.
3 Cowley, *Exile's Return*, p. 282.
4 *Ibid.*, p. 284.
5 *The Dial*, LXXV, 1923, p. 483.
6 *Complete Poems and Selected Letters*, p. 217, and Thomas to Henry Treece, *Letters*, p. 190.
7 Harry Levin, *James Joyce* (Norfolk, 1960), p. 175.
8 Ezra Pound, 'Vorticism', reprinted in *The Modern Tradition*, ed. Richard Ellmann and Charles Feidelson Jr. (New York, 1965), p. 153.

IX

HART CRANE

It was almost inevitable that Hart Crane's poetry should find its most sympathetic reception in *transition*. More than any other contributor to *transition* Crane shared with Jolas the intense desire to find a way to accommodate transcendent experience with the exciting but disappointing potential of the new technological society. In many ways their hopes for respiritualizing America were the same. In addition, the forms, techniques, and the scope of Crane's attempt to present these hopes in *The Bridge* made his work unsympathetic to the editors still so much concerned with the terse emblematic style of imagism or with the down-to-earth Americanism of Sandburg, Robinson, and Frost. Jolas on the other hand was seeking just such new methods.

Crane always had difficulty finding acceptance for his work. As early as 1924 he had declared himself 'deadly sick of manipulating things with magazines.'[1] By January 1927, he was complaining to his friend Allen Tate, 'I've had to submit [The Dance] to Marianne Moore recently, as my only present hope of a little cash. But she probably will object to the word "breasts", or some other such detail. It's really ghastly. I wonder how much longer our market will be in the grip of two such hysterical virgins as *The Dial* and *Poetry*.'[2]

Relief came early in 1927 when Jolas began to solicit Crane's work for *transition*. Jolas's letter requesting a contribution for the magazine and permission to translate several of Crane's poems for his *Anthologie de la Nouvelle Poésie Américaine* was so laudatory that Crane proudly sent it on to his mother. He was not disappointed by the first issue. 'A copy of *transition* 1 has reached me', he wrote to Allen Tate on 27 March, '—and I'm enthusiastic about it. By all means send Jolas some poems—and why not your article on Marianne Moore? It doesn't spoil resale of ms. over here, you know. *transition* has some weak contribs, of course, but the majority is respectable. Joyce, Gertrude Stein, Williams, Winters, Laura [Riding], Larbaud, Gide, MacLeish, Soupault, etc. It's a wedge that ought to be used. Malcolm [Cowley] also ought to send things—and it seems to have a proofreader!'[3]

Two days after the enthusiastic letter about *transition*, Crane again wrote Tate about other hopeful signs. 'The ice is breaking—for both of us, as near as I can see—in several different quarters—and I'm beginning to detect many salutary signals. Apparently our ideas and idiom evokes [sic] some response—however slow.'[4] Crane was too sanguine in his expectations, for the acceptance of his work was grudging and support rare in the years before his death. *The Calendar of Modern Letters*, the only other magazine in which he had much confidence, was defunct by the end of 1927. T. S. Eliot accepted 'The Tunnel' for *Criterion* and later urged him to contribute more, but after a long delay Eliot rejected what Crane did send. In 1927–30, the years when he completed *The Bridge*, Crane's only public support came from *transition*.

In closer connection with his own programme of fostering a modern American romanticism, Jolas made special arrangements to ensure a positive review of *White Buildings*, published sections of *The Bridge* along with relevant background material, and published nearly all of the shorter poems of Crane to appear in magazines between 1927 and his death in 1932. In addition he introduced Crane to Harry and Caresse Crosby who agreed to publish the first edition of *The Bridge* in a luxurious, limited edition and thereby provided the impetus for him to overcome his despair about the poem and finish it.

The editorial response to *White Buildings* in *transition* is in strong contrast to the response in *The Dial* and *Poetry*. In the same letter to Tate in which he praised the first issue of *transition*, Crane complained of the treatment given his book in *The Dial*. Conrad Aiken, *The Dial*'s regular critic, had called the poems 'specious' and 'intellectual fakes'.[5] The review in *Poetry* was highly laudatory, but it was counterbalanced by an announcement dissociating *Poetry* and its editors from the high praise Yvor Winters had bestowed on Crane. Jolas, on the other hand, had taken steps in *transition* to counterbalance a negative review by Kay Boyle with a positive one by Laura Riding.

Miss Boyle, who later became a close friend of Crane's, accused him of being 'done with life' and found his poems 'false', 'dull', and 'humorless' (*t.* 10, p. 136). Though Miss Boyle was a respected friend and contributor, Jolas would never have allowed her negative opinion of Crane to stand unchallenged. He had noticed Crane's early work in *The Pagan* and *Double Dealer* and been impressed by it. As Crane matured, Jolas saw him as an outstanding American poet. In his letters he had called *White Buildings* an 'immense' book.[6] Later he said privately, 'After Crane America has no poets.'[7] His sympathies were with Miss Riding who saw the theatricality of Crane's words not as something false but as a means of exhibiting a deeper expression of self than poets normally do. 'There is', she wrote, 'something heroic, moving, beautiful in this role: the saying self going through a part written by itself for itself—a sacrifice of identity to eloquence. It has a passion which, though theatrical, the discursive saying self cannot match' (*t.* 10, p. 140). Crane was baffled by the exchange; he was irritated by 'Kay Boyle's explosive boil' but unable to decipher Miss Riding's defence.[8]

By the time *transition* began to appear, Crane had left *White Buildings* behind and was struggling to finish *The Bridge*. The first sections of the poem to be published appeared in June 1927. The 'Dedication to Brooklyn Bridge' appeared in *The Dial* while *transition* published 'Harbor Dawn' and 'Cutty Sark'. Four months later *transition* published the 'Van Winkle' section. After the dedication in *The Dial*, Crane probably did not identify poems he sent out as parts of *The Bridge*. Though Crane almost certainly explained to Jolas that the poems were part of *The Bridge*, Jolas did not pass this information on to his readers.

While Crane's friends like Tate, Yvor Winters, and Malcolm Cowley were beginning to raise objections about *The Bridge*, *transition*, without referring directly to the poem by name, was developing a remarkably specific programme to prepare readers for the themes and methods of the poem. The American romanticism which Jolas advocated in the early issues of *transition* had already provided a sympathetic context for *The Bridge*. *transition* had grown out of an urge to renew American art by linking it with the Romantic tradition of Europe. Jolas had seriously considered calling his magazine *The Bridge*.[9] The emphasis was different but the urge to find a means of renewing an inadequate present by joining it to something that transcended it was central to the conception of both men. In 'Suggestions for a New Magic', Jolas had listed Crane as one of those who were showing the way to 'new words, new abstractions, new hieroglyphics, new symbols, new myths' (*t.* 3, p. 179). Crane's 'myth of America', as he referred to *The Bridge*, was an attempt to accomplish for America what Jolas felt necessary for all nations. The problem for both was to counter the negative elements of technological society. As an independent, material factor in life, the machine had been destructive. Linked with a spiritual perspective it could become a great source for renewal. The spiritual values which would redeem mechanization were to be found in the past history of America. The new myth which Jolas sought, and which Crane saw symbolized in Brooklyn Bridge, would form a link between material and spiritual, past and present, present and future.

The reviews and those sections of *The Bridge* which were read appeared in the first issues, the correspondence between Jolas and Crane continued. In *transition* 9 the common hopes of Crane and Jolas were made much more explicit. In that issue Crane published a series of his lyrics which recorded his successful personal struggle to cast off doubts about the possibility of an affirmative vision in the modern world. Jolas's essay 'On the Quest' in that same issue defined his search for a vision in terms almost identical to those Crane had used in his own statement of principles, 'General Aims and Theories'.[10] Jolas calls the problem, 'the attempt to discover a new notion of man' (*t.* 9, p. 191). Crane defines it as 'a reorganization of human evaluations'. To solve the problem they both see the need for 'a new faith' which may take its specific form in America at first but is not necessarily to be confined to American materials. Jolas writes, 'we are struggling for a new faith which may help us create the mythos for which every true artist is waiting today. We hope for an esthetic synthetism in which not only Europe and Asia will coalesce into a new flowering, but to which also the two Americas will bring their vision' (*t.* 9, p. 191). Crane's emphasis is different but his goal is very nearly the same.

> I am concerned with the future of America, but not because I think that America has any so-called par value as a state or as a group of people. . . . It is only because I feel persuaded that here are destined to be discovered certain

as yet undefined spiritual quantities, perhaps a new hierarchy of faith not to be developed so completely elsewhere. And in this process I like to feel myself as a potential factor; certainly I must speak in its terms and what discoveries I may make are situated in its experience.

Both clearly distinguish their new faith from a more shallow futuristic celebration of modern life. Crane declares that his goals cannot be reached 'merely by referring frequently to skyscrapers, radio antennae, steam whistles, or other surface phenomena of our time.' Jolas rejects what he calls 'skyscraper spirituality', as a corollary he also rejects realism as an inadequate 'photographic representation of life' (*t.* 9, p. 194). Crane had referred to realism as 'painting a photograph'. Instead, they seek to achieve a poetry of the absolute through an internalization of the raw material of the modern world: Jolas calls for a 'duality' composed of the physical and the 'hermetic' and Crane refers to it as a 'submission . . . and assimilation of the organic effects' of external phenomena.

The five lyrics which Crane published in *transition* 9 under the title 'East of Yucatan' are the only appearance of this optimistic personal statement. Later in his despair at the failure of America to accept *The Bridge* and achieve the kind of renewal he desired, he tried to conceal the fact that these poems belong together as a single positive statement. It is doubtful that he would have ever exposed his personal hopes publicly at all had he not sensed how close his own aspirations were to those of Jolas.

The poems are the product of his experience on the Isle of Pines in 1926 during the period when his serious doubts that an optimistic poem about modern life could be written had given way to his first period of extraordinary productivity on *The Bridge*. In a letter to Waldo Frank in 1928 Crane identified them as poems belonging together and added 'O Carib Isle' published in *transition* 1 and 'The Air Plant' which was published in *The Dial* in January 1928. The larger poem which Crane planned to make out of these seven poems was never published in any final form, and later editions of Crane's poetry have ignored the unity of the group. Only in *transition* 9 in 'East of Yucatan' are five of the poems arranged to make their underlying themes and images clear.

Many of the events described in the poems actually took place as Unterecker makes clear in his biography, *Voyager*, but they are far more than bits of local colour which 'distracted' Crane from *The Bridge*. He

had sent 'O Carib Isle' to the *Calendar of Modern Letters* along with 'Cutty
Sark' and 'Harbor Dawn' explaining, 'There is a general emphasis on
the marine in all of them, and if you should care to use them all I suggest that the sequence *would chart an interesting curve* of the underlying
element.'[11] At the time when he would have been reworking the poems
for *transition* he wrote to his mother about the similarity between the
tropical scene of 'O Carib Isle' and the 'Ave Maria' section of *The
Bridge*. 'I'm crazy about those Caribbean waters and skies—even if they
are hot! There's a lot of the feeling they give you in the Columbus
poem—don't you think?'[12]

As he was constantly reminding his friends, Crane found the mood
of *The Waste Land* intolerable and conceived of *The Bridge* partly as a
response to it.[13] 'East of Yucatan' is a search for vision couched in terms
of avoiding the parching death from the sun. And as in *The Waste Land*
the symbols of revivification are wind and water, but Crane's poem
ends with an unmistakable rebirth, while Eliot's ends with only a little
hope. Crane uses no anthropological myth for his poem, but adopts as
his metaphor the attempts of a northern visitor to acclimate himself to
the searing heat of a tropical island. Unlike *The Waste Land* which gives
only a sign of relief in distant thunder over the mountains, the tropic
isle of 'East of Yucatan' provides at least a temporary relief of its own
and signs of the greater relief are steadily more evident throughout the
poem.

The first poem of the series to be published was 'O Carib Isle' in
transition 1; it is also the opening poem of the set and would undoubtedly
have been printed first in the series in *transition* 9 had it not already been
published in an earlier issue. It announces the themes of the series in
their most dramatic form. After presenting the white tropic sands as a
scene of death without a single live voice even to mourn, the poet raises
the possibility that by speech 'albeit in another tongue' he may 'gainsay
the unknown death . . .' because 'The wind sweeping the scrub palms,
also is almost kind' (*t.* 1, p. 101). The hope emerges at the end of the
poem that he will be spared the excruciating deaths he has suffered in
the past:

> Let not the pilgrim see himself again
> bound like the dozen turtles on the wharf
> each twilight,—still undead, and brine caked in their eyes,

huge, overturned: such thunder in their strain!
And clenched beaks coughing for the surge again! (*t.* 1, p. 102).

In *The Bridge*, he hoped, the inverted arc of the dying turtle's shell would be replaced by the gracefully arching cables of Brooklyn Bridge rising out of the sea. Even before that poem could be completed, however, the royal palm provided an upward curve of protective shade within the 'East of Yucatan' series itself. But in this first poem of the group there is only hope. The poet must still wait unprotected and not yet enlivened by the force of the great wind which will appear in the final poem. For the present he is 'Slagged of the hurricane' and must 'congeal by afternoons here, satin and vacant.' He has only 'the shell . . . the ember,/Carbolic, of the sun exploded in the sea' (*t.* 1, p. 102),[14] he has only the outward manifestations and diminished former brightness.

'Island Quarry' which appeared as number one of the *transition* 9 version presents the same search for relief and this time the signs are even more promising. At times the island which normally seems so foreboding when it displays its

> . . . fierce
> Profile of marble spiked with yonder
> Palms against the sunset's towering sea, and maybe
> Against mankind.

can change and take on the appearance of a new Atlantis

> In dusk, it is at times as though this island lifted, floated
> In Indian baths.

And when this happens, the path to enlightenment seems open

> At Cuban dusk the eyes
> Walking the straight road toward thunder—
> This dry road silvering toward the shadow of the quarry
> —It is at times as though the eyes burned hard and glad
> And did not take the goat path quivering to the right,
> Wide of the mountain—thence to tears and sleep—
> But went on into marble that does not weep. (*t.* 9, p. 132)

In 'Royal Palm' the images of relief are no longer the straight road toward the thunder and dusk, but the large native tree which gives shade from the hot sun. The 'Green rustlings' of the great palm are 'more-than-regal charities . . . Amid the noontide's blazed asperities' (*t*. 9, p. 133). It is the embodiment of some holy principle because unlike other trees it is beyond the needs of earth.

> Uneaten of the earth of aught earth holds,
> [. . .]
> Forever fruitless, and beyond that yield
> Of sweat the jungle presses with hot love
> And tendril till our deathward breath is scaled—
> It grazes the horizons, launched above
>
> Mortality—
>   (*t*. 9, p. 133)

In addition to the natural shelters like the quarry and the palm, the island offers the northern pilgrim the native population as a symbol of people who have endured the heat. In 'Overheard' the difference between the natives and the foreign visitor who must always seek shelter is treated ironically. The American thinks he is being condescending as he describes two native fishermen. But of the qualities they display he selects just those that make them superior to him. Two of the islanders bought a boat,

> It might as well
> Have been made of—well, say paraffin,
> —That thin and blistered, just a rotten shell.
>   (*t*. 9, p. 134)

Out in the sea among the barracudas the boat stalled and began to leak. Unperturbed, the owners 'sat like baking Buddhas' until the Cayman schooner streaked by and picked them up. Like the speaker of 'O Carib Isle', they are left with a 'shell' vulnerable to the sun (like paraffin) and must wait upon the wind (the sail driven schooner) for their rescue. But their unique blend of patience and high spirits make them indomitable. They come through their exposure untouched.

They're back now on the job at Pepper's.
—Yes, patent-leather shoes, so hot they'd fry
Anyone but these native high-steppers!
(t. 9, p. 134)

Beyond their vitality these island people also have a sublimity described in 'El Idiota'. The poet finds it in a young boy he passes on the way back from the beach. At first he avoids the boy because he is:

. . . daft
With dead lanterns in his head, and it's likely
Fumbling his sex.
(t. 9, p. 135)

But on returning from the hot shore he finds the boy flying a kite:

With a kite-string in one hand, a tin can
In the other, the peeled end tight to his eye.
That kite aloft—you should have seen him scan
Its course, as though he'd clapped midnight to noon sky!
(t. 9, p. 135)

The boy has achieved a kind of miracle of vision that lets him look at the midday sun without being overwhelmed by it. As a result he makes a strong impression on the poet:

I've heard his song
Persist above all reason, and halt serene—
Uncancelled as the stars that sum no wrong.
(t. 9, p. 135)[15]

The wind in the poem does not yet penetrate as it does later in 'The Hour', but it holds the kite aloft and is thus the cause of the boy's vision.

In 'The Hour' the poet has his own vision. Caught in the midst of a hurricane he exalts in the cadence of a crude liturgy made by the blast.

Lo, Lord, Thou ridest!
Lord, Lord, Thy swifting heart

Nought stayeth, nought now bideth
But's smithereened apart!
    [. . .]
Thou ridest to the door, Lord!
Thou bidest wall nor floor, Lord!
               (*t*. 9, p. 136)

Even when he had reaffirmed the success of his struggle for a personal vision by publishing 'East of Yucatan', Crane had still to contend with the possibility that the more public expression of his hopes in *The Bridge* would not be accepted. He feared that his major symbol was not adequate to sum up for his readers all that it did for him. 'However great their subjective significance to me is concerned', he wrote, '— these forms, materials, dynamics are simply non-existent in the world.'[16] A little later he wrote, 'The bridge as a symbol today has no significance beyond an economical approach to shorter hours, quicker lunches, behaviorism and toothpicks. And inasmuch as the bridge is a symbol of all such poetry as I am interested in writing it is my present fancy that a year from now I'll be more contented working in an office than before.'[17]

In *transition* Jolas had gone beyond general statement of the situation facing the American poet to include remarks specifically relevant to *The Bridge* itself. In 'On the Quest' he had forecast indirectly what *The Bridge* would be like. The American poet could 'absorb the rhythms of the indigenous Afro-American and Indian traditions, and find skyscrapers of the fourth dimension he dreams of' (*t*. 9, p. 184). Crane does of course use the indigenous rhythms of America quite consciously in nearly every section of *The Bridge* and he gave his major symbol a mythic dimension beyond its existence in steel and stone. The bridge as it appears in his poem was approached spiritually so as to create what Jolas called in the essay 'a new sense of the vertical' (*t*. 9, p. 192). Crane's own personal sensation of the Brooklyn Bridge was just such a vertical movement: 'I have been able to give freedom and life which was acknowledged in the ecstacy of walking hand in hand across the most beautiful bridge of the world, *the cables enclosing us and pulling us upward in such a dance as I have never walked* . . .'[18] (emphasis added). This was also the feeling he hoped to transmit to his readers. 'The Bridge in becoming a ship, a world, a woman, a tremendous harp (as it does finally)

seems to really have a career. I have attempted to induce the same feelings of elation, etc.—like being carried forward and upward simultaneously—both in imagery, rhythm and repetition, that one experiences
in walking across my beloved Brooklyn Bridge.'[19]
   Even details of the imagery of *The Bridge* appear in 'On the Quest'.
Jolas thinks of the cinema as a possibility for propagating a vision. 'The
cinema, in spite of the imbecility surrounding its present evolution, can
give us possibilities for hallucinations that check successfully the pedan-
try of the puritan' (*t.* 9, p. 195). The first image of a vision in *The
Bridge* is of the movie as an unfulfilled potential for creating a new faith.

> I think of cinemas, panoramic slights
> With multitudes bent toward some flashing scene
> Never disclosed, but hastened to again,
> Foretold to other eyes on the same screen;

Later in his essay Jolas also mentioned the older, historical material that
Crane used. 'The American poet, for instance, to whom his age is a
torture may very well follow the advice of William Carlos Williams
and return to the origins of the American mythology. Here is a species
of American romanticism that evades the dynamism of the present'
(*t.* 9, p. 195).
   Common concerns of Jolas and Crane described theoretically in 'On
the Quest' had been dealt with from the first issue of *transition* in articles
that helped to establish a favourable context for Crane's work. Kay
Boyle reviewed Williams' book *In the American Grain* very favourably
for the first issue. Before Williams, she wrote, 'chronology has been a
matter of national moralities and geographical differences and it has
excluded too much. The only qualities which could authenticize historical fact have gone unrecognized: the contemporaneous sense of
place; the feel of cloth as it must have been, for instance, to fingers
which knew it from their own loom' (*t.* 1, p. 139). In Williams, though,
there is a new immediacy and a whole new approach. For him, the
American tradition has 'four dimensions; and, in incident, dimensions
of an unfixed value which leaves them free to adaption to the manner
of life which existed at the time each incident functioned' (*t.* 1, p. 139).
Crane also saw America as 'four dimensional' and felt the need to rediscover history in a more direct way. Several months after Miss Boyle's

article appeared, Crane wrote his patron Otto Kahn, 'It seemed altogether ineffective from the poetic standpoint to approach this material
from the purely chronological angle—beginning with, say, the landing
of "The Mayflower", continuing with a resumé of the Revolution
through the conquest of the West, etc. . . . What I am after is an assimilation of this experience, a more organic panorama, showing the con-
tinous and living evidence of the past in the inmost vital substance of
the present.'[20]

In the course of her review Miss Boyle also helped to establish
Pocahontas as material for a mythical treatment like that Crane made
of her in *The Bridge*. She quoted a contemporary description of the
Indian princess which Williams had included in *In the American Grain*.
'Pocahuntus, a well-featured, but wanton yong girle . . . of the age of
eleven or twelve years, get the boyes forth with her into the market
place, and make them wheele, falling on their hands, turning their
heels upwards, whome she would followe, and wheele so her self, naked
as she was, all the fort over' (*t.* 1, p. 139). This was the same image of a
vital, young, innocent but strikingly unpuritan figure that Crane presented in the 'Powhatan's Daughter' section of *The Bridge*. He called
her 'The natural body of America-fertility'[21] and described the section
as the 'gradual exploration of this "body" whose first possessor was the
Indian.'[22] Crane had already read Williams' book and written most of
the section by the time Miss Boyle's review appeared, but she must
have expressed much of what he felt himself and caused him to realize
that the description of Pocahontas could itself be incorporated in his
poem. He copied that description as it appeared in *transition* number
one, complete with spelling errors, as the epigraph to 'Powhatan's
Daughter'.

Another figure of the American myth that Crane shared with
Williams was the subject of an article by Laura Riding in *transition* 7.
In her article '*Jamais Plus*' Miss Riding argued that Poe had been mis-
interpreted by Williams who had viewed him as a heroic figure fighting
American puritanism and literary parochialism. Miss Riding was not
willing to accept Poe as archetype of the struggling spirit.

> It is to be suggested that the partiality for Poe in modernist criticism is a con-
> fession of that love of 'magnificent meditation', that morbid taste for desola-
> tion and ill-fatedness which is more appropriate to the boyish, melodramatic
> enthusiasm of the penny dreadfuls than to the philosophical depression of

advanced contemporary poetry and criticism—unless these are willing to confess to internal melodrama, as they apparently are not. (*t.* 7, p. 156)

Whether Crane was ready to confess to melodrama is questionable but his conception of Poe was a great deal like Williams'. He wrote Waldo Frank that Williams 'puts Poe and his "character" in the same position as I had *symbolized* for him in "The Tunnel" section.'[23] At the same time Crane's depiction of Poe in that section was not greatly different from Miss Riding's view of him either. While Poe may have exhibited spirit and rejection of the puritan attitudes as Williams said, he had also been a failure and his ghastly appearance in 'The Tunnel' does not depict Poe's failure as magnificent. The final attitude toward Poe in that section is one of questioning.

> And when they dragged your retching flesh,
> Your trembling hands that night through Baltimore—
> That last night on the ballot rounds, did you
> Shaking, did you deny the ticket, Poe?

Since Crane was depicting the failure of the positive aspects which Williams had noted, he could agree with both Williams and Miss Riding. The essay was, therefore, another helpful step in establishing an almost mythological value for Poe as an archetype of American failure.

Jolas and Crane began a more intensive effort to prepare for the appearance of *The Bridge* when Crane went to Paris in early 1929. As Crane expounded his hopes in long discussions with Jolas and as he began to plan details for the Black Sun edition with the Crosbys, he gained confidence and looked again with optimism to the publication of *The Bridge*. *transition* 16/17 under preparation at the time of Crane's visit to France seems to have been conceived of as the climax of the strategy to acclimate potential readers of the full edition to the symbols and method of *The Bridge*. For his part in the issue Crane wrote to the American painter Joseph Stella asking permission for *transition* to reproduce three pictures—'The Bridge', 'The Port', and 'The Skyscraper'— and an essay on Brooklyn Bridge from his monograph, *New York*. In the end the only material by Stella to appear in the issue were his cubistic painting of Brooklyn Bridge and his essay about it. The skyscraper and harbour motifs, both prominent in *The Bridge* were emphasized in the issue not by Stella's paintings but by photographs from the collection of Gretchen and Peter Powel.

The cover of the issue is a photograph from the Powel series of a sky-scraper emphasizing its vertical lines and the open sky above it. The almost black lower part of the photograph contrasts with the light of the sky above. Written vertically across the right side of the picture is the word 'synthesis'. The picture obviously symbolizes the synthesis of modern civilization with spiritual values just as Brooklyn Bridge does in Crane's poem.

The nature of Crane's own particular symbol is stated quite clearly in Stella's essay. Stella was as ecstatic in his evaluation of the Brooklyn Bridge as Crane was:

> BROOKLYN BRIDGE . . . Seen for the first time, as a weird metallic Apparition under a metallic sky, out of proportion with the winged lightness of its arch, traced for the conjunction of WORLDS, supported by the massive dark towers dominating the surrounding tumult of the surging skyscrapers with their gothic majesty sealed in the purity of their arches, the cables, like divine messages from above, transmitted to the vibrating coils, cutting and dividing into innumerable musical spaces the nude immensity of the sky, it impressed me as the shrine containing all the efforts of the new civilization of AMERICA —the eloquent meeting point of all forces arising in a superb assertion of their powers, in APOTHEOSIS. . . . I felt deeply moved, as if on the threshold of a new religion or in the presence of a new DIVINITY. (*t.* 16/17, pp. 87–8)

Stella defines his symbol in detail and presents it in a context com-pletely in accord with the way Crane used it. His essay, like Crane's poem discusses the painfully negative situation of the modern mechani-cal world and regards the bridge as an escape to something higher. He saw New York as an 'oceanic tragic city' (*t.* 16/17, p. 86) just as Crane saw America as a lost Atlantis. His essay presents Poe and the subway in negative juxtaposition to the bridge much in the same way that they appear in 'The Tunnel'; it describes the war as a manifestation of the failure of a mechanical civilization as Crane also does in 'Cape Hatteras'; it talks of the feelings of confinement caused by the skyscraper; and it is even concerned with the buildings as points of light in the dark as they appear in the opening section of Crane's poem. The essay presents the sounds of the harbour as 'strange moanings of appeal from tug boats, guessed more than seen, through the infernal recesses below' (*t.* 16/17, p. 88) in a tone quite similar to the first stanza of the 'Harbor Dawn'.

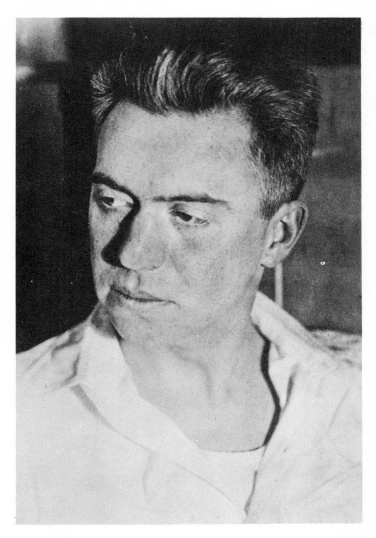

Photograph of Hart Crane by Walker Evans (Courtesy Walker Evans)

'Brooklyn Bridge' by Joseph Stella, which appeared with Hart Crane's 'The Bridge' in *transition* 16/17, 1929

The positive elements of the bridge itself are associated with Walt Whitman whom Stella depicts as a spirit returned to inspire the artist just as Crane does in 'Cape Hatteras'. Even minor details of the bridge, like the traffic lights that shine along its length, are found in Stella's short piece as well as in Crane's 'Proem'.

The aspects of New York which formed a common 'myth' for Crane and Stella were further emphasized in the pictures of Gretchen and Peter Powel which formed the centre section of the issue. They show subway stations, skyscrapers, the harbour, cables stretching upward on great derricks, and lights atop buildings in the night. It is probably not by chance that the opening picture of the series is of an iron fire-escape seen from below with the sky behind it so that it appears to be ascending past the buildings into heaven. Despite the obvious relevance of these materials to *The Bridge* and Crane's part in securing some of them, no mention is made of Crane's poem in the issue. This was probably part of the plan to keep *The Bridge* from too much exposure to criticism until it was completed. It is as if Crane were anxiously preparing an audience but was too unsure of himself to let them know what he was doing.[24]

Beyond publicizing the elements of an American myth and helping to establish Crane's symbols, *transition* also helped to establish the validity of his style. The rejection of his attempt at a new intrinsic form and his radical use of language was a serious hindrance to Crane first in getting his material past editors and before the public and secondly in getting his public to understand. As much as any author Crane was creating a 'Revolution of the Word'. Since he was in Paris when Jolas circulated his proclamation, it was only natural for him to sign. The appearance of the manifesto in the same issue as the material from Stella constituted another part of the *transition* apologia for *The Bridge*. Crane's biographers, Philip Horton and Brom Weber, have said that Crane's signature on this manifesto was the result of a momentary impulse. They go on to argue that it was negated when he repudiated the document by saying that he was drunk when he signed. This private recantation, however, was made back in New York under the pressure of friends like Malcom Cowley, Matthew Josephson, and Gorham Munson who were still in the first flush of their newly discovered social commitment to America and thus antagonistic to the 'mere aestheticism' of *transition*. The explanation that he was drunk does not cover the facts of Crane's relation to Jolas and the manifesto sufficiently. He was in Paris for over a month during which time he became close to Jolas and talked frequently with him. Jolas wrote in his autobiography that in these discussions Crane agreed upon each point of the manifesto.

There is no question that the proclamation presents an aesthetic theory very close to Crane's own. His whole attitude was as the manifesto said that 'The writer expresses, he does not communicate' (*t*. 16/17, p. 13). As he wrote to Miss Monroe, his language frequently depended upon the tangential connotations of words. If people did not have a store of experience that related to his material, the fault was theirs not his. In his poems he sought no descriptive fidelity to the objects of the external world and he made no concessions to the fact that this might cause difficulties for him. Poetry was for him 'a true record . . . of "illumination" ', a means to 'absolute knowledge'[25] toward which he was always working. His poems were true only to the 'a priori reality within' heralded in the proclamation. Thus even when he depicts the real world in detail as in 'The Tunnel' for example, he presents what the manifesto called a 'metamorphosis' of it as it appears through the changed perspective of the visionary. One of Crane's favourite quotations which he repeated to friends was Blake's: 'We are led to believe in a lie/When we see *with* not *through* the eye.'

The pursuit of vision left no room for concern about rules and convention. 'There is only one way of saying what comes to one in ecstasy', he wrote Waldo Frank, 'One works and works over it to finish and organize it perfectly—but fundamentally that doesn't affect one's *way* of saying it.'[26] He was quite willing, as the manifesto said, to 'disintegrate' the words given to him by the 'textbooks and dictionaries' and 'disregard existing grammatical and syntactical laws.' In explaining his poems to Sherwood Anderson, he wrote, 'what I want to get is . . . an "interior" form, a form that is so thorough and intense as to dye the words themselves with a peculiarity of meaning, slightly different maybe from the ordinary definition of them separate from the poem.'[27] He did not, however, go so far as to create wholly new words as did others who published in *transition*. Crane was content to leave words as he found them (he wrote of 'ransacking' the richest writers of the language for words) but to use them in new and unusual combinations. More perhaps than any American poet before him, he wrote from the 'rhythmic hallucination of the word' that Jolas extolled. As he said in a letter to Tate, 'One must be drenched in words, literally soaked with them to have the right ones form themselves into the proper pattern at the right moment. When they come, as they did in "Pastorale" . . . they come as things in themselves; it is a matter of felicitous juggling!'[28]

Like most of the other signers of the manifesto who turned their efforts to connecting external reality with the spirit, Crane too found time 'a tyranny to be abolished.' The whole task of *The Bridge* was to undo history, to redeem the present by linking it with a past that could create a future; to do that he had to make contemporaries of his ancestors. In the poem the unifying mind of the poet inspired by the symbol of the bridge blends modern sailors with Columbus and modern railway bums with Daniel Boone.

Only one of the points of the manifesto was not directly relevant to Crane. He did not in his own work admit the 'litany of words' as an 'independent unit'. He might combine words in response to their connotations but he did not dispense altogether with logical statement. He depended upon what he called 'the logic of metaphor'.[29] In Crane there is always some deliberate referent though it is frequently an extremely personal set of memories or responses at first difficult for the reader to grasp. Crane did not admire the abstract or nonreferential works of others either; while he found Gertrude Stein a pleasant and impressive person, he did not like her work. Probably he accepted this point because he respected such writing as an attempt worthy of defence even though it had failed to affect him personally.

Even more than his adherence to the explicit tenets of the proclamation, Crane's refusal to impose external form and his attitude toward 'the word' as the mode of ultimate experience mark him as one of the major figures of the revolution to create new modes of expression for internal experience.

Crane's use of internal structures as opposed to external structures is illustrated most strikingly in the contrast between *The Bridge* and Eliot's *The Waste Land*. Both poems are attempts to deal with the necessity to find relief from the loss of faith in the modern world. Crane's poem is in many respects a reply to Eliot's. The mythical method which *The Waste Land* did so much to make famous, had also appeared to Crane an important means of dealing with modern material and he had employed it in his poem 'For the Marriage of Faustus and Helen'. But he confessed later in 'General Aims and Theories' that he found that

choice of 'scaffolding' not totally successful. The 'great mythologies of
the past', he said, were 'deprived of enough facade to even launch good
raillery against.' The whole attempt he dismissed as a 'kind of grafting
process that I shall doubtless not be interested in repeating. . . .' In writing *The Bridge*, he had deliberately avoided this kind of external
organization. When Yvor Winters had urged him to impose pre-
existing structures on his poem to make it more easily understandable,
Crane replied, 'The structural weaknesses which you find in my work
are probably quite real, for I could not ask for a more meticulous or
sensitive reader. It is my hope, of course, not only to improve my statement but to extend scope and viewpoint as much as possible. But I
cannot trust to so methodical and predetermined a method of development, not by any means, as you commend.'[30] Instead he took for his
structure the rhythmic rise and fall of his subject itself, the 'intrinsic
myth' as he called it of Brooklyn Bridge that showed the form of the
history and the emotional experiences he was writing about.

The restoration of 'the word' as the medium of truth is one of the
most distinctive aspects of *The Bridge*. In most of his poetry before *The
Bridge* and in some of it written afterwards Crane employs an imagistic
mode of statement. The whole 'East of Yucatan' series is constructed
around single, clear visual images. 'Royal Palm', might stand as an
example of the poem which works almost exclusively by a single
image. But even in this series, there is indication of a growing emphasis
on words as opposed to visual stimuli. The apotheosis comes as a hurricane bringing new air; 'the syllables' that 'want breath' in the opening
poem now have the means of utterance. This is the continuation of a
trend towards exaltation of verbal experience in Crane's work. The
last poem in *White Buildings*, 'Voyages VI', culminated in an image, but
of the sea as 'the imaged word . . . the unbetrayable reply' to the questioning lover. And in 'General Aims and Theories' he had compared
the 'spiritual illumination' possible in poetry as a 'single new *word* never
before spoken and impossible to actually enunciate. . . .' (Crane's
italics).

The titles of *The Bridge* and 'The Broken Tower', Crane's last major
poem, indicate that he did not depart from the technique of a central
symbol in his later works. But there is a significant change in the way
he uses visual images in these poems. The bell tower and Brooklyn
Bridge pervade their respective poems by details given separately.

Neither of them is pictured clearly 'in an instant of time' for the reader to grasp immediately.

In connection with this departure from the instantaneous presentation of a clear image, there is also in these poems a marked tendency to turn the image into words. *The Bridge* is the exact reversal of one of the most common patterns in modern poetry. At the moment of 'illumination' in their poems many modern poets switch from a discursive mode to an imagistic one. After the almost garrulous musings of a 'sixty-year-old smiling public man', in Yeats's 'Among School Children', all his questionings and the implied answers are compounded into the famous images of the chestnut tree and the dancer. In Wallace Stevens's 'Sunday Morning', the poet, having lectured about the beliefs the woman should hold, concludes with the promise of earthly peace implied in the image of pigeons circling down to rest at evening. Most obviously, Eliot in *The Waste Land*, having given the message of the Thunder in words, quickly translates these words into images. ('I have heard the key / Turn in the door once and once only.' 'The boat responded / Gaily, to the hand expert with sail and oar.')

As *The Bridge* reaches its climax in the 'Atlantis' section, attention is focused on the bridge itself and its physical details are depicted. But even as they begin to coalesce into a single picture, Crane is already restating his visual symbol as words. The section begins with a reference to 'the bound cable strands' arching upward. But from these many strands issues a 'whispered rush' of 'Sybylline voices'. Soon the strands change into the 'labyrinthine mouths of history' and the lines of 'the cipher-script of time'. When the bridge is apostrophized as 'Tall Vision-of-the-Voyage', this vision is immediately restated as a voice uttering 'the word'.

> . . . O Choir, translating time
> Into what multitudinous Verb the suns
> And synergy of waters ever fuse, recast
> In myriad syllables,—Psalm of Cathay!
> O Love, thy white, pervasive Paradigm . . .!

In 'The Broken Tower' Crane again equated his attempt at illumination with the word. He questions whether he has expressed the ultimate truth he sought, but he leaves no doubt that the truth is in 'the word'.

> My word I poured. But was it cognate, scored
> Of that tribunal monarch of the air
> Whose thigh embronzes earth, strikes crystal Word
> In wounds pledged once to hope—cleft to despair?

Crane's 'crystal Word' shows how completely the image has been replaced in his view as the symbol of truth. The faith in language demonstrated so clearly in these poems was also implicit in the works of the other major contributors to *transition*.

Crane's connection with *transition* through the publication of 16/17 is an accurate reflection of his still tenuous but nevertheless ascending hopes for *The Bridge*. His ideas and idiom had indeed evoked a response —a favourable and potentially influential one. Later issues reflect the decline from this apogee. Brom Weber suggests that Crane's personal visions had evaporated by the time he was struggling to complete *The Bridge*, and that he pushed on out of obligation to his patron Otto Kahn and his obligation to fulfill the publication agreement made with Harry and Caresse Crosby. The poems Crane published in *transition* 18, November 1929, and 19/20, June 1930, indicate a different story. 'The Mango Tree' in number 18 was begun in 1926 even before the experience of the 'East of Yucatan' poems had been achieved. It was composed as Crane put it, 'on the way to the Bridge', and is a negative commentary on the public response to his ideals. As he worked on his major poem he had been able to look out his window at a mango tree which came to be a symbol of an annunciation that had been debauched. In the poem the rich fruit-giving mango tree is compared to the tree of forbidden knowledge. Though written earlier, it is an ironic counter poem to the positive vision of 'East of Yucatan'. In contrast to the inviolate 'Royal Palm', the mango tree sprouts fruit, and tourists in their American greed ignore its significance for its superficiality. 'It's all like Christmas / When you sprouted Paradise a discard of chewing-gum / took place. . . .' The irony of the poem exists in Crane's own knowledge of the mango fruit's laxative power of which the tourists are ignorant. In explaining the poem to a friend he wrote, 'I'm convinced that the Mango tree was the original Eden apple tree, being the first fruit tree mentioned in history with any accuracy of denomination.'[31]

At one point Crane had planned to use the poem in *The Bridge* after 'Three Songs'.[32] That is the position now held by 'Quaker Hill' another picture of a paradise and a vision despoiled by a greedy public. (This was the Promised Land, and still it is/To the persuasive suburban land agent. . . .) Crane's decision to publish 'The Mango Tree' in November 1929 is a retrenchment from the more optimistic mood of 'East of Yucatan' and an admission that the strategy of preparation in *transition* 16/17 and elsewhere among his friends had not met with great success.

It is important to note, however, that the bitter parody in the poem is directed at the defilers and not at the tree itself as a positive symbol. The tree retains the miraculous combination of sun and dusk which had defined the visionary experience in 'El Idiota', 'Island Quarry', and 'Royal Palm'.

This distinction between the failure of the vision itself and the failure of the public to accept it properly is emphasized in *transition* 19/20 by Jolas's essay, 'The Machine Age and Mystic America', and Crane's poem 'To the Cloud Juggler'. Jolas's essay in a final section entitled 'The Atlantic World' recalling Crane's concern with Atlantis was not as might have been expected a review of *The Bridge* which had just been published, but of Waldo Frank's book *The Re-Discovery of America*, which Crane had read and been inspired by while writing his poem. Jolas uses Edward J. O'Brien's *The Dance of the Machine* as a foil for Frank's book. O'Brien concentrated on the negative influence of the machine which Frank also recognized. Frank, however, had hopeful expectations as well. The essay arrives at the same point that *The Bridge* does—that a new America is possible but is not yet here—but with a different emphasis.

The 'Atlantis' section of *The Bridge* indicates that the 'pardon for this history' is at hand in 'One song, one Bridge of Fire!' Jolas's review emphasizes Frank's realization that the hope for a new 'mystic America' is only 'a poet's vision' and quotes Frank: ' "We are dealing with a world that never yet has been; a world which may come true." ' Jolas adds '[this world] is still far away' (*t.* 19/20, p. 383). It is difficult to prove any direct relationship between the essay and *The Bridge*, but one must exist. Frank's book was two years old; both the elaborate Crosby edition and the Boni and Liverwright trade edition of *The Bridge* had been published since the last issue of *transition*. And Jolas had, after all, been responsible for bringing Crane to Crosby. Probably Jolas's article is an oblique comment; the ecstacy of Crane's final sections showed more optimism than Jolas, who was himself in the midst of disbanding *transition*, could muster.

Jolas had urged Crane to foster his 'poet's vision'. To be completely sympathetic a review of *The Bridge* would have had to agree with the spirit of its optimism. Under the circumstances an honest review that would not have been interpreted as a denial of Crane would have been almost impossible. At most Jolas could only suggest his attitude in terms of another writer. The review was not a denial of the vision or a rejection of the poem, but a frank appraisal of how distant the goals he shared with Crane remained.

Crane's elegy for Harry Crosby, 'To the Cloud Juggler', (*t.* 19/20, p. 223) also exhibits his own admission, inherent in the very form of arcs which dominate his poems, that the visionary perfection he sought could not be sustained. For the first time in his poetry the emphasis is on the downward aspect of the curve, the decline of hopes. He speaks in the poem of the 'falling wonder of a rainbow's trance' and points out that in death Crosby can attain what 'we hold in vision only'. There is in the poem a new note of acceptance of a cyclical pattern of rise and fall. In the final stanza he appeals to the sun to

> Wrap us, lift us; drop us then returned
> Like water, undestroyed,—like mist unburned. . . .

The poem was Crane's last published work before his suicide. Though not one of his best works it is one of the fullest expressions of the trajectory which his experience took and incidentally of the trajectory of his expectations and disappointments as recorded in *transition*.

Notes

1 *Letters of Hart Crane*, ed. Brom Weber (New York, 1965), p. 118.
2 *Ibid.*, p. 289.
3 *Ibid.*, p. 294.
4 *Ibid.*, p. 295.
5 *Ibid.*, p. 294.
6 Unterecker, p. 479.
7 Interview with Maria Jolas.
8 *Letters*, p. 321.

9 'Man From Babel', unpublished autobiography of Eugene Jolas now in possession of Maria Jolas in Paris.

10 *The Complete Poems and Selected Letters and Prose of Hart Crane*, ed. Brom Weber (New York, 1966), pp. 219–222.

11 *Letters*, p. 283.

12 *Ibid.*, p. 291.

13 *Ibid.*, pp. 127, 271, 351.

14 This text from *transition* differs greatly from the later text in *Complete Poems*, but the tone and essential elements are not altered markedly.

15 Here too the *transition* text differs from *Complete Poems*. The last line in the *transition* version, 'Uncancelled as the stars that sum no wrong.' was changed to 'My trespass vision shrinks to face his wrong.' The change in emphasis is in keeping with the progressive difficulty Crane experienced in maintaining the high point of vision he achieved in the summer of 1926. The association of stars with a naive, native vision and Americans as trespassers is much like the presentation of the American Indian as a sometimes unseen but always present star looking down on history in *The Bridge*.

16 *Letters*, p. 261.

17 *Ibid.*, p. 261.

18 *Ibid.*, p. 181.

19 *Ibid.*, p. 232.

20 *Ibid.*, p. 305.

21 *Ibid.*, p. 241.

22 *Ibid.*, p. 305.

23 *Ibid.*, p. 278.

24 This mood of an undesired offering also pervades Crane's poem 'Moment Fugue' in *transition* 15. There a syphilitic flower seller 'bestows his eyes' on every purchaser but they 'like crutches hurtled into grass / Fall phantom-sudden.'

25 *Letters*, p. 237.

26 *Ibid.*, p. 129.

27 *Ibid.*, p. 77.

28 *Ibid.*, p. 71.

29 *Complete Poems*, p. 235.

30 *Letters*, p. 300.

31 *Complete Poems*, p. 217.

32 *Letters*, p. 255.

X

SAMUEL BECKETT

Crane's association with *transition* grew out of a shared interpretation of American history. Samuel Beckett's association was almost exclusively on aesthetic grounds. Beckett came to *transition* through Sylvia Beach and Joyce. Soon after he arrived in Paris to assume a position as exchange lecturer at the *Ecole Normale Supérieure*, he found his way to Shakespeare and Company and through Sylvia Beach, he and Joyce became friends. Joyce liked Beckett's work and showed it to Jolas who printed it. His first published story, 'Assumption', appeared in *transition* 16/17 simultaneously with his essay on Joyce's 'Work in Progress'. At times Beckett was a part of the group of friends around *transition*; he visited Joyce often, helped him with proofreading and other tasks, and sometimes he was a part of the social gatherings held by the Jolases. In 1931 he signed the 'Poetry is Vertical' manifesto. All the same, he led an independent life and in the years between 1927 and 1938 travelled back and forth between London, Paris, Dublin and Germany. To think of him, as has become the popular habit, as 'Joyce's secretary' or always in the Paris group, is a mistake. His publishing association with *transition* was close but by no means exclusive. He published his first criticism, fiction and poetry there but also contributed to other magazines like *The New Review* and *Dublin Magazine* as well.

His contributions to *transition* are basic critical and philosophical statements which define his attitudes and help clarify his relationship to Jolas and the aesthetic and philosophical concerns of the magazine. In *transition* 27 Beckett published a laudatory review of Dennis Devlin's *Intercessions*. The poems, Beckett says, are written 'with his selves on behalf of his selves. *Tour d'ébène*' (*t*. 27, p. 289). They are therefore not to be discussed in the terms of the 'politicians, antiquaries (*Geleerte*) and zealots'. Rather Devlin's poetry is to be discussed in 'Its own terms, that is terms of need' (*t*. 27, p. 289).

There are two kinds of need and the failure to distinguish them has led to 'the common rejection as "obscure" of most that is significant in modern music, painting and literature' (*t*. 27, p. 289). Beckett distinguishes between the social need that 'in its haste to be abolished cannot pause to be stated,' and the personal 'need that is the absolute predicament of particular human identity' (*t*. 27, p. 289). On the one hand, there is the ' "*Unbefriedigt Jeden Augenblick*" the eternally unsatisfied, the need to need ("*aimant l'amour*"),' which drives men like Devlin. On the other hand there are 'the go-getters, the gerrymandlers . . . solution clapped on problem like a snuffer on a candle' (*t*. 27, p. 290). Devlin's poems are the expression of a 'profound and abstruse self-consciousness' and as such they are likely to arouse criticism. But this is to question the probity with which the creative act has carried itself out, a probity in this case depending on 'a minimum of rational interference' (*t*. 27, p. 293). To make such objections is to 'suggest that the creative act should burke its own conditions for the sake of clarity' (*t*. 27, p. 293). With ironic precautions Beckett goes on to suggest that 'art has nothing to do with clarity, does not dabble in the clear and does not make clear, any more than the light of day (or night) makes clear the subsolar, lunar-and-stellar excrement. Art is the sun, moon and stars of the mind, the whole mind. And the monacodologists who think of it in terms of enlightenment are . . . "the sarpego and the sciatica of the Seven Liberall [*sic*] Sciences" ' (*t*. 27, p. 293).

In this review one sees the same rejection of positivism, 'the pragmatic conception of progress', and the same promotion of the 'inner life over the outer life' that appear in the Verticalist manifesto. In his remarks on clarity there is also the denial of 'Esthetic will' in favour of the 'a-logical movement of the psyche' (*t*. 21, p. 148). In referring to the poet's 'profound and abstruse self-consciousness' and the attempt to present 'the whole mind' there is something akin to the leading of 'the emotions [out] of the sunken, telluric depths' (*t*. 21, p. 149). Beckett's own contributions of stories and poems to *transition* show many of the same attitudes that he praises in Devlin. In them he defines 'the absolute predicament of [his own] particular human identity' as he had praised Devlin for doing. For him that predicament is a kind of purgatory brought on by the conflict between his limited nature and his urge for transcendence.

'Assumption' which appeared in *transition* 16/17 was Beckett's first published short story. In a style not yet so elusive as his later pieces, it is the most direct statement of the kind of need which he defined in his review of Devlin. The struggle of the story's main character to give utterance to a cry long pent up in him is clearly labelled as a 'struggle for divinity'. While it is a genuine and unavoidable impulse, Beckett calls it futile and mocks it by portraying it as a meaningless, inchoate scream. He lumps together all impulses toward transcendence in a burlesque of ascending aspiration: 'the blue flower, Vega, GOD'. Still it is not the futility of the struggle that Beckett emphasizes, but the torment that it causes. Instead of the glorious translation of Mary to heaven in the arms of her son as the title might suggest, Beckett ends the story with an ironic pietà—the broken man mourned by the woman whose promptings to acknowledge his spiritual aspirations lead to his death.

In the other works he published in *transition* Beckett elaborates the theme of suffering from metaphysical aspirations into a personal mythology of life as a painfully cyclical motion between the two extremes of metaphysics and gross physicality. Central to this private mythology is the character of Belacqua introduced in 'Sedendo and Quiesciendo' in *transition* 21. The story in *transition* is the only published section of Beckett's first long work, 'A Dream of Fair to Middling Women', in which the character of Belacqua is developed in greater detail. Like his counterpart in Canto IV of Dante's *Il Purgatario*, Belacqua is too lethargic to wish to pursue the flesh of this world or the ideals of the next very actively. He would prefer to sit while others strive for purgation. But like Dante himself Beckett's Belacqua has been urged on by Smeraldina, a kind of ironic, negative Beatrice figure. She destroys his repose by creating unwanted desires in him. Repulsed by her physicality in close and surfeiting contact, he tries to escape into metaphysical contemplation. In her absence her image becomes idealized and he is again lured back to her only to begin the reciprocal process anew.

'Sedendo and Quiesciendo' presents the essence of Belacqua's situation. The title, used ironically, comes from Aristotle's dictum, 'it is by sitting and contemplating that the soul attains wisdom.' Drawn back from refuge in metaphysical speculation by his own idealization of Smeraldina as 'his Vega', 'his blue flower', the same terms he had used in 'Assumption', Belacqua returns to her. No sooner is he with her than he senses the repulsion that caused him to leave her in the first place. As in 'Assumption' but humorously this time, he becomes her victim and she becomes like 'a parrot in a pietà'. He seeks relief by escaping to the toilet. There, presumably seated in the characteristic posture of Dante's Belacqua, he will be free for the time being. It is typical of the predicament defined by Beckett that an urge to escape from the flesh and purgation should only lead to the grossest form of corporeal existence and another kind of purgation. The respite from Smeraldina may be desirable but the suggestion that excretion is the way to the wisdom of the soul is grotesque.

Belacqua is one of the partially purged who cannot escape the earthly purgatory described by Beckett in his essay, 'Dante . . . Bruno, Vico . . . Joyce.' There he wrote 'Hell is the static lifelessness of unrelieved viciousness. Paradise is the static lifelessness of unrelieved immaculation. Purgatory a flood of movement and vitality released by the conjunction of these two elements.' In this kind of purgatory, movement is 'multidirectional and a step forward is, by definition, a step back' (*t.* 16/17, p. 253). The myth of this world as the place of purgation became more personal and more bitter as it developed. In *The Divine Comedy* the mention of Beatrice's name is enough to save Dante from the torments of the devil's cauldron. In Beckett's poem 'Malacoda' (*transition* 24), Belacqua's Smeraldina actually attempts to prohibit his departure from the pain of the world by refusing to allow the undertakers to carry him away after his death.

In 'Ooftish' (Yiddish, 'lay it on the table'), *transition* 27, Beckett published his most bitter rejection of the human condition. Again he uses the terms of the crucifixion but he also adds a Swiftian scorn for the human body. He wants to purge all the ills of the flesh. They are to be spat up into a pot like the expectorations of a tuberculosis patient. 'Spit it all out,' he says, 'it all boils down to the blood of the lamb.' But as always in Beckett the physical suffering is only half the problem. 'Golgatha was only the potegg'—a constant factor like the china eggs British housewives keep in their kettles to collect the residue from the

hard water when it boils. 'Blood of the Lamb' is also the menstrual discharge signifying the failure of soul and body, God and Man, to produce a live birth.

In so far as verticalism designates a downward movement into the
psyche in search of a way upward, Beckett participates. Belacqua is
certainly a personification of the urges and conflicts Beckett experienced
internally. But having made the descent beneath the surface, he did not
find there the great power that had been promised. Though suffering
the same longings for an upward movement suggested by the metaphor
of a vertical line, he did not find the metaphysical consummation, the
union of the 'I and Thou' spoken of in the Verticalist manifesto. So the
urge which the other signers celebrate as positive has become only a
source of woe in Beckett's works. The 'blue flower, Vega, and GOD' of
'Assumption' and 'Sedendo and Quiesciendo' were for Jolas, Arp,
Einstein and the others positive symbols of ideals worthy of quest.
Beckett himself makes the distinction quite effectively when he has
Belacqua say in an unpublished portion of 'A Dream of Fair to Middling Women', 'Behold Mr. Beckett, a dud mystic.' And then comments 'He meant *mystique raté* but shrank always from the *mot juste.*'[1]
Beckett is a ruined mystic—one who feels the need for transcendental
experience, suffers from it, but cannot fulfill it.

Perhaps this is most obvious in the way Beckett expresses the vertical
aspirations. Jolas himself wrote and collected works in which the desire
for metaphysical experience is expressed in the metaphor of flight; for
Beckett that kind of experience is expressed in terms of the wearisome
toil up the Mount of Purgatory or suffering of Calvary.

In their irreverent negative treatment of the interior expression of a
metaphysical longing Beckett's works are almost a parody of the search
for metaphysical experience undertaken by Crane, Jolas, and many of
the other *transition* writers. But by dealing with this subject he was
nevertheless helping to establish the aesthetic principles of the magazine.
No other contributor with the possible exception of Kafka did more to
liberate literature from the demands that it imitate external life and to
re-establish metaphysical situations as a proper concern for twentieth-
century writers.

Belacqua represents an innovation in the use of internal psychology
devoid of any attempt to create the illusion that he exists in a 'real'
world. 'There is no real Belacqua', Beckett wrote, 'it is to be hoped not

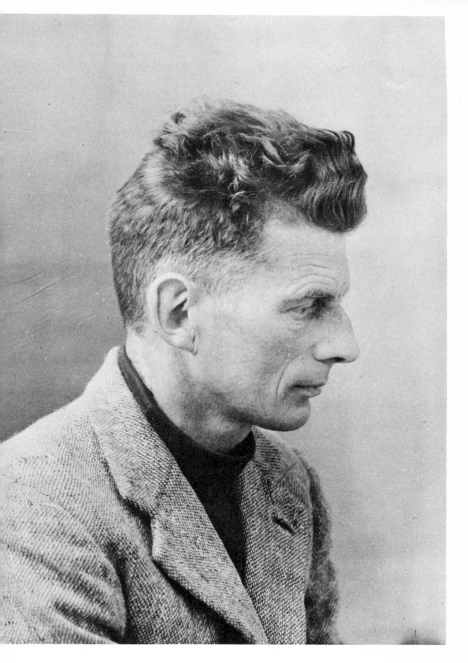

Samuel Beckett, 1950

Photograph taken by Peggy Guggenheim in the garden of her Sussex cottage in May 1938, showing from left to

indeed. There is no such person.'[2] Beckett has no desire to produce more novels like those of Jane Austen or Balzac: 'milieux, race, family, structure, temperament, past and present . . . that tires us . . . the background pushed up as a guarantee, that tires us.'[3] Nor is he interested in the literature of the 'psycho-scientific sleuth'.[4] There is only Belacqua, 'my little internus homo',[5] the creature of Beckett's own mind, and the set of peculiar internal conditions there which produced him.

External plot or structure is equally foreign to Beckett's purposes. If Belacqua's traits come from Dante, or if the poems of *Echo's Bones* follow a metamorphosis like those in Ovid, it may be recalled that Beckett was a student of Romance literature and had internalized Dante and Ovid. His endless reciprocal purgatory is not an assimilation of the external form from Dante but the expression of the internal form of his own experience. Myth, allegory, even logical arrangement are 'extrinsic'[6] and undesirable. 'The mind achieves creation by producing deep castings that brook no schemes.'[7] His characters are not even characters at all but 'refractory constituents . . . they are no good from a builder's point of view firstly . . . because they will not suffer their systems to be absorbed in the cluster of a greater system and then chiefly, because they themselves tend to disappear as systems.'[8]

Beckett reacted strongly to the tendency of modern poets to impose external order through symbol and metaphor. He acknowledges the image as one of the most immediate modes of consciousness but praises Devlin for presenting his images unhindered by his rational faculties. In a review of Pound's 'Make it New' in the Christmas 1934 *Bookman* he brushed aside Pound's 'recipes for an imagist poem' with sarcasm. In his essay on Proust he rejected Baudelaire's use of images as symbols because they were secondary reformations calling them 'discursive' and 'determined by a concept.'[9] He found them the stylistic equivalent of structural allegory which he condemned as extrinsic. The whole idea of summation he looked upon as the business of 'those impostors that call themselves mathematicians.'[10]

Like Joyce and Crane, Beckett is much concerned with the word and its possibilities for expressing the ultimate experience. He consciously presents it in his works as juxtaposed to the image. Several of the poems which appeared in *transition* were part of *Echo's Bones*[11] which without any very tight narrative line nonetheless presents a metamorphosis of the female character from a visible corporeal being to a voice. The pattern in the poems themselves is a progressive dissolution of images. And in technique the poems undergo an alteration from conventional imagism in the opening poem ('The Vulture') through self-conscious reference to this mode as a 'banner' ('Enueg I'—i.e., a consciously arrived at display of meaning through symbols) to rejection and hope for freedom from a 'tempest of emblems' ('Alba').

'Enueg II', one of the three poems from this series which were published in *transition*, deals specifically with the process of forming an image of the human situation. Central to the whole poem is the idea of Veronica's napkin with the outline of Christ's face made by his sweat. The poem begins with a fairly clear image of the face as a grave cloud against the evening. While one might expect this image to be clarified and emphasized, just the opposite occurs. The face crumbles and disappears. The suffering in the poem is associated with that of Christ on the way up Calvary but there is no visual presentation of it whatsoever. The centre which unifies this poem about images is not an image at all, but the words 'Veronica mundi veronica munda' with their play upon the popular etymology, *vera ikon*—true image, and the similarity of the Latin words for world ('mundi') and cleansing and purgation ('munda').

Images of transcendence can be put aside, but words and voices remain as an inescapable residue like the voice of Ovid's *Echo*. In his first treatment of the problem of metaphysical longings Beckett had distinguished between the images—Blue Flower, Vega—of an illusory promise of transcendence and the cry in which the transcendence was supposed to be achieved but which was in reality only the expression of the anguish of the struggle for it.

The female who lures toward transcendence in *Echo's Bones* is at first presented as 'the Logos' in 'Alba'. But as Belacqua realizes that she lures to an impossible goal and tries to extricate himself from her, she is presented as less and less exalted forms of 'the word'. From 'The Logos' she devolves into a folded scroll in 'Dortmunder', 'the final verb' in 'Sanies I'. When the impossibility of freedom from her becomes apparent in 'Sanies II', she turns into the menacing Madame de la Motte (combining French 'mot' and the name of a famous poisoner). Soon she is the overwhelming 'mumbo-jumbo'. His fall again into the spell of her attraction in 'Sanies III' is occasioned by 'the mixed declension of those mamae'. Ultimately in 'Malacoda' she is only an unseen voice saying 'nay'. No longer the illusory blue flower he once hovered near in the form of a butterfly, she has become only the minimal quintessence of the force opposing his release from painful existence.

If Beckett's attitude towards 'the word' is in one sense the inversion of that implied in Crane's 'Crystal word', it is nevertheless clear that for him the ultimate residue of interior experience is verbal. When the images that give false hope or oversimplify experience are dissipated, there will still be words. Beckett contrasted Joyce's faith in words with his own lack of faith that they could express what he wanted. He expressed the desire to be free of 'wordshed' and 'the unalterable whey of Words' ('Cascando'). He has spoken of a desire for a liberation, for the 'unword' which he has in some sense achieved in film. Still the very fact that he is so troubled with persistence of language only confirms how deeply he is concerned with an interior condition that is essentially verbal. As he writes at the end of *The Unnameable*, '. . . words there is nothing else you must say words as long as there are any until they find me until they say me strange pain strange sin.'[12]

In the later works after *Murphy* on which his fame rests the language is distilled. The general verbal exuberance, the exotic vocabulary, multilingual puns, portmanteau words, and unusual syntax which characterized his work in *transition* have largely gone, though any of these early traits of style may reappear briefly at any point. While the style that made his early work seem written expressly for *transition* has disappeared, the rejection of extrinsic matter and form in favour of internal verbal experience which was the heart of the revolution of the word remains central to those works in which Beckett has done so much to change the novel and the drama of the twentieth century.

Notes

1 John Fletcher, *The Novels of Samuel Beckett* (London, 1964), pp. 14–15.
2 Lawrence Harvey, *Samuel Beckett, Poet and Critic* (Princeton, 1970), p. 344.
3 *Ibid.*, p. 340.
4 *Ibid.*, p. 340.
5 Samuel Beckett, *More Pricks than Kicks* (London, 1970), p. 40.
6 Harvey, p. 407.
7 *Ibid.*, p. 342.

8 *Ibid.*, p. 341.
9 Samuel Beckett, *Proust and Three Dialogues* (London, 1965), p. 79.
10 Harvey, p. 333.
11 Samuel Beckett, 'Echo's Bones' in *Poems in English* (London, 1961).
12 Samuel Beckett, *Three Novels* (New York, 1965), p. 414.

XI

DYLAN THOMAS

The place of Dylan Thomas among the important contributors to *transition* is unique. He did not sign the manifestos as did Crane and Beckett. And he was not an imposing established figure like Joyce or Miss Stein. His two contributions, one story and one poem, hardly mark him as a regular contributor. It cannot even be argued that he was 'discovered' in *transition*, for he had already published *Twenty-Five Poems* before his first appearance. Still, the influence the magazine had upon him and the similarities of both his pronouncements and the themes of his poetry to those of the other figures in the magazine establish him as a part of the revolution of the word. It would have been strange if Thomas, whose works moved toward a reliance on the unconscious and a new reverence for verbal experience in the mid-thirties, had had no connection whatsoever with *transition*.

Thomas read Jolas's magazine and found its programme sympathetic. With more talent and perspicuity than other receptive young writers, who have been previously mentioned, he avoided the extravagances of his enthusiasm to produce major works that reflect the attitudes expressed in *transition*. His positive reaction contrasts strongly with that of Robinson Jeffers and Henry Miller, two of his prominent contemporaries who were also exposed to Jolas's theories but rejected them.

Jolas took special interest in Jeffers's attempt to deal with the unconscious, wrote to him, and published a review by Irene Schindler calling him 'an American major poet', but Jeffers declined any close association with the programme of *transition*. Asked about the use of dreams in his work and the need to develop a new language, Jeffers asserted that dreams played no part in his work and that he saw no need to alter language. Though Jeffers *did* present dreams in works like 'Roan Stallion', his overriding concern with the sexual aspects of the unconscious and its relation to character, his use of conventional narrative structures, and his dedication to 'normal' language make it clear that he does not belong with the *transition* writers. In his preface to *Roan Stallion, Tamar and Other Poems* he bemoaned the 'renunciations' made by the successors of the symbolist movement. *transition* is not mentioned by name but the thrust of his remarks is clearly in the direction which the magazine represented. Ideas, meter, imagery, recognizable emotions had been eliminated from poetry. 'Perhaps at last words would have to go or give up their meaning, nothing be left but musical syllables. Every advance required the elimination of some aspect of reality, and what could it profit me to know the direction of modern poetry if I did not like the direction?'[1]

Henry Miller and Anais Nin were subject to the influence of *transition* directly. Together in Paris where Miller was working as a proofreader for the *Chicago Tribune* they came to know Jolas personally. Miss Nin was favourably impressed with Jolas's neo-romantic theories which she praises in her diaries. She urged these same attitudes on Miller by showing him copies of *transition* and suggesting that they get some of its fervour into his writing.[2] Miller was sympathetic to *transition*'s interest in the unconscious and his writing of this period does reflect its influence. Years later Miller acknowledged his debt to Jolas and *transition* with gratitude in a long letter written to Jolas, then suffering from his final illness. But despite the influence *transition* had on him, Miller could not accept all that the revolution of the word implied. His 'Cosmological Eye', a portion of which was published in *transition* 27, uses the metaphor of the 'third eye' to discuss the contact with the deeper forces inside man. However, in 'Max and the White Phagocytes', he attacks Joyce and *transition*. 'Joyce's deformity of vision . . . is depressing . . . it is a defect of the soul . . . Joyce is growing more blind every day—blind in the pineal eye.'[3] A few pages later he castigates Joyce for 'that peculiar failing of the modern artist—the inability to communicate with his audience. . . .' The grounds of Miller's attack, sexuality, becomes apparent when he calls 'Work in Progress' 'ferocious

Dylan Thomas (Courtesy Camera Press Ltd.)

masturbation carried on in fourteen tongues . . . a dervish dance on the peripherie of meaning, and orgasm not of blood and semen, but of dead slag from the burnt-out crater of the mind.' The Revolution of the Word is only the logical outcome of this 'sterile dance of death'.[4] Like Lawrence, whom he juxtaposes to Joyce, Miller conceived of the unconscious as primarily sexual and discounted the importance of words in the mental process.

The reactions of Jeffers and Miller illustrate well the attitudes of those who rejected *transition*. They resented its departure from everyday reality, its concern for verbal innovation, and its obscurity. In effect they wished literature to provide an easily recognizable surrogate for physical experience and were unwilling to allow verbal experience for its own sake.

For Thomas, word and world were so inextricably bound together that he could not separate verbal and physical experience. Though he had contact only through copies of the magazine, he responded far more favourably to the programme offered there. He had read *transition* at least as early as December 1933.[5] According to his friend, J. H. Martin, he 'turned to the extreme avant-garde, to Joyce and the Paris magazine *transition*' as an influence on his work sometime in 1934.[6] He thus came in contact with the magazine during one of the most formative periods of his life, the 'key year' for his work according to one critic.[7] In 1934 he was reworking his manuscript of poems for his first book, developing the dense style that became his hallmark. This was also the period in which he made most of the entries in the 'Red Notebook' from which much of his early prose and many of his most intricate poems were written.

By 1933 *transition* was well into its Verticalist phase and the concept of poetry being advanced by Jolas accorded well with the native Welsh traditions which shaped Thomas's poetry. In Wales the concept of the poet was more primitive, mystical, and romantic than in England. There the bardic tradition was still a strong influence. From this Welsh tradition Thomas incorporated the concept of the poet as bard, the incantatory patterns of *cynghanedd*, the deviations from standard English, and ancient rituals from early Christian and pagan religion. In *transition* he could see similar provincial and primitive cultural backgrounds acclimatised to the thoroughly modern and sophisticated world of internationally famous authors. Ceremonial masks and descriptions of rituals appeared along with the best poets of the day. The compatibility between the Welsh tradition and *transition* may be seen best in the article in *transition* 27 by Keidrych Rhys on the Welsh *cynghanedd*.

It is not surprising to find that Thomas read *transition* closely, was 'fascinated by its published work',[8] and borrowed back issues from his friends. His letters and works of this period gave a picture of Thomas reading the magazine with interest, accepting its major attitudes and adapting parts of what he found there for his own use, while trying to maintain his artistic independence by rejecting the specific approaches of *transition* writers.

To Glyn Jones he identified *transition*'s contributors as examples of various kinds of modern obscurity—seeming to justify them in the process. 'Some poets, like Gertrude Stein, and the French-American Transitionists of Eugene Jolas, have evolved a mathematically precise method of removing the associations from words, and giving language, or attempting to give language, its *literal* sound, so that the word "cat" becomes no more than a one-syllabled word with a hard consonantal ending; others, like Joyce, have magnified words, lengthened and animated them with contrary inferences, and built around them a vast structure of unexpected and often inexplicable associations . . .'[9] His own obscurity, he correctly points out, is different—the result of a private symbolism.

A letter to Trevor Hughes makes clear that the difference is not so large as Thomas, who disliked having his name linked with other writers, indicated to Jones. In discussing the current state of language he said,

> . . . consciousness of such prostitution [of words by use] need not lead us, as it has led James Joyce into the inventing of new words; it need not make us, as it has made Gertrude Stein, repeat our simplicities over and over again in intricate and abstract patterns so that the meaning shall be lost and only the bare and beautiful shells of the words remain. All we need do is to rid our minds of the humbug of words, to scorn the prearranged leaping together of words, to make by our own judicious and, let it be prayed for, artistic selection, new associations for each word. Each word should be a basin for us to cough our individual diseases into, and not a vessel full already of others' and past diseases. . . .[10]

Thomas's particular way of revitalizing words has more in common with Crane than with Joyce and Stein, but there can be no doubt that he was motivated by the same concern for a renewal of language that formed the basis of Jolas's revolution.

His respect for the magazine may be seen in the fact that he did send them 'Then Was My Neophyte', the poem he thought of as his best work, and 'The Mouse and the Woman', the story that had occupied him longer than any of his prose pieces up until this time. The specific influence of *transition* on his own work may be seen in the titles and style of two of his most verbally complex stories, 'Adventure from a Work in Progress' and 'In the Direction of the Beginning'.

In every important respect Thomas shares the assumptions of the transitionists. Like them he rejected the claims of exterior representation and literary convention. 'To hell with all the preconceived notions of short story writing', he wrote to Trevor Hughes, 'Into the sea of yourself like a young dog and bring out a pearl. . . . To hell with everything except the inner necessity for expression and the medium of expression . . .'[11] Poetry was for him specifically a product of the unconscious. In response to an inquiry about Freudian influences in his work he wrote, 'Poetry, recording the stripping of the individual darkness, must inevitably cast light upon what has been hidden for too long, and, by so doing, make clean the naked exposure. Freud cast light on a little darkness he had exposed. Benefiting by the sight of the light and the knowledge of the hidden nakedness, poetry must drag further into the clean nakedness of light more even of the hidden causes than Freud could realize.'[12] This is closer to an explicit statement in agreement with Jolas's theories of poetry as sublimation, but not necessarily sexual sublimation, than can be found in statements made by any of the other major contributors to *transition*.

He regards structure as an equally internal matter. He excoriated the 'mythological' writers as poets 'so aware of the huge mechanism of the past that their poems read like scholarly conglomerations of a century's wisdom, and are difficult to follow unless we have an intimate knowledge of Dante, the Golden Bough, and the weather-reports in Sanskrit.' His own structure was 'based . . . on a preconceived symbolism derived . . . from the cosmic significance of the human anatomy.'[13] Thomas's myth, exploited in most of what he wrote, is the myth of his own internal physical experience: 'Through my small, bonebound island I have learnt all I know, experienced all, and sensed all. All I write is inseparable from the island. As much as possible, therefore, I employ the scenery of the island to describe the scenery of my thoughts, the earthquake of the body to describe the earthquake of the heart.'[14]

Implicit in Thomas's statement about his use of the metaphor of the human body is an approval of the image as a basic form of expression. Images play as large a part in his work as they do in that of any modern poet, but he rejects the current use of one image presented instantaneously as a unifying metaphor. When Henry Treece complained about the lack of any single, easy approach to his poems through images, he responded:

> . . . it consciously is not my method to move concentrically round a central image. . . . A poem by myself needs a host of images because its centre is a host of images. I make one image—though 'make' is not the word, I let, perhaps, an image be 'made' emotionally in me and then apply to it what intellectual and critical forces I possess—let it breed another, let that image contradict the first, make of the third image bred out of the other two together, a fourth contradictory image, and let them all, within my imposed formal limits, conflict.[15]

This is an attitude much closer to the surrealists than to the imagists and it is devoid of the distrust of language that is inherent in their work.

A statement of his 'theory of poetry' to Charles Fisher, leaves no doubt about the importance of words in his aesthetic.

> You asked me to tell you about my theory of poetry. Really I haven't got one. I like things that are difficult to write and difficult to understand; I like 'redeeming the contraries' with secretive images; I like contradicting my images, saying two things at once in one word, four in two and one in six. But what I like isn't a theory even if I do stabilise by dogma my own personal affections. . . . I think [poetry] . . . should work from words from the substance of words and rhythm of substantial words set together, not towards words. Poetry is a medium, not a stigmata on paper.

In this passage one can see the acceptance of words as the medium which itself plays a role in giving form to art. In the same letter, Thomas goes on to show that he regards the poet's ability to work perfectly freely with this medium as most important. 'Men should be two tooled, and a poet's middle leg is his pencil. If his phallic pencil turns into an electric drill, breaking up the tar and the concrete of language worn thin by the tricycle tyres of nature poets and the heavy six wheels of the academic sirs, so much the better.'[16]

Without diminishing the importance of images, Thomas casts off the imagist distrust of language. He revels in both the image and the word. In the title line of one of his poems he exactly equates his basic image with himself, 'I, in my intricate image, stride on two levels', and says of the appearance of this image in the world, 'This was the god of beginning in the intricate seawhirl.' But he could also equate all existence with words, as he did in a letter to Pamela Hansford Johnson in 1934.

All sentences fall when the weight of the mind is distributed unevenly along the holy consonants & vowels. In the beginning was a word I can't spell, not a reversed Dog, or a physical light, but a word as long as Glastonbury and as short as pith. Nor does it lisp like the last word, break wind like Balzac through a calligraphied window, but speaks out sharp & everlastingly with the intonations of death and doom on the magnificent syllables. . . . There must be only a half a world tangible, audible, & visible to the illiterate. And is that the better half? Or is it the wholly ghostly past? And does the one-eyed ferryman, who cannot read a printed word, row over a river of words, where the syllables of the fish dart out & are caught on his rhyming hook, or feel himself a total ghost in a world that's as matter-of-fact as a stone?[17]

This is the same belief in the word which he expressed in 'Especially when the October wind' where his own heart's blood becomes syllables and all the world takes on the form of words

> Especially when the October wind
> With frosty fingers punishes my hair,
> [. . .]
> My busy heart who shudders as she talks
> Sheds the syllabic blood and drains her words.
>
> Shut, too, in a tower of words, I mark
> On the horizon walking like the trees
> The wordy shapes of women, and the rows
> Of the star-gestured children in the park.
> Some let me make you of the vowelled beeches,
> Some of the oaken voices, from the roots
> Of many a thorny shire tell you notes,
> Some let me make you of the water's speeches.[18]

Thomas used the visible signature as a stage between image and pure verbal experience as Beckett did in 'Dortmunder' and Crane did in *The Bridge*. This is an important theme in the 'Altar-wise by owl-light' sonnets. There he expresses ultimate experience in terms that suggest 'The Logos', but he still clings to a visual manifestation. In these poems the word is imprinted on life. The theme is dominant in sonnet VII:

> Now stamp the Lord's Prayer on a grain of rice,
> A Bible-leaved of all the written woods
> Strip to this tree: a rocking alphabet,
> Genesis in the root, the scarecrow word,
> And one light's language in the book of trees.
> [. . .]
> Time tracks the sound of shape on man and cloud,
> On rose and icicle the ringing handprint.

In the final sonnet of this series the illumination toward which the series moves (the perception of an unorthodox kind of Christianity) is expressed both as word and image. The searchers for this revelation

> Spot the blown word, and on the seas I image
> December's thorn screwed in a brow of holly.

This tendency to keep word and image on a par as the joint and equal modes of ultimate experience is a characteristic of Thomas's verse. It is the subject of his poem 'In the Beginning'. The original genesis is first stated as an image:

> In the beginning was the pale signature,
> Three-syllabled and starry as the smile. . . .

Again the theme of words as a mystic signature stamped upon the world is developed.

> And after came the imprints on the water,
> Stamp of the minted face upon the moon;
> The blood that touched the crosstree and the grail
> Touched the first cloud and left a sign.

It appears that in the poem the word and not the image will be the dominant form of ultimate experience.

> In the beginning was the word, the word
> That from the solid bases of the light
> Abstracted all the letters of the void;
> And from the cloudy bases of the breath
> The word flowed up, translating to the heart
> First characters of birth and death.

The poem ends, however, with image and word equal. Before anything else there was the mind, the perceiver of both image and word.

> In the beginning was the secret brain.
> The brain was celled and soldered in the thought
> Before the pitch was forking to a sun;
> Before the veins were shaking in their sieve,
> Blood shot and scattered to the winds of light
> The ribbed original of love.

Man's inner thoughts and visions preceded all. If 'the word' is not paramount in Thomas's scheme, it is at least equal and coextant with the image and the brain like a part of the trinity. With Thomas, as with his contemporaries who were more closely allied with *transition*, the word has regained a place of respect.

Notes

1 Robinson Jeffers, *Roan Stallion, Tamar and Other Poems* (New York, 1935), ii.
2 *The Diary of Anais Nin*, 1934–9, ed. Gunther Stuhlmann (New York, 1967), pp. 165, 202.
3 *The Henry Miller Reader*, ed. Lawrence Durrell (Norfolk, Conn., 1950), pp. 209–10.
4 *Ibid.*, pp. 218–19.
5 *Selected Letters of Dylan Thomas*, ed. Constantine Fitzgibbon (New York, 1966), p. 86.

6 J. H. Martin, Letter to the editor of the *London Times Literary Supplement* (19 March 1964), p. 235.

7 Annis Pratt, 'Dylan Thomas's Prose', in *Dylan Thomas A Collection of Critical Essays*, ed. C. B. Cox (Englewood Cliffs, N.J.), p. 119.

8 Keidrych Rhys, Letter to the editor of the *London Times Literary Supplement* (26 March 1964), p. 255.

9 *Letters of Dylan Thomas*, p. 96.

10 *Ibid.*, p. 91.

11 *Ibid.*, p. 16.

12 Dylan Thomas, *New Verse* II (Oct., 1934), p. 9.

13 *Letters of Dylan Thomas*, p. 97.

14 *Ibid.*, p. 48.

15 *Ibid.*, p. 190.

16 *Ibid.*, p. 151.

17 *Ibid.*, p. 127.

18 This and subsequent quotations from poems are from Dylan Thomas, *The Collected Poems of Dylan Thomas* (Norfolk, Conn., 1950).

XII

GERTRUDE STEIN

Miss Stein never signed any of the *transition* manifestos or had much direct contact with Jolas. Still she has probably been as widely associated with *transition* as any contributor except James Joyce. Her experimental prose is frequently referred to as one of the examples of the kind of innovation with which the magazine was concerned. Unquestionably Miss Stein shared with Jolas and the other writers of *transition* fundamental assumptions which separate them from most of their contemporaries. Her association with the magazine, however, was based on a wide variety of personal and historical considerations which have suggested a closer theoretical relationship than actually existed. Miss Stein shares with Joyce the position of a major figure in the revolution of the word but her position is eccentric and her relations with the magazine were often strained and at the end, after publication of *The Autobiography of Alice B. Toklas*, hostile.

Miss Stein's two books, *Three Lives* and *The Making of Americans*, and some of her shorter works like 'Tender Buttons' had already won her the reputation of a serious avant-garde writer. Her fame, however, was small and rested on the earlier works that had begun to be forgotten. But a series of articles by Elliot Paul in the *Chicago Tribune* in 1926 led to what she called, 'the first seriously popular estimation of her work'.[1] It was only natural that as an editor of *transition* Paul would continue to advocate her cause.

Her appearance in *transition* was not, however, exclusively bound up with her own work. Though never quite the dominant figure on the left bank that she has been made out to be, she was one of the first American expatriates to settle in Paris and establish contacts with the outstanding young artists and writers of several countries. She was thus one of the figures linking European and American literature. In that sense she was the personal embodiment of one of the main objectives of *transition*.

She was further one of the main advocates of radical new attitudes toward art and literature. She argued constantly that no work could ever achieve the stature of a classic unless it differed greatly in style from the classics that preceded it. Even though she often did not like specific examples of experimentation by others, she was warmly receptive to many new departures in painting and writing and made an effort to appreciate them. So by virtue of her contacts, her general attitudes and her own style, she belonged with *transition*.

To its readers, Miss Stein must have appeared to hold a position of great eminence. A note in the eighth issue announced in her own style, 'Whenever she pleases, Gertrude Stein contributes what she pleases to *transition* and it pleases her and it pleases us' (*t.* 8, p. 187). By acknowledging that the editors did not even consider rejecting Miss Stein's pieces, the note gave the impression of unanimous enthusiasm for her work. It is true that nothing of Miss Stein's was rejected by *transition*, but the high regard for her writing was largely limited to Elliot Paul.

Under these conditions almost all of the dealings Miss Stein had with *transition* were left to Elliot Paul. To her he portrayed himself as *the* careful editor of *transition* who chose the contents of each issue with much thought and care. To the Jolases he portrayed Miss Stein as a kind of female Buddha who remained aloof from social and literary contacts. So long as Paul remained, no serious problems arose. Miss Stein appeared to be one of the cornerstones of *transition*. Critics responded violently to her prose, attacking it as a major influence on the magazine. Announcements of future issues featuring Miss Stein's name equally with Joyce's did not dispel the idea. In time the situation was bound to produce conflict between Miss Stein, who thought she held a special position in the magazine, and Jolas, who had no special interest in her work and in some ways saw in it tendencies opposed to his own theoretical orientation.

It was Paul who attempted to explain her work to the magazine's readers. In defending her in *transition* 9 against the attacks of Wyndham Lewis, he discussed the development of her work and identified the type of writing represented in each stage. Her first stage was 'the servant girl epoch' (*t.* 9, p. 171), the period of *Three Lives* which featured Melanctha, the coloured servant girl, and was written in a style that could be appreciated by a servant girl. In the next stage she had condensed 'the life stories of small groups of people into a few pages. . . . Later, in the form of sketches, plays and the like, she put the soft pedal on characterization and gave us characteristic situations to which plots and alternative plots could easily be fitted by the reader, if he was so minded. Then she achieved abstract patterns of words, skillfully rescued from the realm of the specific, which may be enjoyed as music is enjoyed, or abstract painting. There is no telling what she will do next' (*t.* 9, p. 172).

The temporal divisions in Miss Stein's work were not quite so strict as Paul indicated. Her contributions to *transition* do not fit perfectly into the types mentioned. Most of them fall somewhere between the last two types defined by Paul. All of them with the exception of 'The Life and Death of Juan Gris' (*t.* 4, p. 160) have a great deal of verbal abstraction which does not appear directly related to any life story, characterization, or description and yet the pieces as a whole are not totally abstract and do have some vague relevance to real or imagined people or events. 'If He Thinks', for example, is subtitled 'a Novelette of Desertion', implying that it will be the story of the end of a love affair or a marriage. Some parts of the piece appear to be the musings of a woman who has been deserted by her husband just after the birth of a child. But throughout the piece Miss Stein is also using words to make abstract patterns as in the last paragraph.

> In finishing we say ram lamb sheep or mutton, mutton lamb sheep or ram, sheep ram lamb and mutton, mutton ram sheep or lamb. When this is said everything is said. When everybody sings nobody sings. When nobody pleases. You please if you please he will not go so far readily and in anger. To finish. (*t.* 10, p. 13)

Also quite similar in the mixture of implied characterization and plot with abstract passages are 'As a Wife has a Cow' (*t.* 3, p. 9), 'Studies in Conversation' (*t.* 6, p. 75), 'One Spaniard' (*t.* 4, p. 152), 'Four Saints in Three Acts' (*t.* 16/17, p. 39), and 'Dan Raffel A Nephew' (*t.* 12, p. 51).

Two other works, 'Made a Mile Away' and 'Descriptions of Literature', mix criticism with abstraction. Her mixture of description and abstract word play in the section on El Greco from 'Made a Mile Away' is typical of the style of these works.

> So much longer and seen, feel seen fell seen, fell saw saw it saw him, saw him sell him, see him, seen. As seen a scene. So and seen, seen so, seen as as much longer and seen as so much and as seen and so long. Not good-bye but so long. Longhi. Very nice and quiet I thank you. (*t.* 8, p. 156)

The passage obviously records Miss Stein's reaction to the elongation of figures in El Greco's paintings, but the play between 'long', 'so long', and 'good-bye' as well as the play between 'feel' and 'fell' and 'scene' and 'seen' stem more from the sounds of words than they do from the experience of seeing the painting.

'Descriptions of Literature' does much the same thing as 'Made a Mile Away' but it does not mix reference, abstraction, or description of the thoughts within one passage. Instead it is divided into discrete sentences each describing a kind of book. Some of the sentences are directly referential like 'A book which places the interest in those situations which have something to do with recollections and with returns.' Others are deliberately abstract: 'A book describing six and six and six. A book describing six and six and six seventy-two.' And a few appear to be the product of Miss Stein's own personal musings: 'A book and a bookstore. A book for them. Will they be in it' (*t.* 13, pp. 51–3).

The abstract side of Miss Stein's work was presented more obviously in 'Tender Buttons' a series of 'still lifes' divided into sections on 'Objects', 'Food', and 'Rooms'—'the basic subject matter of the cubists.'[2] Her descriptive note for the *transition* publication of the work helps to explain her techniques. 'It was', she wrote, 'my first conscious struggle with the problem of correlating sight, sound and sense, and eliminating rhythm . . .' (*t.* 14, p. 13). An example of this may be seen in her section entitled 'Apple'. 'Apple plum, carpet steak, seed clam, colored wine, calm seen, cold cream, best shake, potato, potato and no no gold work with pet, a green seen is called bake and change sweet is bready, a little piece a little piece please' (*t.* 14, p. 37). The mention of seeds, the red of wine, the allusion to the difference between green baking apples and sweeter ones deal with the 'sense' of words, and visible characteristics of apples. Cold cream may also suggest the inner whiteness and coolness

of an apple, but sound accounts for the continuation of the 'o' sound in
'cold' to 'potato' and 'gold'. If there is no specific reference in the piece
to a definable situation, there is still a great deal of specific meaning to
the words that do recall associations with apples.

'Tender Buttons' first appeared in 1914 and Miss Stein had since
developed her manipulation of language as an abstract medium even
more by the time she began contributing to *transition*. As her note to
'Tender Buttons' went on to explain, 'now I am trying grammar and
eliminating sight and sound' (*t.* 14, p. 13). The difference between her
earlier and her later method may be seen in the opening segment of
'Dan Raffel A Nephew'. 'Arthur two our age chance will tree behaviour
for finally left come to such now their stability compress in union
against made hence for the close of establishment leak and forfeit a
plenty of ununited practice of their popularity just now goes as made
a piece of inclined to their fairly restrain collapse rectitude . . .' (*t.* 12,
p. 51). Several things about this passage are immediately evident in
comparison to the description of the apple quoted above. There are
almost no physical referents to give the passage any power of specific
suggestion. Far from building her works around images, Miss Stein was
consciously trying to expunge the image in order to accentuate the
purely verbal awareness of her audience. Moreover, there is no pattern
of sound like the 'o' in the apple passage. The passage does not form a
single clear sentence or a grammatical series. In reading it, one must
concentrate upon trying to organize it into intelligible, or at least
recognizable, units. In this process one becomes actively involved in the
perception of grammatical forms and syntax. 'Tree', for example,
stands out not only because it is a noun in the position of a verb, but
also because the reader is looking so hard to find a verb. The number of
suffixes designating function ('ly', 'ilty', 'ess', 'ion', 'ence', 'ment', 'iet',
and 'ty') is extremely high in the passage. Whether the reader clings to
these consciously or not, they are the abstract elements which Miss
Stein manipulates almost like the geometric shapes in cubist painting.
The words have lost their referential value by being placed in 'nonsense' arrangements, but the passage is not a random assortment of
words. Miss Stein has quite consciously emphasized the relationships
among them.

The differences in Miss Stein's method from work to work did not
alter the basic aims of her technique: the pieces she published in *transition*

were all abstract to a greater or a lesser degree. If there were real figures
or situations behind them sometimes, that was not the point. One simply
read the works and responded to them. Explication and 'understanding'
in the usual sense were not possible.

The only kind of critical discussion relevant was a general description
of her methods and the presentation of techniques similar to hers in
other arts. Elliot Paul provided both kinds of commentary. If one dis-
counts the extravagance of his views about the relative merits of the
various media for art, Paul's description of her method in 'K.O.R.A.A.'
(*t*. 3, p. 173) is among the best introductions to her work of this period.
It repeats Miss Stein's own position more directly than she would have
put it herself.

> . . . She discovered that a phrase, if it can escape being specific, has an absolute
> or static quality which is more intricate and significant, as art, than a like
> composition in sound or color. . . . [Her works] are as undecipherable as
> Bach fugues. They are abstract patterns. . . . To such as can enjoy abstract
> art, they offer unique pleasure, but do not attack them as a species of modern
> Sanskrit. (*t*. 3, p. 175)

Paul's article on Miss Stein's favourite artist, Juan Gris, entitled 'A
Master of Plastic Relations', defines quite well the theory of abstract art
that Miss Stein shared with Gris and other contemporary artists. Gris is
'interested in relations, not objects, in examples rather than explanations.' To him 'the unfailing instinct of the spectator to find a representative significance in the abstract colored forms, appeared the most
natural thing in the world. Thus a pale ellipse might become a plate
with no harm done and considerable speculation avoided.' Both artists
allowed reference to existing reality to appear if it arose naturally, but
never allowed it to determine or overshadow the abstract patterns from
which they began.

In an article on Picasso in *transition* 14, Paul made the connection between Miss Stein and cubism explicit. After describing Picasso's great
achievement in liberating himself 'from representation or comment',
Paul quoted Miss Stein on his importance. Picasso, she claimed,
'organized the aesthetic world as Napoleon organized the political
world of his day, and with an effect quite as permanent' (*t*. 13, p. 141).

In maintaining the right of the artist to be free of the pre-existing
external reality as a determinant for art, in seeking new form derived

exclusively from the internal considerations of her material, and in her diminishing of the image in favour of attention to the purely verbal aspects of words, Miss Stein was affirming attitudes central to the revolution of the word. It is difficult to assess her achievement in winning for words the same kinds of freedom she saw exercised in abstract art, but for the present her works remain as some of the most far reaching assertions of a revolutionary kind of verbal experience.

But if Miss Stein's work was central to the revolution of the word in its broadest aspects, it was also quite different from the particular revolution conceived by Jolas and manifested in the other major contributors. As Jolas wrote in his autobiography, 'Her attitude was remote from anything I felt or thought. For not only did she seem to be quite devoid of metaphysical awareness, but I also found her aesthetic approach both gratuitous and lacking in substance. . . . The little household words so dear to Sherwood Anderson never impressed me . . . I wanted . . . new words, Millions of words.'[3] The 'absolute' quality which Paul found in Miss Stein's work was quite different from the absolute of the deepest personal mental experience which Jolas sought and with which Joyce, Crane, Beckett, Thomas and the writers of the European movements presented in *transition* dealt in their various ways. There may have been for Miss Stein an 'a priori reality' to which her works were faithful, but if so it existed exclusively in the formal potential of her medium and not 'within ourselves' as Jolas said. Any belief like that in the verticalist manifesto that poetry was an approach to a source of creativity that transcended the individual was simply not a part of her aesthetic. It was precisely upon this point that Braque claimed, in 'Testimony Against Gertrude Stein', that she misunderstood cubism.

In its strictest sense only one article of the manifestos applied to Miss Stein—the one defending the 'litany of words as an independent unit'. But even in this point, the religious overtones, the suggestion of the use of obvious rhythms and the heightening of emotional response to words is not like the purely formal relations Miss Stein was exploiting.

Even apart from aesthetic differences, Miss Stein and Jolas were not kindred spirits. They had first met at Ernest Hemingway's in 1925 when she and Miss Toklas came 'visiting like two maiden aunts.' After they were introduced, Miss Stein posed the inevitable question, 'What are you doing in Paris?' And Jolas replied with the familiar and awkward but honest answer that he was 'trying to write poetry.' Miss Stein made no attempt to hide the fact that this answer left her unimpressed and responded with silence. As the embarrassment grew, Miss Toklas looked on and smiled. Suddenly, Miss Stein left the room brusquely, said goodbye to the Hemingways and departed leaving the long silence between her and Jolas unbroken. Later when the first issue of *transition* was being put together, Sherwood Anderson brought Miss Stein and Miss Toklas for an evening at the Jolases. She was less abrupt than she had been at the Hemingway's but still the conversation was awkward and the evening not a complete success. Miss Stein's petulant reaction a few weeks later to the printer's error in 'An Elucidation' added further disharmony to her relationship with the Jolases.

Ironically Miss Stein played for a brief time a more prominent role in *transition* after Paul left in the beginning of 1928 than she had while he was still co-editor. While Paul was editor, he had made the selection of her works to be published from a large stack of previously unpublished manuscripts in her possession. Most of the selections he made were shorter, less ambitious pieces. When Paul left, Miss Stein herself began to make the selection of works for publication and she requested Jolas to print longer pieces by her. This led to the appearance of 'Tender Buttons', 'Four Saints in Three Acts', an accompanying critical article by Ralph Church repeating the points made by Paul in 'K.O.R.A.A.', and a bibliography of her published and unpublished works up to 1928. The special American issue number 14 even opened with a photograph of her.

Jolas, though willing to oblige Miss Stein by publishing the works she requested him to, did not show the same enthusiasm in dealing with her that Paul had shown and he did not solicit contributions from her regularly. When he did ask her for a manuscript in the spring of 1930, she reproached him with neglecting her reputation in favour of Joyce's. 'Joyce is a third-rate Irish politician', she said, 'The greatest living writer of the age is Gertrude Stein.'

'When Paul edited *transition* things were different.'

'When did Paul edit *transition*?' Jolas asked. In the end Jolas left 'mentally slamming the door.' For his part the alliance was over.

Eighteen months later when it was rumoured that *transition* was about to resume publication after its dormant interval, Miss Stein renewed contact with Jolas by a phone call: 'Jolas, I have just put in a new telephone and I am phoning friends to test it. You're the first one.' That

With the

Compliments

of

CALDER & BOYARS LTD

18 BREWER STREET

LONDON W1R 4AS

TELEPHONES 734 1985 6900 3786 3787

year Miss Stein even sent a copy of her 'How to Write' with the inscription 'To Maria and Eugene Jolas with affection and appreciation for what they are and what they do.' As a result of Miss Stein's efforts, one short piece by her, 'She Bowed to Her Brother', did appear in *transition* 21. And in the same issue she responded to 'The Metanthropological Crises' inquest. She dismissed the problem that Jolas felt was so important with a typical solipsism 'I don't envisage collectivism. There is no such animal, it is always individualism, sometimes the rest vote and sometimes they do not, and if they do they do and if they do not they do not' (*t.* 21, p. 136).

In 'A Play without Roses' published in *Portraits and Prayers* in 1934 Miss Stein gave a portrait of the Jolases during this short period of *entente*. Much of it is abstract, but the tenor of the relationship as Miss Stein saw it is clear. In the first section she evokes the tension in a meeting of herself and Alice B. Toklas with Eugene and Maria Jolas. 'We need not be nervous if we are anxious. They will be more than ever ours or forward.' By part two the feeling is dissipating, 'I do not as anxious feel a really anxious moment coming.' At the end there is a note of good will on Miss Stein's part toward the Jolases. 'Let me think splendidly of Eugenes . . . And they will be well wish. And Eugene and Maria Jolas.'

Neither of the Jolases saw a copy of 'A Play without Roses' until after 1935. But they did see *The Autobiography of Alice B. Toklas* published in that year which displayed quite a different attitude toward *transition* and its editors. In *The Autobiography* Miss Stein insisted on repeating the fiction that Elliot Paul had been the chief editor of *transition* even though the whole situation had been explained to her several times by both Eugene and Maria Jolas.

As she told the story, she first heard of *transition* one day when Paul had come to her for advice: 'A proposition had been made to him to edit a magazine and he was hesitating whether he should undertake it. Gertrude Stein was naturally all for it. After all, as she said, we do want to be printed. One writes for oneself and strangers but with no adventurous publishers how can one come in contact with those same strangers.'[4]

Finally, she mentions the Jolases as if they had come into the picture long after the founding of *transition*. 'Elliot Paul slowly disappeared and Eugene and Maria Jolas appeared.' She implies that Jolas was a poor influence on the magazine and caused its death. '*Transition* grew more bulky. At Gertrude Stein's request *transition* reprinted "Tender Buttons," printed a bibliography of all her work up to date and later printed her opera, *Four Saints*. For these printings Gertrude Stein was grateful. In the last numbers of *transition* nothing of hers appeared. *Transition* died.'[5]

To Eugene and Maria Jolas, Miss Stein had committed a personal affront by relating as fact things about *transition* that she knew to be untrue. She had, as Jolas said quoting Madame Matisse, 'presented the epoch "without taste and without relation to reality." '[6] Besides Jolas, Matisse, Georges Braque, André Salmon and Tristan Tzara all shared the belief that Miss Stein misrepresented them in her book. To correct the record, Jolas organized 'Testimony Against Gertrude Stein' as a supplement to *transition* 23. The small pamphlet would, Jolas hoped, prevent 'the regrettable possibility that many less informed readers might accept Miss Stein's testimony about her contemporaries.'

Maria Jolas stated *transition*'s case against Miss Stein. The magazine was not, 'conceived by Eugene Jolas as a vehicle for the rehabilitation of her own reputation, although it undoubtedly did do this. Nor was her role in its development different from that of many other well-wishing contributors.' The problem was with Miss Stein who could 'tolerate no relationship that did not bring with it adulation. This was undoubtedly lacking in our otherwise entirely correct and cordial attitude towards her, so when the moment came to play the mad queen in public, our heads had to come off with the others, despite the very real service we had rendered to her.'

Matisse, Braque, and André Salmon were concerned with Miss Stein's pose as an expert on the intricacies of the modern movements in painting. Matisse pointed out that it was not Gertrude Stein but her brother Michael's wife, who had first noticed his paintings. Miss Stein had also distorted other facts. In describing a picture of Cézanne in Matisse's possession she had misrepresented it badly. A scene between Matisse and his wife that Miss Stein had used to illustrate his attitude while painting had been totally misunderstood. These and other events, though each of them was minor in itself, showed how poor Miss Stein was in her observation, memory and understanding of the art circles she moved in.

The most important criticism made by Matisse was that her account

Photograph of Gertrude Stein, which appeared in *transition* 14, 1928.

Photograph in the cubist manner, which appeared in *transition* 11, 1928

Painting by Pablo Picasso which appeared with the cubist photograph, by courtesy of Gertrude Stein, in *transition* 11, 1928

of the origins of cubism was distorted. Picasso 'created cubism,' Miss Stein wrote bluntly. Matisse responded,

> According to my recollection it was Braque who made the first cubist painting. He brought back from the south a Mediterannean landscape that represented a sea-side village seen from above. In order to give more importance to the roofs . . . he had continued the designs that represented the roofs in the drawing on into the sky and had painted them throughout the sky. This is really the first picture constituting the origin of cubism and we considered it as something quite new about which there were many discussions.

Braque himself claimed that Miss Stein 'entirely misunderstood cubism which she sees simply in terms of personalities.' 'In the early days of cubism, Pablo Picasso and I were engaged in what we felt was a search for the anonymous personality. We were inclined to efface our own personalities in order to find originality. . . . Miss Stein obviously saw everything from the outside . . . she never went beyond the stage of the tourist.'

André Salmon charged that Miss Stein had misunderstood as serious a great deal of the joking among the surrealists and cubists whom she knew. Like Braque he laid much of the blame on her poor French.

Tristan Tzara attacked the very idea of the autobiography. He was displeased by Miss Stein's proclamation of her own genius and particularly by the collection of personal accounts which was amassed to build up the picture of literary-artistic cenacle with Miss Stein at the centre. '. . . Underneath the "baby" style . . . it is easy to discern such a really coarse spirit, accustomed to the artifices of the lowest literary prostitution, that I cannot believe it necessary for me to insist on the presence of a clinical case of megalomania.' He closed with a typical revolutionary attack against 'the depraved morals of bourgeois society' which he saw opposed only by 'a few rare beings who have posited the problem of man's destiny and dignity with a gravity . . .'

The inaccuracies of *The Autobiography of Alice B. Toklas* were probably more the result of a subjective point of view thinly disguised by making Miss Toklas the ostensible author of the book than of any malice or desire to alter the truth. But it had the effect of a hostile attack and the response left little room for reconciliation. The alliance between *transition* and Gertrude Stein was never resumed. While it lasted, it had been mutually beneficial. *transition* gained by publishing one of the most famous and controversial American writers. Miss Stein profited by finding an outlet for works not readily accepted elsewhere. And as Jolas had concluded despite her many differences from the magazine her fundamental departure from prevalent literary attitudes meant that she 'belonged' with *transition* more than with any other group of writers.

Notes

1 Gertrude Stein, *The Autobiography of Alice B. Toklas* (New York: Vintage), p. 252.
2 Donald Sutherland, *Gertrude Stein* (New Haven, 1951), p. 85.
3 Jolas, 'Man from Babel', p. 201.
4 Stein, *op. cit.*, p. 240.
5 *Ibid.*, p. 241.
6 Jolas, *op. cit.*, p. 202.

XIII

'WORK IN PROGRESS' IN *transition*

There was nothing illusory about the enthusiasm shown in *transition* for Joyce. Jolas opened the magazine to him completely. *transition* became, as the French critic Marcel Brion said, *'la maison de Joyce'*. Joyce dominated the magazine in almost every respect except determining what work by other contributors would appear. More pages of *transition* were devoted to 'Work in Progress', defence and explanation of it than to any other author. Jolas's theories, while frequently not shared exactly by Joyce, took their direction from his writing. At the peak of celebrity caused by *Ulysses*, Joyce was by far the most famous of the regular contributors, his reputation rivalled only slightly by Gertrude Stein. Later evaluations of *transition* have also tended to centre on Joyce almost to the exclusion of other writers.

Indeed, the name Joyce became so synonomous with *transition* that attackers could or would not tell them apart although the editors and Joyce tried to make distinctions clear. While *transition* opened its pages to Joyce, he reciprocated by devoting ample space to it in *Finnegans Wake*.

Joyce came to publish 'Work in Progress' (*Finnegans Wake*) in *transition* only after a series of almost unbelievable difficulties with other magazines. Ford's *transatlantic review* had given him proofs so 'grotesque' that he asked for a delay while the printer learned his trade. At *This Quarter* Ernest Walsh, dying of consumption, delayed publication for many months, lost the manuscript, and worst of all was unable to answer Joyce's inquiries. Printers for *The Calendar of Modern Letters* refused to set the 'Anna Livia Plurabelle' episode.

Joyce had, despite these difficulties, managed to get his first three sections introduced in the order he had chosen. However, as he explained in a letter to Harriet Weaver, he wanted his pieces 'to appear slowly and regularly in a prominent place' and had not yet found such a place.[1] T. S. Eliot, the first to solicit a section, remained sympathetic to 'Work in Progress' but solicited no second installment for *Criterion*. Even if Joyce had been willing to continue contributing to the *transatlantic review* and *This Quarter* after his first bad experiences with them, neither of them would have provided the regular prominent place of publication he was looking for. The *transatlantic review* was defunct by the spring of 1925. *This Quarter* published only one more issue before Walsh's death in 1927 and did not begin again until 1929. The one issue which did appear in 1927 contained a lengthy attack on 'Work in Progress'. *Le Navire d'Argent* which had published the 'Anna Livia Plurabelle' section was a French review and did not reach the audience Joyce required. Moreover, Joyce's friend, Valery Larbaud, who edited the review for Adrienne Monnier lost his early enthusiasm for the new work and spoke of it privately as a *'divertissement philologique'*.[2] Probably he did not request further contributions either. Joyce was now forced to take the initiative in finding a place to publish. By September of 1925 he was finishing the four watches of Shaun and looking for a place for them to appear. He decided to offer them to Marianne Moore, the editor of *The Dial*. He had high hopes that in *The Dial* he could find the regular, established mode of publication he desired. While waiting for a reply from Miss Moore he described himself as being 'as diffident as a young lady of nineteen'.[3] At last Miss Moore cabled an acceptance offering $650.00 for the contribution computed at the rate of one half cent per word, upon the condition that she might sée the text first. When she read the text, she asked Joyce to delete about one third of it. He refused, and *The Dial* withdrew its offer. The rejection upset Joyce and dejected him so that he wrote to Miss Weaver, 'I suppose no other review will take abcd but I will give it to anyone who will print it.'[4] Joyce was disappointed, but other possibilities still seemed open. Wyndham Lewis had plans for a new as yet unnamed critical–philosophical review. As a matter of principle Lewis intended to accept only criticism but he wanted to make an exception to the policy so that he could include a contribution by Joyce. Joyce agreed 'with great pleasure' to give him the four watches of Shaun. Sylvia Beach sent Lewis the typescript with the understanding that it would appear in the first issue of the new review. For months no review appeared and Lewis refused to respond to Joyce's inquiry. Not until January 1927 when Lewis published the first issue of *The Enemy* containing 'The Revolutionary Simpleton', a violent attack on Joyce, was there an answer.

In early November 1926, Pound, who was also planning a new literary magazine, *The Exile*, asked Joyce for the typescript of a new instalment. Joyce again complied willingly and hopefully, but Pound disappointed him also. He did not publish an attack like Lewis, but he did reply with a letter which despite its tone of goodwill contained harsh criticism. 'Nothing', Pound wrote, 'short of divine vision or a new cure for the clapp can possibly be worth all the circumambient peripherization.'[5] (Pound's criticism was intensified in January and February, 1927, by Miss Weaver's suggestion that Joyce should accept his verdict on his work and stop 'wasting his genius.'[6]) The complete reversal in the attitudes of his former champions was difficult for Joyce to accept, for, as he complained to Miss Weaver later, he needed encouragement in such a vast and difficult enterprise.

At the end of this series of disappointments and rejections came the request for Joyce to contribute to *transition*. Negotiations were begun in early December of 1926. First Sylvia Beach sent the manuscript to the editors and then Joyce invited them to a reading of the opening pages which he must have hoped would help to make the nature of 'Work in Progress' clearer. The reading was a success. He expressed his general relief in finding an audience which voiced approval at his reading in a letter to Miss Weaver, perhaps hoping that some of the enthusiasm would be contagious. 'I enclose your piece. I read it a few days ago to a small audience. Though I was partly smothered by a cold and in a state of exhaustion it seems to have made an impression for the next day also I received letters and bouquets!'[7] There was a second reading and then an agreement was reached for *transition* to reprint the pieces which had appeared earlier in *transatlantic review*, *Le Navire d'Argent*, and *Criterion* and then to continue with further instalments in each issue of *transition*.

After his dealings with other editors, Joyce could only have been pleased with the way in which this agreement was carried out. Both

Jolas and Paul were experienced and competent newspapermen who knew the mechanics of publication thoroughly. With them Joyce had no problems of lost manuscripts or months of delay in publication. The editors understood Joyce's need for several revisions of proofs with un-limited additions. Once Joyce received as many as five different sets of proofs. When his eyes got worse, his contributions were set up in out-size proofs so that he could correct them himself. On a few occasions the presses were stopped while the printer waited for Joyce's late revi-sions, heralded by a last minute telegram, to arrive by special mail. The practice grew so frequent that the printer began to use 'Joyce, *alors*' as a swear word modelled on '*merde, alors*', a fact which amused Joyce immensely. In *Finnegans Wake* Joyce refers optimistically to the print-ing of *transition* in the little town of St Dizier. 'I hope have of Sam Dizzier's feedst' (*F.W.*, p. 408).

While co-operating with Joyce on the practical arrangements, Jolas also offered the enthusiasm and understanding which Miss Weaver and others had been unable to muster even though they wished Joyce well. This enthusiasm and Jolas's uncompromising attitude toward censor-ship assured Joyce that he would not be asked to make changes in his work to suit editors, customs officials or printers.

From quite early in the relationship Joyce showed his confidence and gratitude. He formed the habit of dropping by the Rue Fabert office for informal visits, he referred to Paul and Jolas as 'my editors', and in July, 1927, when the arrangement was only three months old, he gave Paul and Jolas each copies of *Pomes Penyeach* in the special large paper edition of which only thirteen copies were printed. Later, he showed his friend-ship by starting a subscription to help Robert Sage who was ill and having financial difficulties. Joyce's greatest display of confidence was in entrusting to Jolas a copy of the general plan of *Finnegans Wake*, a document about which Joyce was even more secretive than his plan of *Ulysses*.

Even in a situation where his extreme suspiciousness brought on by so many earlier betrayals was activated, Joyce preferred to trust Jolas rather than break with him. In an effort to secure an American copy-right for 'Work in Progress' Elliot Paul called in his friend Donald Friede. Friede assumed a great deal of confidence on the part of Joyce and drew up arrangements that left the copyright in his name instead of Joyce's. This, combined with his request to publish all of 'Work in

Progress' and a delay in the copy for *transition* 12 which Joyce wanted
to send to America for copyright in his own name, led Joyce to fear
that Friede might publish part of 'Work in Progress' first and claim the
rights to it. Sylvia Beach, Joyce's then business manager, had a 'set-to'
with Jolas, but Joyce, aware of the value of a good editor, would not
take part in any accusations against Jolas.

   transition had advantages for Joyce beyond its editors. Its position as
an American magazine published in France was also helpful in the
matter of United States censorship. The editors were determined that
copies should reach subscribers and book stores in America and merely
printed and reshipped large numbers of copies to offset the numbers
confiscated. The price of a single issue was raised from 50 to 60 cents to
cover the cost of extra copies. Delay and slightly higher price were the
only obstacles placed between Joyce and his readers by the attempts at
censorship. Meanwhile European readers were still receiving their
copies usually without hindrances from the authorities. In comparison
with his previous difficulties this was negligible.

   transition also offered the advantage of political neutrality, or as Joyce
called it, 'the positive absence of political odia' (*F.W.*, p. 108). By 1927
both Pound in his review *The Exile* and Lewis in *The Enemy* were
already adopting dogmatic positions calling for political partisanship
which Joyce had resisted from his earliest days and with which he did
not want to be associated even indirectly. In the following years communism and fascism came more and more to demand allegiances from
writers and journals which began to be described as of the left or of the
right. In this situation *transition* carefully avoided becoming associated
with either camp. Joyce could publish in *transition* without giving up
the apolitical stance so important to him.

   Finding a suitable place for 'Work in Progress' to appear was only
part of the problem of introducing it. *transition* was also valuable to
Joyce as a means of teaching readers how to approach this bafflingly
different sort of book. Difficulty and indirection were part of Joyce's
method which he would not compromise to meet the demands of
readers, not even his former supporters like Ezra Pound and Harriet
Weaver. Nor was Joyce willing to explicate his works publicly as he
did privately to his friends. He was not, however, deliberately trying to
confuse the public. If he refused to lead readers easily and directly to his
'meaning', he was careful to point out the roads they should follow to

arrive there on their own and to make sure that some of them would follow the suggested route.

The first step after getting the sections published was to get them into the hands of those who would be able to understand them best. On his visits to the *transition* office Joyce would look over the list of subscribers to see who was receiving 'Work in Progress'. When he thought of names that he felt should be added to the list, he suggested that they be sent circulars inviting them to subscribe. Sometimes he would simply request that copies be sent to people whom he felt should be interested. He also made sure that Sylvia Beach circulated copies of *transition* to those like Professors Bernard Fay and Louis Cazamian whom he thought capable of understanding it. In January 1928 Joyce reported in a letter to his brother, Stanislaus, that he had been spending four hundred francs a month to keep a list of readers supplied with free copies. At the regular price of ten francs a copy his list would have included forty names.

Once the proper circle of readers was established, there remained the problem of overcoming the negative criticism which had met the sections published earlier and of providing the background necessary to read his book. Joyce watched the public reaction to his work carefully and became quite disturbed when the clipping service subscribed to by Sylvia Beach showed the public hostile to 'Work in Progress'. Meanwhile letters deploring his collapse poured into the *transition* office. By May, 1927, Joyce was considering more active ways of gaining wider acceptance for his work. He wrote to Harriet Weaver 'I will try to think out some other plans. . . . I have tried to keep off the stage as much as possible in the interest of other people's finer feelings but evidently it is not enough.'[8]

The plan which Joyce devised consisted at first of a series of articles by friendly critics in *transition*. Later he arranged with Sylvia Beach to publish the *transition* essays and three other pieces in *Our Exagmination Round his Factification for Incamination of a Work in Progress*. Joyce seems clearly to have had four major concerns in mind: to make specific answers to hostile critics, to present the public with an outline of the structural principles of the work, to establish that 'Work in Progress' was a development within literary tradition and not a flaunting of it, and to provide an explanation and justification of the linguistic innovations. Since the direct attacks to be answered were unpredictable, the response to them is *ad hoc* and interspersed throughout the series of articles. The other lines of defence are carried out in a systematic manner which is evident when they are read in order of their appearance in *transition* rather than in the alphabetical order in which they appear in *Our Exagmination*.

Before Joyce had time to put his plan into action an unexpected defence of 'Work in Progress' came from William Carlos Williams. Pound had written to Williams denouncing Joyce's book as 'backwash' and urging him to have nothing to say to it. Willams had responded with the article, 'A Note on the Recent Work of James Joyce', which appeared in *transition* 8 along with the announcement that it was 'the first of a series of articles by various writers, each considering a phase of this work' (*t.* 8, p. 183). While stressing the Catholic element of 'Work in Progress', Williams answered Pound's private criticism that it was a falling off from *Ulysses*. To the question 'Has he gone backward since ULYSSES?' Williams replies that the style of the new work is 'richer' than that of *Ulysses* and 'more able in its function of an unabridged commentary upon the human soul, the function surely of all styles" (*t.* 8, p. 151).

Joyce was soon to explain and defend his linguistic innovations, but he sought first to correct the imbalance of attention to that aspect by having Elliot Paul write 'Mr. Joyce's Treatment of Plot' for the December issue (*t.* 9). The first part of the book had been completed by the segment in the previous issue, the 'general plan' and 'innovations . . . more fundamental and original than the distortion and combination of words and blending of languages . . .' could now be considered (*t.* 9, p. 197). The book's plot is circular. Events are not ordered chronologically or spatially but instead are telescoped according to similarities among them as seen by Joyce's mind. The major motif is the fall and the two major characters H.C.E. and A.L. are avatars of Adam and Eve. Original sin is a continuing element of the plot. The article also points out the relation of many legends such as 'The Ballad of Persse O'Reilly', the birth of Isaac, the story of Finn MacCool, the murder of Abel by Cain, and Tristan and Isolde to the theme of the fall.

Jolas's 'The Revolution of Language and James Joyce' (*t.* 11), was the first of a series establishing links between 'Work in Progress' and previous works of literature. Joyce was pleased with the article and called it 'very good'. It stressed the continuity of Joyce's work with that of his

French and German contemporaries who had experimented with language. Marcel Brion's article 'The Idea of Time in the Work of James Joyce' for the next issue stressed the continuity between the use of time in 'Work in Progress' and its use in Joyce's own earlier works. In passing, Brion concedes Wyndham Lewis's point that 'Work in Progress' is like *Ulysses* a 'time novel', but argues that this is a strength and not a weakness. In 'James Joyce and Old Norse Poetry' Frank Budgen continued the attempt to show that Joyce's new work had literary precedents by comparing his attitudes and techniques to those of the scops of early Nordic poetry who had coined words and phrases freely as 'leverage applied to the imagination' (*t.* 13, p. 209). Again Joyce was pleased and wrote to Budgen, 'Many thanks, I like it very much. I am sure it will make a good effect. It is all to the point.'[9]

Stuart Gilbert was the next to associate Joyce's experimental writing with its forerunners. Joyce was difficult for exactly the same reason that Thompson and Crashaw were difficult: he had chosen for his subject an 'ideal history' as suggested by Vico in *La Scienza Nuova* (*t.* 13, p. 68). And in such a work in which the heroes of many ages are treated as one it is natural that the style would 'reflect the kaleidoscopic permutations' (*t.* 13, p. 68).

The attempt to establish 'Work in Progress' as traditional continued with a short article by Thomas McGreevy, then a young Irish Catholic poet who like Beckett taught at the *Ecole Normale Supérieure* and occasionally helped Joyce with typing. McGreevy's 'Note on Work in Progress' written at Joyce's request points out that the structure and subject matter of 'Work in Progress' is purgatorial and owes something to Dante (*t.* 14, p. 216). Joyce thought the article 'useful'. It was obviously written with less relish than the others and McGreevy later refused to write a second article.

While their emphasis was on other aspects of the defence, the articles by Paul, Jolas, and Gilbert had made reference to linguistic theory to justify the density of style in the new work. With John Rodker's contribution in the fourteenth issue, 'The Word Structure of Work in Progress', the apologia took a new turn by emphasizing linguistic theory. The method of 'Work in Progress' which had its theoretical roots in the theory of the origin of language given by Vico in *La Scienza Nuova* appeared to be confirmed by contemporary linguistic discoveries. Both C. K. Ogden in the *Meaning of Meaning* and the

Parisian Jesuit Abbé Marcel Jousse in his lectures at the *Collège de France* had developed theories which recognized that words contained several layers of meaning beneath their more obvious use as conventional symbols. Here were recognized thinkers whose findings could be used to show that Joyce's unique style was not merely a personal whim. Ogden's work was more widely known than that of Jousse and Vico so his *Meaning of Meaning* provided the argument for a number of articles on Joyce's use of language which culminated in Ogden's own preface to the March, 1929, Black Sun Press edition of *Tales Told of Shem and Shaun*.

In his article Rodker points out that Ogden has shown that words are more than symbols for objects or ideas; they also have affective overtones, vestigal etymological meanings and they act as stimuli toward attempts at physical reproduction of the sounds associated with them. Joyce has used words with full consciousness that these often unrecognized aspects will work upon his readers just as they have worked upon him in selecting them. 'Work in Progress' thus establishes a new 'symbiosis' between author and reader. That is its meaning—an 'attempt to make the unconscious conscious' (*t.* 14, p. 232).

Jolas continued the linguistic argument in number fifteen with his article 'The New Vocabulary'. Sean O'Faolain had launched a series of attacks upon Joyce's use of language in 'Work in Progress' culminating with an article entitled 'Style and the Limitations of Speech' in *Criterion* VIII. An attack from Eliot's direction, even if not from Eliot himself, was disturbing to Joyce and could not go unanswered. O'Faolain had argued that the eloquence of language is limited because 'our vocabulary is not of our manufacture' and 'liberty to invent, and add to, and replace, is . . . denied us' (*t.* 15, p. 171). Jolas counters this objection by showing that words (his example is 'title') have changed their meaning by being used in new contexts and that they gather multiple suggestions and meanings in the process. In the same issue Robert McAlmon's 'Mr. Joyce Directs an Irish Prose Ballet' emphasized another aspect of Ogden's theory—the evocative aspect of language which exists independently of 'meaning' in the traditional sense. The dance, music, painting, sculpture, and architecture have been granted value independent of any 'utilitarian, descriptive, [or] literal' meaning and it is just such a value that is claimed for 'Work in Progress' (*t.* 15, p. 126). The younger generation, which 'may demand less explanation about the meaning of meaning' (*t.* 15, p. 130), will likely understand this better than their elders.

In November, Stuart Gilbert, who had had the benefit of Joyce's own explication of passages (often running to five minutes on a single phrase), provided readers of *transition* 16/17 with a specific application of the theory of multiple meaning to a passage by explicating the many suggestions within single words or phrases. The passage was not included in *Finnegans Wake*, but the method of explication which Gilbert illustrated was applicable to almost all of the book.

Samuel Beckett's 'Dante . . . Bruno . . . Vico . . Joyce' in the same issue was an intentional summary and culmination of all the preceding lines of argument. It summarized *La Scienza Nuova* and clarified the relationship of the linguistic arguments for Joyce's style to the structural principles of the book. The remainder of Beckett's defence of 'Work in Progress' is a comparison between Joyce and Dante. The part of the defence which lay in showing that the structure of Joyce's work was not arbitrary is concluded by Beckett's comparison of Dante's conical purgatory, in which time is transcended, to Joyce's circular purgatory, in which time is recurrent. He sums up the discussion of linguistic innovation by showing that Joyce's rejection of standard English in favour of an artificial synthesis of several languages was like Dante's rejection of Latin for a language composed of parts of several Italian dialects. The critics of those innovations will, he says, be silenced by time as the critics of Dante have been. The whole rather detailed comparison with Dante offered one of the best proofs that there were literary precedents for Joyce's kind of experimentation and thus gave an impressive conclusion to the line of defence based on literary tradition.

Joyce was generally pleased by this series of articles and yet the necessity for a group effort by friends who were themselves still struggling to understand the uncompleted work left both Joyce and them open to attack. He tried to ward off some of the expected reaction by treating their effort to explain with irony in the *Wake*. There he says, 'Imagine the twelve deaferended dumbbawls of the whowl above-beugled to be contonuation through regeneration of the urutteration of the word in pregross' (*F.W.*, p. 284). The writers of *Our Exagmination*, in other words, were twelve not very perceptive authors who were so immersed in deference to Joyce and in the defence of his work even while it was being written that they appear deaf and dumb. Their comments might be regarded as bugling or howling. Still the reader must imagine them to be a kind of re-creation of the first utterances of the work, or in other words spokesmen for Joyce. Later Joyce has one of the inquisitors in the *Wake* ask, 'His producers are they not his consumers? Your exagmination round his factification for incamination of a warping process. Declaim!' (*F.W.*, p. 497). Joyce's friends were Finnegan's producers in that accounts of their actions and fragments from their conversation went into the *Wake*; they were his consumers in that they were at first almost the only audience able to read 'Work in Progress' with much success. In telling the prisoner to 'Declaim!' the inquisitor is also commenting on the style of the articles which was frequently defensive and declamatory. The 'warping process' is both 'Work in Progress' which does warp words to make new suggestions and *Our Exagmination* which, though official, could not give back Joyce's ideas without some distortion.

This first stage of Joyce's attempt to explain his book was separated from other attempts by almost two years of silence. In the spring of 1929 while he was finishing Part III and marshalling his defence of it, Joyce's eyes worsened. With number 18 Parts I and III had been published complete in *transition*, providing a convenient stopping point. Since no more parts were finished, Joyce had fulfilled the loosely agreed upon oral contract to publish all of the parts completed. A note at the end of 18 announced that because of his eyes Joyce was suspending publication in *transition*—hopefully temporarily. Freed from the demands of periodical contribution, he experienced both a sense of relief and a letdown. At first he wrote to Miss Weaver that he was 'no longer bound to *transition*.' Later he wrote to her, 'when I ceased contributing to *transition* I felt a sudden kind of drop. . .'.[10] The demands, though constraining, had also given him the impetus to continue a difficult and not very well-received undertaking.

Jolas's suspension of *transition* coincided with Joyce's rest from work on Part II. When publication of *transition* was resumed in 1931 the situation had changed so that Joyce could count on more approval from outside critics and had to depend less upon his own friends.

After *Our Exagmination*, Joyce had planned a second defence in the form of a book with four long essays each dealing with an aspect of 'Work in Progress'. Three topics were chosen—the treatment of night, mechanics and chemistry, and humour. The fourth topic was never decided upon. Harry Crosby, who owned a copy of the Egyptian *Book of the Dead*, was to do the essay on night. After Crosby's suicide in December 1929 the project was not carried out. But Jolas's *The Language of Night* begun in 1930 probably did receive some impetus from Joyce's plan. No series of articles dealing at length with the three topics of the proposed second book of essays ever appeared under Joyce's direction.

After 1929, the role of official commentator shared by the contributors to *Our Exagmination* fell to Jolas almost exclusively. Instead of being treated in essays by various hands the topics of the second planned defence were treated briefly by Jolas in his 'Marginalia to Work in Progress' in *transition* number 22. There Jolas emphasizes the essentially humorous tone of the work and calls attention to the use of *The Book of the Dead* and the division of the night into watches. In addition to mentioning the aspects which Joyce had thought to include in the second book of essays, 'Marginalia to Work in Progress' also provides an introduction to Part II. It notes the change in emphasis from the myths of the 'all-father', and '*Magna Mater*' to the myth of the 'infancy of mankind' (*t.* 22, p. 101), indentifies the characters in their new manifestations, and locates the time and place of the action. It also continues the explanation of the book's language by pointing out that some of the changes in words in this section are based on attempts of Sir Richard Paget to recreate the language of children. Finally the essay informs the reader of the presence of autobiographical material and use of numerology in the book.

After this introductory article to Part II no other 'official' commentary appeared until the final issue of *transition* in 1938. Jolas's essay, 'Homage to the Mythmaker', in that issue served the dual purpose of a valedictory to 'Work in Progress' and an introduction to the forthcoming Faber and Faber *Finnegans Wake*. In it Jolas answers the question 'what will the finished book be like?' with an extremely concise recapitulation of most of the points already made in earlier essays. The density of the references to the principles upon which the book is based and the detailed enumeration of characters and themes suggest that the article was planned systematically to include all of the important facts Joyce thought necessary to begin a reading of the book. There is also evidence that part of the essay constituted Joyce's own response to praise from the Vatican and official attacks from Russia and Nazi Germany.[11] It is certain that the essay is based upon the knowledge and understanding of the book which Jolas got from reading Joyce's early plan, helping in the stages of composition, and talking to Joyce about the work. Though the statement is in Jolas's terms and much of it comes from him and not from Joyce, the article is by far the closest thing to a final summary statement by Joyce on *Finnegans Wake* that exists.

The official *transition* apologia did not grow to the same proportions after 1932 as it did between 1927 and 1929 because friendly critics not connected with *transition* began to take a more serious interest in 'Work in Progress'. Joyce could, after all, leave some room for 'the finer feelings of others' to work. But having seen them work, Joyce could not resist the temptation of making sure that others had also seen them. A number of articles by people outside Joyce's Parisian circle, like Armand Petitjean's 'Joyce and Myth', were sent to *transition* and appeared for the first time there. Other articles like Carola Giedion-Welcker's '*Die Funktion der Sprache in der heutigen Dichtung*' which had been published elsewhere were reprinted in *transition* so that readers of 'Work in Progress' would not miss them (*t.* 22, p. 90).

There is no question as to the value of Joyce's campaign to use *transition* as a vehicle to explain 'Work in Progress'. As Edmund Wilson, one of the best early critics of *The Wake* put it, 'It is, in fact, rather doubtful whether without the work done by *transition* it would be possible to get the hang of the book at all.'[12]

Joyce's direct involvement with material which appeared in *transition* did not stop with the instalments of 'Work in Progress' and the articles of criticism about it. *transition* also served Joyce as a place where other matters of interest to him could be brought to the attention of the public. *transition* aired its protest against Samuel Roth's piracy of *Ulysses*, denounced the Japanese piracy of *Ulysses*, and published correspondence concerning the mistaken attribution to him of a story by Michael Joyce in *Die Frankfurter Allgemeine Zeitung*. In 1933 when Joyce began to tire of his self-imposed debt to Edouard Dujardin for the *monologue intérieur*, a short piece by Jolas distinguishing between the interior monologue and the interior duologue appeared. The chapter of Gilbert's *James Joyce's Ulysses* dealing with the Aeolus episode was printed in *transition* 18 to attract Joyce's readers to Gilbert's book. Occasionally Joyce directed the works of those who had requested his help in finding a publisher to *transition*. Italo Svevo, Arthur Power, and

Samuel Beckett were all published at Joyce's suggestion. By far the most curious of Joyce's contributions to *transition* was 'Fluviana' (*t.* 16/17), a collection of photographs of pieces of wood resembling various animals found in the Salzach river near Salzburg. Joyce had seen the collection when he visited Raitenhaslach in Austria in August 1928 and had purchased the photos of them.

Joyce's influence on Jolas was marked, but he was not always able to arrange things in the magazine as he wished. *transition* 21, the first issue after the two year suspension, was particularly troublesome to him in this respect. 1932 was the hundredth anniversary of the death of Goethe and also the year of Joyce's fiftieth birthday and the tenth anniversary of the publication of *Ulysses*. Groups were making plans to celebrate both dates. Carl Einstein thought Goethe a bad influence on German literature and could not bear to let the predictable flow of platitudes about Goethe go unquestioned, so he conceived the idea of an issue of *transition* in which Joyce would be praised at Goethe's expense. Jolas agreed, though he did not dislike Goethe as Einstein did and later read Goethe's *Farben Lehre* to Joyce. Einstein organized the attack on Goethe in a piece entitled 'Obituary 1832: 1932' and Jolas assembled the Joyce material.

When he perceived what was happening, Joyce tried to bargain with Jolas to soften the contrast by including a portrait of Goethe and a caricature of himself and by printing several recent personal attacks on him without comment. Jolas agreed but in the end the comparison was only heightened. Jolas did comment and the juxtaposition of the picture of Goethe with the caricature of Joyce, did even less to restore the balance between Joyce and Goethe. The portrait chosen for inclusion shows Goethe in an obviously posed, rigid posture, a manuscript in his right hand, and a stern look on his face. The eyes are averted to one side so that the whites of them are overaccentuated. Beneath the picture is the title 'The Olympian'. César Abin's caricature of Joyce was done at Joyce's own direction (after Joyce had first rejected the idea of being portrayed in black robes with a stack of books at hand) and emphasizes the unheroic aspects of his life. His long body is bent in the form of a question mark over the world, as if to mock the obscurity of his books, his black hat bears the number thirteen to show his ill luck, his dark glasses show his semi-blindness, his clothes are patched to show his poverty, and in his pocket is a copy of the song 'Let Me Like a Soldier

Fall' suggesting his ill-health and his penchant for sentimental Irish music. By itself the caricature might have had some effect in deflating the homage to Joyce, but compared with the portrait of 'The Olympian' it could only work to the detriment of Goethe. Goethe emerges from the contrast as a cold, artificially solemn man with bovine eyes, while Joyce appears a man with human failings who is beset by human ills. The contrast was softened only slightly by Stuart Gilbert whose statement of homage to Joyce lessened the 'Revolutionary Romantic' attack on Goethe's classicism by noting that Joyce too had classical elements.

Joyce placed the episode in a comic perspective by referring to it in the *Wake* as 'Contrastations with Inkermann' (*F.W.*, p. 71) a play on *Conversations with Goethe*, the famous biographical work by J. P. Eckermann. He alludes to the eye in the portrait by calling Goethe 'goatheye' (*F.W.*, p. 344) at one point. He burlesqued Einstein's onslaught on Goethe at another point by having Shaun denounce Shem's writing as 'Worse nor herman dororrhea' (*F.W.*, p. 283), a reference to Goethe's long pastoral poem 'Hermann und Dorothea'. The 'Jubilee issue' was the only case in which Joyce and Jolas differed seriously about the practical problems of what material should appear in *transition* concerning Joyce.

The two basic statements of Jolas's principles, 'The Revolution of the Word Proclamation' and 'Poetry is Vertical' manifesto, contain much that appears to describe 'Work in Progress'. Linguistic experimentation and the use of dream material are the most dominant themes of Jolas's manifestos and the most salient traits of Joyce's work. However, the concept held by Jolas of the part played by the unconscious in writing was quite different from Joyce's.

When Jolas calls for the primacy of the hallucinatory forces in 'Poetry is Vertical' he makes it clear that the sources of the literature he was most interested in were in the writer's own unconscious; the dreams and visions of his own works are not fictional. 'I Have Seen Monsters and Angels' he declared in one of his titles; the subtitle of 'Chimera' is 'words of sleep and half sleep'. He differs from the surrealists only in that he is willing to allow more intervention by the conscious mind than they do. He is essentially of their company in so far as the source of his material is concerned.

Jolas himself seems to have been well aware that he and Joyce

approached the unconscious in quite different ways. About Joyce he
wrote, 'Joyce had a passion for the irrational manifestations of life. Yet
there was nothing in common between his attitude and that of the surrealists and psychoanalysts. Nor did his experiments have anything to
do with those of the German romantics who explored the mysticism of
the individual world.'[13] These sources with which Jolas felt Joyce had
'nothing in common' are the very sources that Jolas refers to most
frequently in expounding his own theories. The attitudes of the surrealists, psychoanalysts, and the German romantics have the common
tendency to begin with the irrational manifestation of the mind, dreams,
automatic outpourings of thought and individual fantasy as a basic
source of material. For all three groups the material they use is
valuable primarily because it is the work of irrational segments of the
mind.

Joyce was interested in his dreams. He talked of them, interpreted
them, and even kept notebooks of them. But there is no indication that
the notebooks he used in writing *Finnegans Wake* are the same ones in
which he recorded his dreams. *Scribbledehobble the Ur-Workbook of
Finnegans Wake* records material from reading, conversation, and
phrases invented by Joyce while he was conscious, but no automatic
writing or accounts of dreams.

Rather than an attempt to record his own subconscious, *Finnegans
Wake* was a conscious attempt to produce a fiction that would depict
everybody's dreams. It is significant that Jolas chose to compare
Finnegans Wake not with the work of Novalis who used his own
dreams in his writing, but with Gerhart Hauptmann's *Hanneles
Himmelfahrt*.

> ... for the first time in any literature, the attempt is successfully made to
> describe that huge world of dreams. ... (To be sure, Gerhart Hauptmann in
> *Hanneles Himmelfahrt* attempted to present a dream-state, but it remained
> bound in the old literary conceptions as far as the actual expression was
> concerned.)[14]

Hauptmann's work is dramatic, not lyrical; the dream that he depicts is
that of a dying girl and not to be confused with any dream that Hauptmann himself might have had. Joyce's aim was similar to Hauptmann's.
His techniques on the other hand were quite different. The difference
lay in Joyce's use of the unconscious as a deliberate part of his means of

presenting the dream. Joyce did exploit the unconscious in writing, but he did so as a technique of presentation and not as a source of material to be presented.

In words that might well have been suggested by Joyce himself, and must in any case have grown out of conversation with him, Herbert Gorman describes *Finnegans Wake* as an attempt 'to break the bounds of formal speech and achieve that plane where the word, no longer a much-handled and partially-defaced token to arouse in the reader's mind an approximation of the thing meant, became the thing meant itself.'[15] This penetration to a 'plane' where language operates in a special way is the penetration of the unconscious which made Joyce's new style necessary. Joyce's revolution in language came not because the material which he was trying to depict came into his mind in the form of psychological distortions of everyday perceptions, but because he desired to create an effect in the reader. This effect was the symbiosis of reader and author which Rodker had written of in his *Exagmination* article, 'The Word Structure of "Work in Progress" ' (*t.* 14, p. 229).

The means by which the plane described by Gorman could be reached was explained by the theory of language which begins with the assumption that words are derived from gestures. This theory, to which Joyce gave adherence according to his friend Mary Colum,[16] was advocated in Vico's *La Scienza Nuova* and Marcel Jousse's *Le Style Oral.*[17] These works, combined with Ogden and Richards' *The Meaning of Meaning*, provided the rationale for Joyce's attempts to use language to penetrate the unconscious. In the articles which made up the *Exagmination* series, attention is called to Vico, Ogden, and Jousse, but the emphasis is upon Ogden's work. This emphasis is understandable since neither Vico nor Jousse had been translated in 1929, whereas Ogden wrote in English and had a much greater popularity than either of the other two. Furthermore, Ogden had taken an interest in Joyce's work, had asked him to record it, and had written a preface for a selection of it. It was only natural that the linguistic defence should have centred around his work. However, though *The Meaning of Meaning* will explain much about Joyce's method, it is not the best explanation and it does not appear to have been as important a source in determining the technique of *Finnegans Wake* as the works of Vico or Jousse.

Joyce had been acquainted with Vico's linguistic theory at least as early as 1913 when he remarked to one of his Berlitz pupils that Freud had been preceded by Vico in offering the theory that slips of the tongue are caused by unconscious motivations. Vico's theory of language seems to have assumed special importance for Joyce as he neared the completion of *Ulysses*. The 'Oxen of the Sun' episode has definite Viconian overtones. There the birth of Andrew Purefoy and the 'language of the future' are simultaneous with a clap of thunder. In Vico's theory the first clap of thunder after the great flood is the cause and the signal of the birth of a new stage of humanity and of language. Later, in the 'Circe' episode, Stephen Dedalus who has been quoting Vico earlier in the episode says '. . . gesture, not music, not odours, would be a universal language, the gift of tongues rendering visible not the lay sense but the first entelechy, the structural rhythm.'[18]

In *Ulysses* the language of gesture remains for the most part a thought in Stephen's mind. In *Finnegans Wake* it is the starting point of a stylistic revolution. According to Vico's *La Scienza Nuova*, language had evolved through three basic stages. The first means of communication had been through mute actions and bodies having natural connections with the ideas which they wished to indicate. This direct, sensual mode of expression was thus inseparable from the thing referred to. From this first stage man had developed the ability to make sound gestures as well as visible gestures. In this second stage language was more abstract but still visual as well as vocal. In the third stage language had become exclusively vocal and the connections with the physical situations out of which it originally arose had been pushed into the background so that it became even more abstract.

It was the residual, sensual element in language that Joyce wanted to exploit in *Finnegans Wake*. In the teachings of Marcel Jousse, Joyce found the most explicit and detailed exposition of the theory that modern language stemmed from gesture language and that it acted upon the senses at a subliminal level of consciousness. Jousse compiled quotation after quotation from psychologists, linguists, and physiologists to prove that language was as much a function of the senses as of the intellect. '. . . There are not [he wrote] in our consciousness any states which are uniquely intellectual awarenesses, these states are accompanied by movements and also by tendencies to action . . .'[19] According to Jousse, it is impossible to perceive anything without registering it permanently in our bodies as well as in our intellect. 'At every perception of an object, our whole body reacts by a gesticulation more or less visible and strikes an attitude which imitates it. This inter-play of the nerves . . . has a significance of which we can hardly grasp the importance. . . . Everything that we see is projected instantaneously in our musculature.'[20] Thus any time we hear a word the motor re-sponses associated with it come into play again. 'It is this infinity of past gestures held under the threshold of consciousness and setting off each other which renders the total revivification of past states and the mul-tiple rapports among them.'[21] Here was a powerful part of each word which might be called into play. For the most part, Jousse said, it had been neglected in Western book cultures in which language tended to become more and more abstract, but in the oral cultures of the East some knowledge of it had remained. In the Aramaic spoken by Christ and in the Hebrew of the *Old Testament* the physical gestures from which words sprang are still quite evident beneath the abstract mean-ings of words, and rhythm and sound are used to accentuate them. The true style of Christ's teaching was not the literary style of the Greek *New Testament*, but an oral style, in which words were used not only as abstract symbols but as physical gestures mimicking in some way by sound, rhythm, or order the things to which they referred.

Sometime in late 1926 or early 1927 Mary Colum accompanied Joyce to a lecture-demonstration of this oral style which she has described.

It took the form of a little play, based on the Gospels. Around the lecturer was a group of girls, who addressed him as 'Rabbi Jesus'. The words spoken —one of the parables, I think—were, I gathered, in Aramaic, and what was shown was that the word was shaped by the gesture. Joyce was full of the subject and talked to me about the lecture as we went along to the café where my husband was waiting for us, but I can't remember what he said.[22]

Mrs Colum did later remember enough of the conversation to tell David Hayman that Joyce had said to her 'if you understand that [Jousse's lecture-demonstration], you understand the aim of *Finnegans Wake.*'[23]

In *Finnegans Wake* itself Joyce also makes clear the importance which the theory of Jousse had for him. In presenting his material Jousse had played upon the famous 'Logos' passage in St John 1:1-14: 'In the beginning was the Word. . . . And the Word was made flesh, and dwelt among us.' Jousse had written, '*Au commencement était le Geste*'[24] and later he had said, '*Il n'est point de pensée qui ne soit incarnée dans un élément moteur, réactionnel ou reviviscent.*'[25] Joyce (perhaps remembering his own lines from *Portrait of the Artist* in which Stephen Dedalus thinks of his villanelle as the incarnation of the spirit into poetry and says 'In the virgin womb of the imagination the word was made flesh')[26] was struck by Jousse's formulation and translated it to his friends often as 'In the beginning was the rhythmical gesture.'[27]

In the *Wake* Shaun, the antagonist of the section, is about to depart from the girls of St Bride's, he promises to send a comforter, his brother Shem the protagonist. To give an indication of what this comforter will be like he quotes him: 'In the beginning was the gest he jousstly says, for the end is with woman, flesh-without-word.' (*F.W.*, p. 468) At another point Shem is said to have 'learned to speak from hand to mouth till he could talk earish with his eyes shut' (*F.W.*, p. 130). As in many cases in the *Wake*, history is progressing in two directions at once in this statement. The way Shem learns to speak is a recapitulation of the development of the spoken language out of gesture as well as the account of how Joyce developed the night language of Finn out of the theory of gesture. Earwicker himself is also described as speaking a language which owes something to Jousse. His speech is 'reconstricted out of *oral style* into the verbal . . . with ritual rhythmics' (*F.W.*, p. 36) (emphasis added).

Joyce's interest in the unconscious, based as it was upon the linguistic theories of Vico, Ogden and Richards, and Jousse, contrasted strongly with the attitude of the psychoanalysts who sought to extract something from the unconscious instead of using it to achieve a new kind of communication. As if to emphasize this difference for his readers Joyce juxtaposes his concept of words calling up responses of the whole body with the psychoanalytic preoccupation with the unconscious as a form of confession. He has HCE's interrogators say

> You're a nice third degree witness, faith! But this is no laughing matter. Do you think we are tone-deafs in our noses to boot? [i.e. from head to foot] Can you not distinguish the sense, prain, from the sound, bray? [i.e. can't you distinguish the purely semantic components of words from their physical effects] You have homosexual catheis of empathy between narcissism of the expert and steatopygic invertedness. Get yourself psychoanolised! (*F.W.*, p. 522)

HCE replies 'O, begor, I want no expert nursis symaphy from yours broons quadroons and I can psoakoonaloose myself any time I want'

(*F.W.*, p. 522). As one of the names of his protagonists, 'Pierce Orrielle', suggests, Joyce's interest was not in 'soaking loose' what was in the unconscious but in a conscious use of language to pierce beneath the normal level at which we respond to words.

'The Revolution of the Word' proclamation was intended to refer to Joyce even though he was not a signer and did not contribute an instalment of 'Work in Progress' to the issue in which the manifesto appeared. The basic differences in their use of the unconscious, however, make it necessary to apply the statements of the proclamation to Joyce with caution.

The *transition* manifestos offered as metaphysical and psychological reality, what Joyce accepted only as the working fictions of *Finnegans Wake*. The mind capable of dreaming all the many manifestations of HCE and his family has much in common with the 'transcendental I with its multiple stratifications reaching back millions of years . . . [a mind] related to the entire history of mankind, past and present' (*t.* 21, p. 148). And often in the dream this mind is represented by the 'hallucinatory irruption of images.' In fact, however, Joyce put very little faith in the Jungian notion of a collective unconscious. He told Carola Giedion-Welcker that he found Jung's thought 'confused and self-contradictory'.[28] To the Danish writer Tom Kristensen he said, 'my imagination grows when I read Vico as it doesn't when I read Freud or Jung.'[29] The 'universal history' which *Finnegans Wake* depicts has a different type of universality from the 'collective reality and totalistic universe' described by the manifesto.

Joyce has not tuned in upon the unconscious of his race; he has simply learned a prodigous amount of history and noted the recurrent patterns of human life. The sensation that the reader is being exposed to a mind that transcends the limits of individual memory located in time and space is deliberate. Joyce noted in *Scribbledehobble*, 'dream thoughts are wake thoughts of centuries ago.'[30] That is the impression that the reader of the *Wake* is supposed to have. But it is all illusory. As Jolas explained to an American reader of *transition*, Joyce's universality was 'literal'.[31] By the use of puns, rhymes, rhythms, catalogues, etc. he made each reference as inclusive and suggestive as he could. The reader, confronted with so many varied referents located within the context of such basic mythological structures as the stories of Adam and Eve and Cain and Abel, has the sensation of reading a work which is in touch with an impersonal source of poetry. The real source, however, was Joyce's own conscious mind and the material it collected, not any collective unconscious. In this respect Joyce's attitudes are in strong contrast to the whole orphic orientation of the latter stage of *transition*.

Even with these important differences in mind it is clear that Joyce was centrally involved in the revolution announced in *transition*. No work had ever concentrated on the representation of an internal state to the exclusion of external representation as *Finnegans Wake* did. It is ostensibly the dream of a Dublin pub-keeper, but we never see enough of the dreamer in his own persona to even speculate about his waking life. It does not even bear any acknowledged connection to the waking life of its author as the works of the surrealists do. The dream exists only as itself.

The form is equally determined by internal rather than external models. Old myths may abound in *Finnegans Wake* but no one of them, including the song which gives the title, explains the development of events. One of the most prevalent oversimplifications about *Finnegans Wake* is the assertion that Vico's cyclical theory of history determined the structure of the book. The four-stage pattern of Vico's 'universal history' is evident throughout, but as Joyce himself made clear, the cycles overlap and the *Wake* is not the recapitulation of one pattern. Vico's four ages are no more prevalent as a structural element than the myths of Cain and Abel, or the Tower of Babel. No single, pre-existing structure determined the events of the book. Joyce's own concept of the way the unconscious structures dreams and his own private myth of HCE, Anna Livia, and their children are the closest thing to a model for the structure of the book, but it is really the possibilities and suggestions of the medium itself that determined what Joyce would write and how. That is one of the main suggestions of the title under which the segments were published in *transition*—it is inconceivable that a dream should have a pre-existing form independent of the progressive stages of its own development.

And of course the work is paramount in every respect in the *Wake*. There more than anywhere else the new spirit of verbal indulgence successfully replaced the careful restraint and distrust of eloquence and rhetoric that characterized the previous quarter century. And there more than anywhere else the word—through puns, portmanteau words, and the rhythm of passages—was developed into a powerful vehicle for the concentration of thought and emotion. For Joyce, it is not the image which is the primary pigment equatable with our most basic consciousness, but the word which is as he puts it comically, the 'Ding hvad in idself id est' (*F.W.*, p. 611). And not only is this word the beginning for Joyce it is also the end, or rather it is Alpha and Omega, end and beginning. Through words experience remains forever with us ready for a kind of eternal return. At the climax of the *Wake* as Anna Livia is waking and regretting that all that has passed must be forgotten she says, 'What has gone? How it ends? Begin to forget it. It will remember itself from every sides, with all gestures, in each word. Today's truth, tomorrow's trend. Forget, remember!' (*F.W.*, p. 614). It is difficult to imagine a larger claim for the power of words. Joyce might have protested with reason, but the personal revolution he had carried out was bound to attract followers and bound to be seen in connection with others who were making similar departures from common assumptions. It was impossible for friends and critics alike not to see him as the leader of the movement.

Notes

1 *Letters of James Joyce* I, ed. Stuart Gilbert (New York, 1957), p. 245.
2 'Man from Babel'.
3 *Letters of James Joyce* I, p. 243.
4 *Ibid.*, p. 245.
5 *The Letters of Ezra Pound*, ed. D. D. Paige (New York, 1950), p. 202.
6 Richard Ellmann, *James Joyce* (New York, 1959), p. 603.
7 *Letters of James Joyce* III, ed. Richard Ellmann (New York, 1966), p. 149.
8 *Letters of James Joyce* I, p. 255.
9 *Letters of James Joyce* III, p. 177.
10 *Letters of James Joyce* I, pp. 288, 290.
11 Joyce's hand is evident behind several parts of the essay. The Nazis -had declared Joyce degenerate; Klaus Mann had asked him to contribute to *Mass und Werk*, his anti-Nazi anthology. Joyce had declined. The essay pointedly underscores Joyce's neutrality, 'Joyce does not take sides. He tells the pessimistic story of mankind's internicine war with a smile of irony and sometimes pity. He has no ethical axe to grind.' Joyce had discussed communist party spokesman Karl Radek's accusation that he lacked 'social consciousness'

with Jolas. Jolas repeated his defence that he represented the struggles of the 'proletarized lower middle-class' with understanding. The official voice of the Vatican, *Osservatore Romano*, had on the other hand praised 'Work in Progress' as an attempt to 'open new paths for the expression of human sentiments.' Joyce proudly exhibited the clipping for friends to read. Jolas includes a translation of the notice and adds the Joycean comment, 'the Catholic Church is apparently far removed from the philistinism and hypocrisy of some of the orthdoox literary crtiics of Dublin, London and New York.'

12 Edmund Wilson, 'The Dream of H. C. Earwicker', in *James Joyce Two Decades of Criticism*, ed. S. Givens (New York, 1963), p. 326.

13 Eugene Jolas, 'My Friend James Joyce', in *James Joyce Two Decades of Criticism*, p. 15.

14 *Ibid.*, p. 14.

15 Herbert Gorman, *James Joyce* (New York, 1940), p. 334.

16 Mary and Padraic Colum, *Our Friend James Joyce* (New York, 1958), p. 87.

17 Marcel Jousse, *Le Style Oral* in *Archives de Philosophe* II, iv (Paris, 1925).

18 James Joyce, *Ulysses* (New York, 1946), p. 425.

19 Jousse, *Le Style Oral*, p. 438.

20 *Ibid.*, p. 454.

21 *Ibid.*, p. 23.

22 Colum, *Our Friend James Joyce*, p. 87.

23 David Hayman, *Joyce et Mallarmé*, I (Paris, 1956), p. 161.

24 Jousse, p. 20.

25 *Ibid.*, p. 23.

26 James Joyce, *A Portrait of the Artist as a Young Man* in *The Portable James Joyce*, ed. Harry Levin (New York, 1947).

27 Colum, p. 87.

28 Interview with Carola Gideon-Welcker.

29 Ellmann, p. 706.

30 *James Joyce's Scribbledehobble: The Ur-Workbook for Finnegans Wake*, ed. Thomas E. Connolly (Evanston, 1961), p. 104.

31 Mrs Anna Braune of Chapel Hill, N.C. made notes of a conversation with Jolas on her copy of 'Anna Livia Plurabelle' (*Criterion Miscellany*, no. 15, 1929). 'According to Jolas . . . Joyce attempts

universality in a literal sense. That is, he packs into the stuff allusions to ancient and modern history, biology, etc., etc.' This copy of 'Anna Livia Plurabelle' is now in a private collection.

XIV

transition IN THE WAKE: FRIENDS AND THE ENEMY

As one of *transition*'s major and most experimental contributors, Joyce was implicitly involved in the controversy surrounding it. Joyce's associates at *transition* made no demands that he become directly embroiled in its literary disputes but the reaction of the public and critics soon made it clear that Joyce could not remain totally aloof unless he was willing to allow serious misunderstandings about his work to remain uncorrected. The appearance of Joyce, Gertrude Stein, the dadaists and the surrealists in the same magazine led to the widespread assumption that there was collusion among them. By the third issue, even before Jolas had issued any manifestos at all, there was so much negative criticism linking Joyce and Miss Stein together as the leaders of a cult of 'unintelligibility' that Elliot Paul had responded with the article, 'K.O.R.A.A.' ('Kiss Our Royal American Ass', after the heading 'KMRIA'—'Kiss My Royal Irish Arse' in *Ulysses*). The article is a serious attempt to distinguish the aims and methods of Joyce from those of Miss Stein. Wyndham Lewis added to the tendency to equate Joyce with the other experimenters who were appearing in *transition* by writing a series of pieces which he first published as essays in *The Enemy* in 1927 and 1928 and later enlarged and modified until they were published in his *The Diabolical Principal and the Dythyrambic Spectator* in 1931. In them Lewis insisted that *transition* was the work of a communist-surrealist group headed by Joyce and Stein. Meanwhile V. F. Calverton in the *Modern Quarterly* was charging that Joyce was culpable for leading the Paris group away from social revolution which Calverton felt to be more important than literary revolution.[1] In addition Harold Salemson, who had written for *transition* and signed the 'Revolution of the Word Proclamation', left Paris and returned to New York where he wrote a series of rather lurid articles about life in Paris which gave the impression that Joyce, Stein, and surrealism were part of a single-minded Parisian literary society. F. R. Leavis in *Scrutiny* even proclaimed that since Joyce had made no public statements specifically repudiating his connection with the manifestos and other contributions in *transition*, it must be assumed that he was in agreement with all that appeared in *transition*.[2]

The two earliest attempts to correct the misconception that *transition* was the work of a clique with identical literary and political aims were editorials. 'K.O.R.A.A.', was followed by 'First Aid to the Enemy', the joint work of Jolas, Paul, and Sage. It was a direct response to Lewis's charge of a conspiracy. In it the three editors denied any conspiracy or identity of aims and theory with either the communists or surrealists, but did admit to a sympathy for the revolutionary spirit of both movements. The drawbacks of efforts like these became apparent to Joyce at once when Lewis (in *The Enemy* no. 3) pounced upon the two denials as *prima facie* evidence that the conspiracy was even more subversive than it had appeared at first.

Where argument had failed, ridicule seemed a better weapon. Joyce's regular contribution to *transition* number 6 had already been completed when the third issue of *The Enemy* appeared. Joyce nevertheless wanted to publish a reply as soon as possible. He worked steadily and rapidly to prepare his first long response to Lewis and when *transition* number 6 had already gone to press an urgent telegram from Joyce arrived at the printer's office announcing that a large addition to Joyce's contribution would follow. Six extra pages (106a–106f) were required to accommodate the addition; the issue was delayed, and the printer was greatly inconvenienced, but Joyce's reply to Lewis was included. It was 'The Mookse and the Gripes', the first of two fables in the *Wake* in which Lewis is satirized.

The title is based upon Aesop's fable of the 'Fox and the Grapes'. Joyce becomes the 'gripes' instead of the Grapes because he was the cause of Lewis's annoyance. Lewis becomes a 'Mookse', a mixture of fox and monkey because of the title of two of his books. The idea of characterizing Lewis partly as a monkey came from his *Apes of God*, a satirical novel about literary pretenders which Lewis used as another part of his wide attack upon the whole situation in art and literature after World War I. The characterization of him partly as a fox came not only from Aesop, but also from Lewis's fictional account of Shakespeare, *The Lion and the Fox*. At times in the fable he is called Leo, as well. Lewis appears elsewhere in the *Wake* in the guise of all these animals. 'The Mookse and the Gripes' deals more with Lewis's attacks on *Ulysses* and 'Work in Progress' than upon the rest of *transition*. To display the criticism of 'Work in Progress' Joyce has the Gripes ask the Mookse to tell him all about Anna Livia. This simple question precipitates a vituperative onslaught from the irate Mookse. The even simpler question, 'What time is it?' provokes an even more violent response. Here Joyce is referring to Lewis's attack in 'The Revolutionary Simpleton', *The Enemy* II, where he first denounced *Ulysses* as a 'time book'. In the face of this behaviour, the Gripes remains quite eventempered and admits that the Mookse 'had reason' (*F.W.*, p. 158). The moral to Joyce's fable was that the general nature of Lewis's criticism was unfounded and that his hostility was unwarranted. 'That Mooksius with preprocession and with proprecession, duplicitly and diplussedly, was promulgating ipsofacts and sadcontras' (*F.W.*, p. 156). The whole quarrel is ultimately shown to be folly. The exchange of epithets between the two opponents is 'bullfolly' answering 'volleyball' (*F.W.*, p. 157). 'Nuvoletta' (*F.W.*, p. 157) [the new literature, 'Work in Progress'] meanwhile is ignored by both combatants.

The 'Mookse and the Gripes' showed that the technique of using the *Wake* itself as a vehicle for defence was successful. The structure of the book was well suited for carrying its own defence. Much of the action takes place between characters representing pairs of varying opposites. To dispel accusations Joyce had only to insert them into the many quarrels and associate them with the unpopular figures or exaggerate them to the point of being comic. By couching his polemics in this comic mode Joyce gained a great advantage over Lewis. As Geoffrey Wagner, Lewis's biographer, notes, the contrast between Lewis's malicious essays and Joyce's comic response make Lewis appear wrongheaded and Joyce appear 'heroically generous.'[3]

Lewis's main complaints against *transition* were that it was communist, nihilistic, and diabolic. In the course of his pieces in *The Enemy*, however, Lewis managed to find in *transition* examples of almost every-thing he disliked. Joyce ridicules Lewis's disdainful view of *transition* by having the 'lair' (*F.W.*, p. 183) of Shem the penman appear odious. 'Smatterafact, Angles aftanon browsing there thought not Edam reeked more rare' (*F.W.*, p. 183). Lewis, the Englishman on the side of the angels using only a smattering of fact, and after not reading very care-fully (Lewis admitted in *The Diabolical Principle* that he had not read all of the issues of *transition* which had been published), found Joyce's literary company unpleasant. The lair itself is full of things that Lewis associated with *transition*. It contains 'telltale stories, sticky-back snaps' (fiction and photographs), 'alphybettyformed verbage', 'imeffible tries at speech unasyllabled' (experimental writing), 'flue-foul smut' (salacious material), 'borrowed brogues' (literary borrowings), 'ompiter dictas' (critical pronouncements), 'fallen lucifers' (diabolism), 'neverworn breeches' (Carl Sternheim's 'The Pair of Pants' which Lewis had said represented the ideal of the magazine), 'unused mill and stumpling stones' (pieces by Gertrude Stein), 'cans of Swiss condensed bilk' (Dadaist writings), 'fresh horrors from Hades' (works like those of Lautréamont and Drieu La Rochelle) (*F.W.*, p. 183), and 'war moans' (the latter's *The Young Europeans* which the editors pointed out was born out of the despair created by World War I.) '. . . to which, if one has the stomach to add the breakages, upheavals distortions, inversions of all this chambermade music ['Work in Progress'] one stands, given a grain of goodwill a fair chance of actually seeing the whirling dervish' (*F.W.*, p. 184). Lewis obviously lacked the goodwill that it would have taken to see beyond his distaste for other contributors in order to find the distinguishing characteristics of Joyce's work.

One of the most malicious of Lewis's assertions was that 'the *transi-tion* camp' was led jointly by Joyce and Gertrude Stein. Lewis had ample opportunity from his personal contact with Joyce to know that this assertion was not true; he nevertheless repeated the charge often. He spoke of his series of articles as 'my considerable expedition against Stein and the *steinizing* foreign garrison in Paris'.[4] He refers to the writers of *transition* as 'Joyce, Stein, *et hoc al*.'[5] Worst of all from Joyce's point of view he indicated that Joyce and Miss Stein were imitating each other and that she was the originator. 'Stein should scratch Joyce's back as he has scratched hers and repay him by taking a leaf out of his polygluttonous volume (always "in progress"—Continuous Present) and get out of English.'[6] Joyce turned this confusion of his aims and methods with Miss Stein's into an elaborate joke which appears somewhere among almost all of the accusations at the various inquisitions which go in the book.

The first mention comes when the hog caller who had been abusing Joyce's hero, HCE, ends his diatribe with a final act of insult. 'That more than considerably unpleasant bullocky before he rang off drunkishly pegged a few glatt stones, all of a size, be way of final mocks for his grapes' (*F.W.*, p. 72). The anticipation of the 'Mookse and the Gripes' identifies the caller with Lewis. The English-German pun, 'Stein-stone', is one which Joyce repeated frequently. By making the stones 'all of a size' Joyce is able to ridicule Lewis's inability or unwillingness to acknowledge that differences existed. The reference, depending as it does upon a pun and an allusion to a later part of the book, might easily have been missed by readers, but Joyce calls attention to it several pages later. The speaker, 'conscious of enemies', refers to 'broadsteyne 'bove citie' and adds '(Twillby! Twillby!)' (*F.W.*, p. 75). The short passage refers to the fact that Joyce has already commented on Lewis's confusion of him with Gertrude Stein (' 'bove citie'—cited earlier) and that in the coming pages '(Twillby! Twillby!)' he will reply to the 'broadside' (Lewis insisted on calling his rather lengthy discourses 'pamphlets') in which the accusation was made. The passage also makes humorous reference to Miss Stein's corpulence ('Broadsteyne') and Picasso's famous retort 'Never mind, she will', when told that Miss Stein did not resemble his portrait of her.

Joyce's first actual denial of his connection with Miss Stein, other than that contained in the phrase 'unused millstones' in the description of Shem's lair, comes as HCE is being examined in court. He swears most solemnly, 'that was no steal and that, nevertheless, what was deposited from that eyebold earbig noseknaving gutthroat, he did not fire a stone either before or after he was born down and up to that time' (*F.W.*, p. 91). The allusion to Miss Stein's large features and the harsh play on her first name, Gertrude-'Gutthroat' (cutthroat, visceral enunciation), do not make it appear that he was fond of her.

There is a similar accusation and denial in the Glugg and Chuff section (a section which according to Jolas was an extension of 'Mookse and the Gripes', *t*. 22, p. 102) but this time it is possession of a stone and not throwing one which is in question. 'Have you monbreamstone?'

(moonstone and brimstone) Glugg demands of Chuff. 'No', he answers, 'Or Hellfeuersteyn?' 'No' (*F.W.*, p. 225). Joyce here disclaims both the association with Miss Stein and charge of diabolism which Lewis raised against *transition*. In another passage Joyce, remembering Miss Stein's public quarrel with her younger brother Leo, has Shem take on the form of 'Dolph, dean of idlers, meager suckling of gert staon' who 'coached rebelliumtending mikes of his same and over his own choirage of Backlane Univarsity' (*F.W.*, p. 287).

By bringing Miss Stein's quarrel with her brother into the matter Joyce is also referring to his own disputes with Stanislaus. In April 1931 Stanislaus Joyce had written a letter to his brother in which he had complained 'It riles my blood to see you competing with Miss Stein for the position of Master Boomster.'[7] Though the letter did not accuse him of taking his ideas from Miss Stein, it did accuse him of trying to assert himself as the major representative of the new writing. The passage is thus partly an answer to Stanislaus as well as to Lewis.

Aside from the fact that they were both in Paris, wrote for *transition*, and had experimented with style, the only specific similarity that Lewis mentioned was that Joyce's work, 'continually in progress', owed something to Miss Stein's 'Continuous Present'. Joyce responded to this by using the phrase 'continuous present' to describe the writing of Shem the Penman, 'this Esuan Menschavick and the first till last alshemist wrote over every square inch of the only foolscap available, his own body, till by its corrosive sublimation one continuous present tense integument slowly unfolded . . . transaccidentated through the slow fires of consciousness into a dividual chaos, perilous, potent, common to allflesh, human only, mortal) but with each word that would not pass away the squidself which he had squirtscreened from the crystalline world waned' (*F.W.*, pp. 185–6). It is clear from this that it is not Miss Stein's theory of a single moment of consciousness with which the writer keeps 'beginning again' that makes his book continually 'in progress' but the fact that it is partially autobiographical— the revelation of a 'squidself' behind a shield of ink—and as such must be in progress so long as it continues to be made up out of the events of Joyce's life. In case there should be any doubt about the part that consciousness and intention play in his writing, Joyce emphasizes that his works must pass through 'the slow fires of consciousness.'

Joyce had almost more reason to fear that Lewis's attempts to link

him with the surrealists would be taken seriously than he had to fear
that he would be associated with Miss Stein. Surrealism had grown out
of the dadaist movement that flourished in Zurich during the time he
lived there and even before Joyce had started 'Work in Progress' or
published in *transition*, his name had been associated with dadaism. He
wrote Stanislaus in September 1920 to complain of the rumour that he
'founded in Zurich the dadaist movement which is now exciting
Paris.'[8] The rumour, while troublesome, was also one he enjoyed
repeating. The dadaists took a delight in destruction of all things held
sacred by the past; HCE, though he is the protagonist of all past history,
is also the embodiment of a new future and thus represents a threat to
the conservative powers of the world. He is, as 'The Ballad of Persse
O'Reilly' describes him, 'fafa-father of all schemes for to bother us'
(*F.W.*, p. 45). Or as Joyce put it in the advertisement he wrote for the
Faber and Faber edition of *Haveth Childers Everywhere* and *Anna Livia
Plurabelle* he is 'the grand-dada of all' (*t.* 21, p. 258).

At another point Joyce plays with the rumour that he was the founder
of the dadaist-surrealist movement by making HCE the focal point of
a literary salon attended by dadaists and surrealists. The topic is introduced by the announcement that the conversation is getting on to
'dadaddy again, as them we're ne'er free of . . .' (*F.W.*, p. 496). There
follows a description of the 'salon de espera' (*F.W.*, p. 497), a literary
group founded upon the hope for a better world that grew out of the
despair about the old one. It is a place where there are 'lodes of ores
flocking fast to Mount Maximagnetic, afeerd he was a gunner but
affaird to stay away' (*F.W.*, p. 497), probably an allusion to *Les champs
magnétiques*, the first official piece of surrealist writing composed jointly
by André Breton and Philippe Soupault, and perhaps also to Max
Ernst who called himself 'dadamax'. This allusion is strengthened later
when the speaker says 'We are again in the magnetic field' (*F.W.*,
p. 501). The salon is attended by 'Merrionites' (followers of Marinetti,
the founder of futurism which influenced the early dadaists for a while),
'Dumstdumbdrummers' (the works read at the Cabaret Voltaire were
often accompanied by loud, rhythmical drumming), 'Cabraists' (those
who took part in the dadaist activities of the Cabaret Voltaire in Zurich
where dadaism was founded), and 'Ballymunites' (followers of Hugo
Ball, one of the founders of dadaism). 'Munites' suggests the comical
tendency of dadaists and surrealists to band together in communities

WL.
1920.

Drawing of James Joyce. 1920.
by Wyndham Lewis.

Portrait of James Joyce by Wyndham Lewis, 1920.

Caricature of James Joyce by César Abin, which appeared in
transition 21, 1932

falling hair and for would be joybella to sing sadly ringless hands.
The dame dowager to stay kneeled how she is as first mutherer
with cord in coil. The two princes of the tower royal, daulphin and
devlin, to lie how they are without to see. The dafe dowager's duffgerent to present wappon and about wheel without to be seen of
them. The infants Isabella from her coign to do obeisence toward
the duffgerent as first futherer with drawn brand. Then the court
to come in to full morning. Herein see ye fail not
— Vidu Porkeg Ili vi rigardas Returnu, Porkego Maldeji-
kat

Hummels! That crag! Those hullocks! What have you therefore? I fear lest we have lost ours respecting these wildy parts.
How shagsome all and beastful! What do you show on? I show
because I must see before my misfortune so a stark pointing
pole. Can you read the verst legend hereon? To the dunleary
obelisk via the rock what myles knots furlongs; to the general's
post office howsands of patience to the Wellington memorial half
a league wrongwards to sara's bridge good hunter and nine to
meet her to the point, one yeoman's yard. He, he, he! At that do
you leer? I leer because I must see a buntingcap of so a pinky on
the point. It is for a true glover's greetings and many burgesses by
us uses to pink it in this way. Do you not have heard that the queen
lying abroad her king shall come tomorrow, michaelmas? He shall
come by jubilarian with — who can doubt it? — His golden bea-
gles and his white elkox terriers for a hunting on our littlego ill-
come faxes meynhir mayour, our boorgomaister, in best bib and
tucker, surrounded by his full cooperation and all our pueblos,
shall receive acm king at broadstone barrow with a keys of good-
morrow onto his pompey cushion. It will give piketurns on the
tummlipplads and crosshurdles and dollmanovers and vicqvious
tyrolyphics at darkfall for our fancy ladies. You do not have
heard? I have heard anyone tell it yesterday how one should
come on morrow here but it is never here today. Well but remind
that it is always tomorrow in that place. Amen.
True! True! Is rich Mr. Pornter always in his such strong health?
I thank you for the best, he is exceedingly herculeneous. One
sees how he is lot stoutlier than of formerly. One would say him
to hold whole a litteringture of kidlings under his aproham. Has
handsome Mr. Pournter always been so long married? O yes Mr.
Pournter families has been marryingman ever since so long time

Final proof of 'Work in Progress' for *transition* 18, 1929, with Joyce's corrections

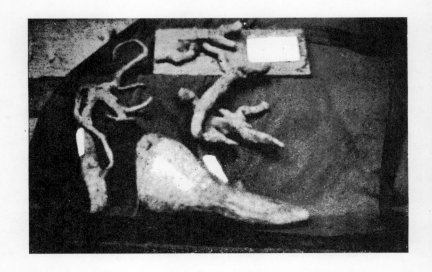

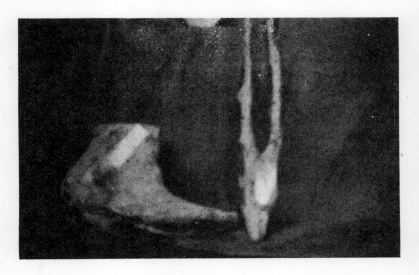

'Fluviana' (photo Fischer, Salzburg), a collection of objects which
appeared by courtesy of James Joyce in *transition* 16/17, 1929

James, Nora, and Lucia Joyce in Austria in 1932; from left to right: daughter of waitress, Lucia Joyce, waitress, James Joyce, Nora Joyce

Eugene Jolas and James Joyce at Joyce's flat in 1939; Jolas is holding the first impression of the last issue of *transition*

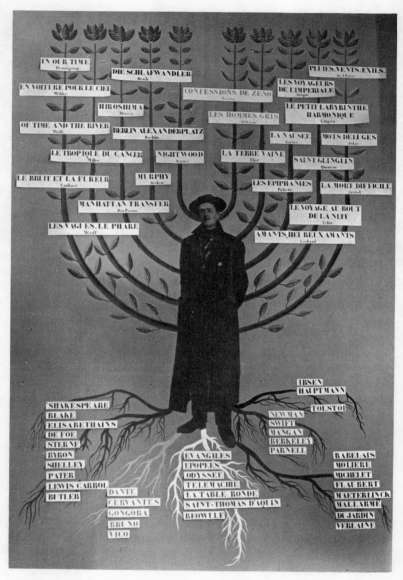

'Roots and Branches': James Joyce pictured with literary ante-cedents (below) and progeny (above); executed by Johnny Fried-lander and Zao-Wou-Ki from a marquette by Bernard Gheerbrant especially for the first Joyce exhibition held in Paris (La Hume Gallery, October, 1949)

(*F.W.*, p. 497). These visitors come 'for to comtemplate in manifest and pay their firstrate duties before the both of him' (*F.W.*, p. 497). Joyce is referring here to the tendency of surrealists and dadaists to write manifestos and partake in joint exercises in automatic writing. The group is entertained in 'the licensed boosiness primises of his delhightful bazar and reunited magazine hall, by the magazine wall, Hosty's and Co, Exports' (*F.W.*, p. 497) referring to the fact that *transition* welcomed both dadaists and surrealists and was instrumental in introducing these essentially European movements to America. This association of HCE with the surrealists is discredited because this is a hearsay report from one of the hostile inquisitors of HCE.

Even when he is not being accused of being the leader of the group HCE must be continually contending with his connections with surrealism during his arraignment. At one point HCE 'soaked in methylated, appeared in dry dock, appatently ambrosiaurealised' (*F.W.*, p. 85). In other words he appears drunk. Like the effects of liquor which law abiding citizens so often think they notice in those accused of crimes, the taint of surrealism is obvious on HCE. To those who judged Joyce without knowing the facts, it was 'patent' that he was a surrealist. A reference to the serialization of HCE is also contained in the passage, as well as a comment on the 'ambrosiaurealised' or too dreamy reports of surrealistic writing.

In the midst of HCE's trial there is an aside about a sugar daddy. The passage obviously owes something to the celebrated case of Papa Browning and his girlfriend Peaches which titillated newspaper readers of the late twenties, but it also contains a number of references to surrealism and its serves as Joyce's most specific disclaimer of sympathy with the surrealist movement. 'dadaddy' of the previous passage had also been described as having done 'something seemly heavy in sugar' (*F.W.*, p. 496). Joyce seems to have enjoyed making the dadaists into sugar daddies. The passage begins with a warning to the common man that his leg is being pulled. 'Come on, ordinary man. . . . Your machelar's mutton leg's getting musclebound from being too pulled' (*F.W.*, p. 64). It then goes on to give the account of the affair between an old man and two young girls. The 'old geeser', perhaps reflecting the surrealists' interest in 'la femme enfant', 'vows her to be his own honeylamb, swears they will be papa pals . . . combing the comet's tail up right and shooting popguns at the stars. . . . For dear old grumpapar, he's gone on the razzledar, through gazing and crazing and blazing at the stars' (*F.W.*, p. 65). References to stars, planets, and celestial panoramas occur continually in the writing of the dadaists and surrealists. Jolas's friend, Paul Eluard, for example, was given by the surrealists the title 'The Nurse of the Stars'. The young girl, however, is not impressed and declares, 'you're too dada for me to dance (so off she goes!)' (*F.W.*, p. 65). (cf. André Breton's description of a woman who no longer wants to dance in 'Discourse on the Dearth of Reality' in *transition* number 5, p. 136). The old geezer is not bothered by this brush-off because he has 'gel number two . . . and he would like to canoodle her too some part of the time' (*F.W.*, p. 65). Ideally though, he would be happiest if 'they all were afloat in a dreamlifeboat hugging two by two in his zoo-doo-you-doo . . . in his tippy, upindown dippy, tiptoptippy canoodle' (*F.W.*, p. 65). The attempt of the old man to keep two affairs going at once in his unstable 'dreamlifeboat' is a humorous allusion to the attempts of the surrealist movement to accommodate widely disparate attitudes among its members, and the bitter conflicts among Breton, Aragon, Tzara, and others that they occasioned. In the course of those doctrinal struggles, charges and countercharges of various heresies were exchanged, people were arraigned before kangaroo courts, and there were even formal excommunications. Surrealism was indeed a tippy canoe.

The aside continues with a further description of the boat and its passengers: 'Ack, ack, ack. With which clap, trap, and soddenment, three to a loaf, our mutual friends the fender and the bottle at the gate seem to be implicitly in the same bateau' (*F.W.*, p. 65). The reference to the fender and the bottle does not appear to refer to surrealism but the other parts of this description call to mind a number of the major concerns and statements of the surrealists. 'Clap' is likely an allusion to René Crevel's statement in the second issue of *La Révolution Surréaliste* that 'everyone is more or less syphilitic.' 'Three to a loaf', and 'soddenment' refer to the unfounded charge of Paul Claudel in his *Il Secolo* interview that surrealism and dadaism meant only one thing: 'pederasty.' His remark evoked the surrealist reply, 'Open letter to M. Paul Claudel, French Ambassador to Japan'.[9] In other writings and manifestos, like 'Hands off Love', the surrealists defended sodomy and all other sexual permutations as necessary to the kind of freedom they were trying to establish (*t.* 6, p. 155). 'Bateau' alludes to the importance that the early surrealist statements ascribed to Rimbaud's 'Le Bateau Ivre', which they declared an exemplary text. It is probably from their interest in this work and recurrence of boats in their poetry that Joyce got the idea of presenting them in a boat. The boat bears 'several of the earmarks of design' (*F.W.*, p. 66). Georges Ribemont-Dessaignes, a frequent contributor to *transition* and a friend of Joyce, had been a member first of the dadaist group and then later of the surrealist group.

The speaker of the passage is rather unimpressed by the whole situation and comments 'the amount of all those sort of things . . . has been going on onceaday in and twiceaday out every other nachtistag among all kinds of promiscious individuals at all ages in private homes and reeboos publikiss and allover all and elsewhere throughout secular sequence the country over and overabroad has been particularly stupendous' (*F.W.*, p. 66). Joyce has in mind here the many public disturbances for which the surrealists became noted. The matter is summed up by calling the group 'Federals' Uniteds' Transports' Unions' for Exultations' of Triumphants' Ecstasies' (*F.W.*, p. 66). The 'Surrealist Central', was an office not unlike a trade union branch where meetings were held, members signed up, and propaganda distributed. The office was at 15 rue de Grenelle in 1924 when Joyce lived in the Square Robiac at 192 rue de Grenelle. He must have passed the office frequently since it lay between his home and St Germain des Prés.

One of the main charges that Lewis brought against the 'conspiracy' of Joyce with Miss Stein and surrealism was that they were all nihilistic. Much of his attack on *transition* was devoted to a discussion of the articles by Jolas and Paul in which they applauded the destructive literature of Lautréamont and Pierre Drieu La Rochelle. To Lewis this amounted to 'a return to the feverish "diabolism" that flourished in the middle of the last century in France, and which reached England in the "nineties", with Oscar Wilde and Beardsley as its principal exponents.'[10] 'All that is new, therefore, is that a band of communizing journalists, living in Paris, have chosen to found a political school for middle-class Anglo-Saxon and French students, mainly art-students, and *fils à papa*, upon the diabolic text of the famous authors mentioned above.'[11] Joyce had even less in common with Lautréamont and Drieu La Rochelle than he did with Miss Stein and surrealism. But *transition* had given much prominence to Drieu La Rochelle in the early issues, and Jolas had advocated acknowledgement of 'the diabolical principle', the irrational, destructive part of the mind. Lewis overstated the case against *transition*, but he was not entirely wrong in his accusation. Because his strictures contained some truth it was necessary for Joyce to defend himself from the allegation.

He resorts again to the method of repeating the charges in a manner so comic as to discredit them. When the Mookse sets out on the way to meet the Gripes, he comes 'upon the most unconsciously boggylooking stream he ever locked his eyes with. Out of the colliens it took a rise by daubing itself Ninon. It looked little and it smelt of brown and it thought in narrows and it talked showshallow. And as it rinn it dribbled like any lively purliteasy: *My, my, my! Me and me! Little down dream don't I love thee!*' (*F.W.*, p. 153). This stream which is associated with the unconscious and sings 'little down dream don't I love thee' (cf. Lewis's sarcastic remark in *The Enemy*, 'Good old "dream" how handy you are!'[12]) has a name composed of a double negative. Surrealism and nihilism appear to be joined. Joyce seems to be determined that the Mookse will find the Gripes' surroundings just as Lewis imagined Joyce's to be.

The accusation is alluded to again in a passage containing a more specific reference to Drieu La Rochelle when in the trial of HCE in part III a witness is forced to admit that a war that has gone on for years 'twill cling hellish like engels opened to neuropeans' (*F.W.*, p. 519). Lewis had, with no basis whatsoever, accused *transition* of advocating war and favouring communism and he carried out his critical attack in terms of war. The passage joins suggestions of diabolism in 'hellish', and Communism in 'engles', with suggestions of Drieu La Rochelle's *The Young European* and the 'new nihilism' which were combined in 'neuropeans'. The passage may also be read as a description of Lewis's attack itself. It sounds like an Englishman opening up on the new, or young, European. In either case the war described is in part at least the war between Lewis and *transition*. The address at which Shem lives also identifies him as a diabolical nihilist. He lives at 'Haunted Inkbottle, no number Brimstone Walk' (*F.W.*, p. 182). This cottage is described also as a 'rose-schelle cottage by the sea' (*F.W.*, p. 179) again bringing Drieu La Rochelle in specifically.

Joyce does not stop with the comic repetition of the accusations. He also links dadaism and surrealism with Drieu La Rochelle and makes his own opinion of them clear. HCE 'boasts him to the thick-in-thews the oldest creater in Aryania and looks down on the Suiss family Collesons whom he calls *les nouvelles roches*' (*F.W.*, p. 129). The 'Swiss' dadaists were bent on destroying old values and attitudes. They had advocated writing by glueing together random words cut from newspapers. In a passage which appears two pages later but is still a part of the catalogue of HCE's 'cognomen' Joyce mentions this manner of composition more explicitly. HCE, he says, 'can be built with glue and clippings' (*F.W.*, p. 135). The phrase 'He'll resemble she' (*F.W.*, p. 135), which immediately precedes this description of HCE, identifies it as a specific reference to Tristan Tzara's '*Pour faire un poème dadaiste*' in which Tzara concludes detailed instructions for cutting up a newspaper article and glueing together to make a poem with the remark '*Le poème vous ressemblera.*'[13] HCE not only preceded them, he is no new-nihilist, but he disapproves of them. This disdain for *Les nouvelles roches* is a mockery of Lewis's disdain for what he called 'new Philistines'. Joyce also must have had in mind Lewis's description of the age of *transition* as 'the New Stein Age'.

The saintly editors

Joyce did not hold Paul and Jolas guiltless of having provoked some of the criticism. He refers to them several times in this connection as comic versions of St Peter and St Paul, an idea he may have gotten from Lewis who referred to the 'New Nihilism' as 'the New Paul's creed' and the 'Paul's gospel'. Paul had written the first of the pieces on the 'New Nihilism' and Joyce seems to have placed much of the blame for starting the trouble on him personally. HCE is an invincible and infallible king until he is felled by a lion. His 'Tiara of scones [the crowned head] was held unfillable till one Liam Fail felled him in Westmunster; was struck out of his sittem when he rowed saulely to demask us and to our appauling predicament brought us plagues from Buddapest' (*F.W.*, p. 131). 'Saulely', 'demask us', and 'appauling' all allude to Saint Paul, but include Elliot Paul as well. In 'The New Nihilism' Paul had challenged the established values of Christianity and humanism. 'Humanists cannot fail to realize they are now on the defensive. The disciples of the Nazarene, as poet and philosopher, must feel that the burden of proof is on them.' (*t.* 2, p. 168)

Lewis had replied in *The Diabolical Principle*, 'I am not a humanist, I am an outsider who has deliberately intervened out of *pure malice* to show up all Paul's tricks, and what I consider often are Stein's.'[14] Drawing upon the title of Lewis's book *The Lion and the Fox*, Joyce makes Lewis the lion who haunts 'Westmunster', the stronghold of established Western, Christian values. There is also a play on the German word *'munster'*—pattern. Lewis saw in himself the pattern to be followed by those who wanted the same stern values. Paul and Jolas had referred to this aspect of his criticism in 'First Aid to the Enemy' by saying that Lewis's ideas were those of a 'solid M.P.' (*t.* 9, p. 165). Lewis roared ('rowed') solely to un-mask Paul. Perhaps he is called Buddha pest ('Buddapest') because he had prefaced *'The Diabolical Principle'* with a passage from Lao-Tze, the founder of Taoist religion whose propagandists annoyed the Buddhists greatly by claiming that Lao had travelled to India and converted Buddha himself. Just before this passage describing his downfall HCE is called 'first of the fenians, *roi des fainéants*' (*F.W.*, p. 131), the earliest agitator and king of the 'do nothings.' Paul, Jolas, and Sage had claimed in 'First Aid to the Enemy' that they ran *transition* 'purely and simply, to amuse ourselves' (*t.* 9, p. 175). Lewis made much of the statement by repeating it sarcastically several times and expanding on it by stating that *transition* was run for and by leisured Anglo-Saxon and French art students in Paris.

Having associated one of *transition*'s editors with St Paul, it was not a large step to make the other St Peter. Joyce liked the humour of seeing himself as the master and his friends as disciples well enough to arrange for twelve contributors in *Exagmination*. The idea of Paul and Jolas as joint apostles must have also pleased him because he used it at least three times in the *Wake*. The voice of Justice which harangues Shem says, 'you was bad no end . . . so whelp you Sinner Pitre and Sinner Poule, with the chicken's gape and *pas mal de siècle*, which, by the by, Reynaldo, is the ordinary emetic French for the grenadier's drip' (*F.W.*, p. 192). Joyce has been considered 'evil' because of the 'help' of Paul and Jolas, those great sinners according to Lewis. 'Whelp' suggests that they are responsible for 'bringing out' what Joyce produces. It also recalls Lewis's assertion that the revolutionary attitude of *transition* was an 'Adolescent State-of-mind'. The editors thus became in Lewis's opinion mere 'whelps', who are 'evil to no end' but merely revolting for the sake of revolt.

Paul is described in the passage as 'Sinner Poule'. The pun on the French *'poule'* ('chicken' and slang for 'mistress') connects him with 'chicken's gape'. Joyce is defining Paul's kind of 'evil' as nothing more than the vice of chasing women. It was part of Paul's public posture to play up his affairs with women, and Joyce was annoyed by this aspect of his personality. There was perhaps too much of Stephen Dedalus in Joyce and too much Buck Mulligan and Blazes Boylan in Paul for them not to react strongly to each other. Paul's response to Joyce was in some ways reciprocal. He thought Joyce too staid and conservative and referred to him privately as 'Camphor Jim', implying that his views were old and smelled of moth balls.[15]

Jolas became 'Sinner Pitre'. '*Pitre*' is French for clown, indicating that the great to-do about 'evil' is only foolishness. '*Pas mal de siècle*' alluded to Jolas's attempt to define the temper of the age in his editorial where he had written, 'call it a new *mal du siècle* if you wish, it is none the less a real thing' (*t.* 9, p. 193). He had gone on to maintain that this new feeling of disillusionment was a good thing because it could lead to the destruction of the old values that impeded the formulation of the new ones which were in his opinion so badly needed. The '*mal*' or 'illness' thus became '*pas mal*', not bad.

In the aside 'which, by the by, Reynaldo, is the ordinary emetic French for grenadier's drip', Joyce addresses Lewis. Already associated with foxes from 'the Mookse and the Gripes' and *The Lion and the Fox*, Lewis gets the name Reynaldo here. The 'illness of the century' which is the bone of contention amounts to nothing more momentous than venereal disease. By calling it 'grenadier's drip' Joyce may be echoing Paul's claim that it was produced by the war. In any case, the terms in which he presents it show that he considers the importance attached to this 'illness' exaggerated.

Paul and Jolas appear again as Peter and Paul in Juan's sermon to the girls of Saint Bridgits. This time, however, they are no longer presented as Saints, but as journalists, as they had been before starting *transition*. Just as the previous references to them indicated that they tried to exaggerate a not very earthshaking vice into a crisis of world values, this passage also shows them exaggerating the evil in the things they write about. Juan in warning the girls about the danger of letting newsmen learn about their activities, 'It would be a whorable state of affairs altogether for the redcolumnists of presswritten epics, Peter Paragraph and Paulus Puff, (I'm keepsoaking them to cover my concerts) to get ahold of for their balloons and shoot you private by surprise' (*F.W.*, p. 438).

In calling them 'redcolumnists' Joyce is parodying Lewis's statement quoted above, that *transition* was 'a band of communizing journalists'. Calling them 'Peter Paragraph and Paulus Puff' probably refers to Lewis's categorization of them as ' "drummers" or Letters' who write in 'the most up-and-coming stale journalese of somebody else's mother tongue that I have ever encountered.'[16] The parenthetical aside '(I'm keepsoaking them to cover my concerts)' is perhaps an allusion to Paul's habit of giving musical names like 'Rondo', 'The Concert', and 'Enharmonics' to his stories. The implication is that Paul is somehow duping ('soaking') the public. In part this passage seems to reflect Joyce's self-consciousness about having his work discussed in the controversial editorials and it serves to distance him from the editors a bit. Coming as it does from the fanatically prudish and pious Juan, the warning against journalists also points out the exaggeration of Lewis's ill-tempered personal attack on the editors.

When it came to dealing with the 'Revolution of the Word' specifically, Joyce realized that he was in danger of hurting feelings and he included an apology. In a passage which appears in *Finnegans Wake* just before the beginning of 'The Mookse and the Gripes' but was inserted after the 'Revolution of the Word' was announced, Joyce claims that he is acting only in self-defence. Dr Jones, the pedantic commentator on Biddy Doran's letter who is partly Lewis and partly Joyce, says, 'I need not anthrapologise for any obintentional (I must here correct all that school of neoitalian or paleoparisien schola of tinkers and spanglers who say I'm wrong *parcequeue* out of revolscian from romanitis I want to be) downtrodding on my foes' (*F.W.*, p. 151). The parenthetical remark contains a number of allusions to statements made by Lewis in *The Diabolical Principle* which identify the passage as a comment on *transition*. The group to be corrected is the 'neoitalian or paleoparisien schola of tinkers and spanglers'. They are neo-Italian because Lewis had charged that they were a new upsurge of Machiavellianism, they are *paleo*parisian (my emphasis) because much of Lewis's attack is devoted to proving that the claims of the Paris group to be 'new' were fraudulent. Lewis had also quoted a long passage from Oswald Spengler's *Decline of the West* to show how similar Paul and Jolas were to Spengler in their idea that Europe was decadent.

The ambiguity of 'revolscian' which contains both 'revolution' and 'revulsion' suggests a need to be independent of the revolution fostered by Jolas and Lewis's revulsion from it. To defend himself against his enemies, Joyce seems to be saying, it may be necessary to step on his friends' toes. If that gives offense he wants it known that it is unintentional.

When the emphasis in *transition* began to shift to verticalism with its stress on the connection with the past offered by dreams and its theories of lost powers residing in a 'third eye', Joyce again demonstrated his independence with comic allusions. When, for example, Jolas published material on *Die Seherin von Prevorst* (*t.* 25, p. 171), a woman who claimed to have had prophetic visions, Joyce included the phrase 'scherinsheiner' (*F.W.*, p. 221) reducing her claim to special vision to a 'black eye'. Much of the theorizing about the lost 'parietal organ' or third eye had been based on the work of Karl Gustav Carus. In one place Carus and eye are brought together as a comic breakfast—'a carusal consistent with second course eyer and becon' (*F.W.*, p. 406). The passage depends upon two puns: 'ei' (German 'egg') and 'eye', and 'beacon' and 'bacon'. 'Second course eyer' contains the suggestion of a 'second sight', as well as the idea that these theories represent a second stage in the development of *transition*.

Joyce's summary of the whole later phase of *transition* comes in a rather long description of a cult which was founded by Dolph, one of the manifestations in which Shem appears.

> that same galloroman cultous is very prevailend up to this windiest of land-havemiseries all over what was beforeaboots a land of nods, in spite of all the bloot, all the braim, all the brawn, all the brile, that was shod, that were shat, that was shuk all the while, for our massangrey if mosshungry people, the at Wickerworks, still hold ford to their healing and byleave in the old weights downupon the Swanny, innovated by him, the prence di Propagandi, the chrism for the christmass, the pillar of the perished and the rock o'ralereality, and it is veritably belied, we belove, that not allsods of esoupcans that's in the queen's pottage post and not allfinesof greendgold that the Indus contains would overhinduce them, (o.p.) to steeplechange back once from their ophis workship and twice on sundises, to their ancient flash and crãsh habits of old Pales time ere beam slewed cable. . . . (*F.W.*, pp. 288–9)

This description of the cult was not written originally as a commentary on the late *transition*: most of it had appeared in *transition* 11. The most obvious reference to the later stage of *transition*, the phrase 'ophis workship' echoing the subtitle 'An orphic workshop of the imagination',

which *transition* adopted in March 1932, was a later addition. By
including the reference at this place Joyce indicates that the material
around it, though composed earlier, is applicable to it. According to the
passage, the cult founded earlier is still prevailing in what was formerly
a 'land of nods'. This suggests that a new religious emphasis had replaced the psychological interest in the dream. The cult prevails even
up to the present in spite of all 'bloot', 'brawn' and 'braim' that have been
shed. The mass of angry people still hold to their healing activities (a
reference to 'First Aid to the Enemy') and believe in the rites innovated
by the 'prence di Propagandi' (the one who prints the propaganda) who
is among other things 'the pillar of the perished' (an exponent of diabolism) and the 'rock of o'ralereality' (founder of surrealism). Even 'allsods
of esoupcans that's in the queen's pottage post' have not wrought a
change in them. That is, not even all sorts of condensed versions of
Aesop, like the Mookse and the Gripes, that have appeared in *transition*
can affect them. Nothing, it seems, would induce them to 'steeple-
change back once from their ophis workship.' Nothing could draw
them away from the commitment to the orphic view of poetry into
which they rushed like a 'steeple chase'.

Friends at the Wake

While he was careful to maintain his independence intellectually, Joyce
basically looked upon his involvement with *transition* and the Jolases
with fondness and gratitude throughout the long association. Over the
years a closer and closer friendship developed between the two families.
They dined together frequently at Fouquets, Les Trianons, or Chez
Francis. Long evenings over wine became customary for the two husbands. Sometimes the mood was gay like the occasion when Jolas
guessed the title *Finnegans Wake* to win the one thousand francs Joyce
had promised to the first of his friends to discover his secret. 'Ah Jolas',
Joyce said almost sadly at first, 'You've taken something out of me.'
In parting that night, however, he embraced his friend and danced one
of his intricate steps. The next day Joyce, in good spirits, brought round
a bag of ten franc pieces which he told Jolas's daughters to serve their
father for lunch.[17] But as Joyce worked to finish *Finnegans Wake* the
rise of fascism and the imminence of war cast a gloom over Paris that
affected those around *transition*. And as the fate of Europe grew darker
the tone of Joyce's personal life also darkened.

The group of friends in Paris could only continue to surround him with friendship. They organized dinners and parties at which they marked birthdays, holidays and other special occasions. Over them all there hung the sense that a phase of their lives, and of their civilization, was coming to an end. A Russian musician spoke of *Finnegans Wake* as the 'most beautiful requiem that had ever been written for a civilization.' Joyce, himself, comments at several points in the *Wake* upon the darkness of his situation. 'Diremood is the name is on the writing chap' (*F.W.*, p. 125), he wrote in one place. In another he said, 'It darkels . . . all this our funnaminal world' (*F.W.*, p. 244).

It is in the context of growing darkness that the major personal references to the Jolases occur in *Finnegans Wake*. Most of them are in Parts II and IV, the last parts to be written. In one case, though, Joyce made an addition in an earlier section so that it included Eugene Jolas. At the end of Part III, when Shaun is about to depart from home to carry Shem's letter, Shem bids him farewell in an affectionate manner. When the passage was first published in *transition* 12, it contained little to suggest that Shaun was to be associated with Jolas and was probably not intended to apply to him. The final version of the passage as it appears in *Finnegans Wake* adds reference to the dark hour and expands the description of Shaun to make it fit Jolas. The additions are indicated by italics in the following quotation.

> Well, (*how dire do we thee hours when thylike fades!*) all's dall and youllow and it is to bedowern that thou art passing hence, mine bruder, able Shaun, with a twhisking of the robe, *ere the morning of light calms our hardest throes*, beyond cods' cradle and porpoise plain, from carnal relations undfamiliar faces to the inds of Tuskland where the oliphants scrum till the ousts of Amiracles where the toll stories grow proudest, more is the pity, but for all your deeds of goodness you were soo ooft and for ever doing, manomano and *myriamilia even to mulimuli* as our humbler classes, whose virtue is humility, can tell, it is hardly we in the country of the old, Sean Moy, can part you for, oleypoe, you were the walking saint, you were, tootoo too stayer, the graced of gods and pittites and the salus of the wake. Countenance whose disparition afflictedly fond Fuinn feels. *Winner of the gamings, primed at the studience, propredicted from the storybouts, the choice of ages wise! Spick-spookspokesman of our specturesque silentiousness!* Musha, beminded of us out there in Cockpit, poor twelve o'clock scholars, sometime or other anywhere you think the time. Wisha, becoming back to us way home in Biddyhouse one way or either anywhere we miss your smile. (*F.W.*, p. 427)

In the original description Shaun is the carrier of the letter, a great helper, and a faithful companion. Earlier in this chapter Shaun is depicted as the person most able to understand and explain Shem's letter (*F.W.*, p. 425). Joyce's relationship to Jolas as it developed over ten years was quite similar to the relationship of Shem to Shaun. As publisher of the magazine in which 'Work in Progress' appeared, he was like Shaun, the means of delivery of the all-important letter which is the *Wake* itself. By one of those coincidences that delighted Joyce, what he had written as fiction had predicted reality. Jolas did perform many services for Joyce and he was a solace to him while he was writing the *Wake*. Jolas, who had some of the characteristics of Shaun, began also to have a career like Shaun's. In Joyce's description of him as St Peter he did become a 'walking saint'. And most remarkable, he did depart for America, however temporarily, in 1935 leaving friends and family behind.

Since Jolas had in a way merged with Shaun naturally, Joyce acknowledged the fact that he was 'propredicted from the storybouts' (*F.W.*, p. 427), predicted by the story and made the description apply to him even more specifically. He is 'winner of the gamings' (*F.W.*, p. 427). The great game which Joyce played with his friends was the challenge to guess the title of his book and Jolas had been the first to do so.

He is 'primed at the studience' (*F.W.*, p. 427) because Joyce had showed him the plan of the *Wake* and had discussed it with him in connection with his articles for *transition*. He thus becomes 'Spickspook-spokesman of our specturesque silentiousness!' (*F.W.*, p. 427) because he has been Joyce's spokesman, and in a very loose sense Joyce had 'ghost written' parts of the articles making Jolas a 'spookspokesman'. The reason for calling him 'choice of the ages wise!' is less specific than the others; it probably is an acknowledgement that the decision to publish in *transition*, which Joyce made ten years earlier was a good one.

The addition of the phrase 'myriamilia even to mulimuli' balances with 'manomano'; both are mock Latin like that spoken in *Portrait of the Artist*. To the English 'man' Joyce has added the 'o' ending of the dative and ablative cases. The addition of endings accentuates the dative. The word 'manomano' would translate as 'man to man'. To this description of masculine kindnesses he adds a similar description of feminine kindnesses done 'mulimuli'. The root of this word is the Latin 'mulier', woman or wife. Joyce shortens this to 'muli', the ending, however, is correct Latin for the dative singular of a third declension feminine noun. 'Mulimuli' would then mean woman to woman, but would also suggest that the women involved were the wives of the men in the first part of the phrase. 'myriamilia' identifies one of the women as Maria and emphasizes that she is a kind of *mater familia*. The spelling 'myria' suggests 'my Maria' and gives the passage a further note of personal affection.

While changing the passage to refer explicitly to the Jolases, Joyce also set it within the context of a dark hour. This is partly to emphasize the fact that Shaun's journey is divided into the watches of the night, but it is also a part of the pattern of autobiographical reference to the friendship of the Jolases. References to darkness and an impending doom also overshadow the passages Joyce composed later dealing with the Jolases and parties they gave.

Maria Jolas had introduced the American holiday, Thanksgiving, into the calendar of the occasions traditionally celebrated by the group of her friends in Paris. And in 1933 when the mood of the group was particularly sombre, and the American depression at its height, she organized a *bal de la purée*, or ball of tramps and down-and-outers. These parties are alluded to in *Finnegans Wake* in the context of the drinking in the pub of King Roderick O'Conor.

> Morya Mortimor! Allapalla overus! Howoft had the ballshee tried! And they laying low for his home gang in that eeriebleak mead, with fireball feast [Christmas or the Fourth of July] and turkeys tumult [Thanksgiving] and paupers patch to provide his bum end [*bal de la purée*]. (*F.W.*, p. 316)

As the night in Roderick O'Conor's pub is drawing to a close and the last round of drinks is being served, Joyce includes a passage which is composed of details from the Thanksgiving dinner of 1937.

> So anyhow, melumps and mumpos of the hoose uncommons, after that to wind up that longtobechronickled gettogether thanksbetogiving day at Glenfinnisk-en-la-Valle, the anniversary of his finst homy commulion, after that same barbecue beanfeast was all over ... King Roderick O'Conor ... after the socalled last supper he greatly gave in his umbrageous house of the hundred bottles with the radio beamer ... overwhelmed as he was with black ruin like a sponge out of water, allocutioning in bellcantos to his own oliverian society. ... (*F.W.*, p. 380-1)

The 'getogether' is 'longtobechronickled' because it had been celebrated in a 'come-all-ye' and now in *Finnegans Wake*. The 'bellcantos' are the songs which he and Maria sang together. The affair is called the 'anniversary of his finst homy commulion' for two reasons: it was a celebration of a religious holiday centered around wine and food that resulted in a community of those who partook. Joyce may also have had in mind the earlier occasion of his fiftieth birthday celebration where he had used the words of the mass to address a similar group of friends as he cut the cake: '*Accipite et manducate ex hoc omnes: Hoc est enim corpus meum.*'[18] And the occasion is also a 'homy commulion' in that it was a gathering of husbands with their wives (commulion cf. mulimuli) in a family setting.

The curious form of address, 'melumps and mumpos', extends the reference beyond Thanksgiving day to the *bal de la purée* again. 'Lumpe' is the German word for tramp while 'to mump' means 'to beg.' When Joyce says 'thanksbetogiving', he is expressing his gratitude to the Jolases not only for this one holiday dinner but for many similar occasions on which they brought him together with his friends.

Maria Jolas appears prominently in all of these descriptions of brief attempts at gaiety and friendship in the midst of a situation moving toward an unhappy conclusion. After the *Wake* was completed, she retained this figure in Joyce's mind. On Christmas Day, 1939, after Joyce had remained troubled and silent throughout dinner, he turned to Mrs Jolas after dinner and asked her to dance saying, 'come on . . . you know very well that it's the last Christmas.' And they danced spiritedly. The same sort of associations with her must have been in Joyce's mind when he composed the ending for *Finnegans Wake* where she is again connected with a thought of happiness in the midst of a sad parting. As Anna Livia is passing out to sea, to be replaced by her daughter Izzy in the affections of her husband Finn, she says 'Carry me along, taddy, like you done through the toy fair!' (*F.W.*, p. 628). The remark is based upon a conversation that Joyce had with Maria Jolas. He had asked her what her earliest childhood memory was and she had told him of the power and contentment she had felt at being carried on her father's shoulders through a Kentucky fair amid the reflected light of kerosene lanterns. As she reaches the last sad moment of life, Anna Livia's memories are going back to the first memorable, triumphant moment of childhood. As the mother and wife figure is being replaced by the daughter, she returns to her father. Through this memory Anna Livia's life like all others in the *Wake* becomes circular, and the end is the beginning.

Both Joyce and Jolas knew that number 27 marked the end of 'Work in Progress' as well as the end of *transition*. Jolas's valediction to Joyce was his article 'Homage to the Mythmaker'. Joyce's contribution to the last issue seems also to have been a kind of valediction to the ten year partnership. As Butt, a soldier in HCE's pub, describes his experiences in the war to Taff it becomes evident that Joyce is also describing his experiences as part of *transition*'s revolution. Throughout a long passage of more than two pages there are scattered references to the quarrel with the enemy. Several references near the end make it unmistakably clear that the enemy in the war Butt describes is Lewis. 'bung goes the enemay the Percy rally got me', (*F.W.*, p. 352) Butt says, alluding to Lewis's full name, Percy Wyndham Lewis. A few lines later Butt speaks of a gun 'to parrylewis', i.e., to paralyze Lewis. The passage is the culmination of the long comic battle in which he had been engaged with Lewis.

The passage begins with the usual soldier's complaint about his food and living conditions. 'I had my billyfell of duckish delights the whole pukny time on rawmeots and juliannes' (*F.W.*, p. 350). The 'raw meat' that he has had to eat is also raw *mots* (French for words). He has been 'feeding and sleeping on the huguenottes' and 'raiding revolations over the allbegeneses' (*F.W.*, p. 350). Both 'huguenottes' and 'allbegeneses' contain references to Jolas's first name, Eugene. Joyce has been beholden to Jolas for a place to publish and this has involved him in a revolution so that everyone could be 'Genes', that is be like Jolas, or so that everybody could be a 'genius'. In addition to Jolas's revolution Joyce also alludes to Robert McAlmon's ironically titled autobiography, *Being Geniuses Together*,[19] in which Joyce, Jolas, and their friends appear. These things Butt considers the hardships of war.

Butt goes on to point out that a camaraderie developed which made the hardship worthwhile. 'Yet still in all, spit for spat . . . every warson wearrier kaddies a komnate in his schnapsack.' (*F.W.*, p. 350). Even though weary, the soldiers each carry 'a komnate' i.e., a comrade, a communist, and a mate. Butt, though tired, had carried his comrade, and Joyce, though weary of Lewis's charges of communism and collusion, has also done his part. In his enthusiasm for the camaraderie Butt

has almost forgotten about fighting itself. 'Unlist I am getting foegutfulls of the rugiments of savaliged wildfire I was gamefellow will-
mate . . .' (*F.W.*, p. 350) and so he brings his remarks back to that
topic. 'And send us victorias' (*F.W.*, p. 351). The passage applies somewhat differently to Joyce than it does to Butt. Except when he had a
'gutfull' of *The Enemy* ('foegutfulls') alleging that he was part of the
new-nihilism or new barbarism ('savaliged wildfire') he was a 'gamefellow' and willing to be associated with others. When angered, he
responded to *The Enemy* and won a kind of victory for *transition*.

As he continues to talk, Butt gets more and more nostalgic about the
war. 'Renborumba! Then were the hellscyown days for our fellows,
the loyal leibsters, and we was the redugout rawrecruitioners. . .' (*F.W.*,
p. 351). 'Hellscyown' and 'redugout' echo once more the charges of
Lewis that *transition* was 'diabolical', 'communist' and not new (i.e., 'redugout', and re-cooked from a pun on the French word *cuit*, 'to cook').

Butt begins next to boast of the wild living in which the soldiers have
indulged. For several lines the passage does not relate specifically to
transition, then when Butt describes one of the soldiers with a special
ability at swearing, the passage returns to *transition*. Butt boasts that
'our Chorney Choplain, blued the air' (*F.W.*, p. 351). Charlie Chaplin's
young wife had sued him for divorce on the grounds that he had asked
her to practice fellatio with him. He thus becomes 'Choplain'. When
the surrealists had made the case a *cause célèbre*, their manifesto 'Hands
Off Love' appeared first in *transition* (*t*. 6, p. 155). The manifesto, which
was deliberately intended to be a shocking affront, becomes a streak of
curses. Butt swears a little himself to show how impressive Chorney
Choplain was. One of his oaths is 'S. Pivorandbowl' (*F.W.*, p. 351)—
St Peter and Paul—another allusion to Paul and Jolas as his dual apostles,
included because Paul and Jolas had signed the manifesto. Butt next
relates how the soldiers passed their time by listening to the radio. 'We
all tuned in to hear the topmast noviality' (*F.W.*, p. 351). 'Noviality',
in addition to suggesting novelty and news, contains the name of the
artificial international language Novil, devised by the Danish gram-
marian, Otto Jesperson. The people connected with *transition* kept
abreast of the new literature and of linguistic innovation too. 'Work in
Progress' was itself a kind of 'topmast noviality' in that it was the major
attraction of *transition* and was written in a language using new words
made up from many languages.

Butt is soon declaring his love for his comrades. 'And tig for tag. Togatogtug. My droomodose days Y loved you abover all the strest. Blowhole brasshat and boy with his boots off and the butch of our bunch and all' (*F.W.*, p. 351). Tit for tat, pulling together (I dream of those days) I loved you above all the rest, all of the bunch. In spite of all the stress it has caused him, the overriding emotion is affection for those connected with *transition*.

Butt returns to the subject of his part in the fighting. 'I was a bare prive without my doglegs . . . I could always take good cover of myself . . . I did not care three tanker's hoots . . . for any feelings from my lifeprivates on their reptrograd leanins . . .' (*F.W.*, p. 351). Though only a private, Butt cares little about the opinions of others. Joyce, too, was only a private individual. He cared little about the leanings of *transition* toward communism which Lewis alleged, nor did he share their interest in Gertrude Stein (*petro*-rock).

Butt ends his account by describing his encounter with one of the enemies. 'And, by Jova, I never went wrong nor let him doom till, risky wark rasky wolk, at the head of the wake, up come stumblebum (ye olde cottemptable!), his urssian gemenal, in his scutt's rudes unreformed and he went before him in that nemcon enchelonce with the same old domstoole story and his upleave the fallener as is greatly to be petted (whitesides do his beard!)' (*F.W.*, pp. 351–352). Butt has encountered a Russian general in the act of attacking *transition*. As Butt tells what led him to shoot at the Russian general, Joyce tells why he rebuked Lewis. The attack by Lewis had begun very early, 'at the head of the wake'. Since he accused them of being politically oriented like Tolstoy as well as being communists, one of the charges made might have been expressed, 'urssian gemenal' (you're Russian, Jim and all). 'Scutt's rude unreformed', sounds a good bit like 'Gertrude's unreformed', another of the charges made by Lewis. Joyce was also offended by the fact that Lewis gave the 'same old domstoole story' i.e., the same old story that Joyce was part of a school of writers who might have been found on bar stools at the *Café du Dome*, the well-known Parisian hangout of artists and would-be artists. The piety of Lewis's tone and his attempt to lift up the fallen who are greatly to be pitied also irritated Joyce.

When Butt sees the general in this compromising position, he takes his revolver and shoots him.

... and I seen his brichashert offensive and his boortholomas vadnhammaggs
vise a vise them scharlot runners and how they gave love to him and how he
took the ward from us ... and, my oreland for a rolvever, sord, by the
splunthers of colt and bung goes the enemay the Percy rally got me, messger,
(as true as theirs an Almagnian Gothabobus!) to blow the grand off his
aceupper. Thistake it's meest! And after meath the dulwich. We insurrectioned and, be the procuratress of the hory synnotts, before he could tell
pullyirragun to parrylewis, I shuttm, missus, like a wide sleever! Hump to
dump! Tumbleheaver! (*F.W.*, p. 352)

When Joyce saw 'The Enemy' face to face with *transition* his anger was
aroused, 'and how they gave love to him and how he took the ward
from us' recalls 'First Aid to the Enemy' in which the editors had pre-
tended to treat Lewis with kindness, and the way Lewis had then used
it in further attacks in *The Diabolical Principle*.

When the shot is actually fired, it is not clear whether it is Joyce or
Lewis who has fired it. 'Bung goes the enemay,' Butt declares, indicating that the shot was fired by Joyce, but the next phrase 'Percy rally got
me' indicates that Joyce was hit by Lewis's attack. The matter is not
cleared in the next phrase when it is announced that the purpose of the
shot was 'to blow the grand off his aceupper.' Both Lewis, the ondt,
and Joyce, the gracehopper, are included.

What began as a single shot turns out to be a whole revolution, 'And
after meath the dulwich. We insurrectioned.' This particular insurrec-
tion appears to be the 'Revolution of the Word'. In a limerick written
for Jolas when he published *Mots Déluge*, a book of poems in French,
Joyce had once before played upon the phrase *Aprés moi, le déluge* in
connection with Jolas's literary activities.

> There's a genial young poetriarch Euge
> Who hollers with heartiness huge:
>   Let sick souls sob for solace
>   So the *jeunes* joy with Jolas!
> Book your berths! *Aprés mot, le déluge.*[20]

Whatever reservations he may have expressed elsewhere, Joyce is now
wholeheartedly a part of the revolution and at its forefront. Before any-
body else could 'pull a gun' ('pullyirragun') to 'parrylewis', he had done
it. 'I shuttm, missus (I shot him; I shut him up; he missed us). Like Butt
Joyce has been part of the uprising and he does not regret it.

The camaraderie which soldiers talk of over drinks must always be discounted a little, and yet the fidelity of comrades in arms expressed here is genuine. This is a typical Joycean affirmation. He declares his fidelity through a drunken soldier and thus establishes the ironical perspective that allows him to undercut the emotions even as they are expressed. But the irony underscores the importance of the affirmation. It is necessary to assure that the sentiment is unclouded by sentimentality or oversimplification and to protect it from the ridicule of others.

Though Butt's speech is the last comment on this subject to appear in *transition* itself, it is not Joyce's final comment in *Finnegans Wake*. In section four, which was not published until the complete book appeared, Joyce wrote his final appraisal of *transition*. 'Benedicted be the barrel . . . a hygiennic contrivance socalled from the editor' (*F.W.*, p. 596). A number of connections are united and brought to a culmination in this reference. Joyce had depicted Jolas earlier as Shaun the Post. In Section III Shaun becomes a barrel of Guiness stout floating down the Liffey. He remains the valuable but separate and distinguishable mode of conveyance for the material he delivers. *transition* was also associated with a waterborne conveyance earlier in a number of incidental passages in which it appears as a ship. In passages already discussed, Joyce had referred to the 'ophis work*ship*' and called 'Work in Progress' a 'top*mast* noviality' in the context of a discussion of *transition*. In another of the passages summing up his combat with Wyndham Lewis, Joyce wrote, 'I was a bad boy's bogey but it was when I went on to sankt piotersbarq that they gave my devil his dues' (*F.W.*, p. 549) ('Give the Devil His Due' was the title of the section of *The Diabolical Principle* in which Lewis dealt with Jolas's article 'Enter the Imagination', a discussion of Lautréamont).

The references to *transition* as a floating vehicle for his work was another of the details of 'Work in Progress' that Joyce began as fiction and which turned into fact. *transition* 26 was printed in Cincinnati, Ohio by the Ebbert and Richardson Printing Company. The Ohio River flooded in January 1937 destroying the first set of copy and thereby delaying the appearance of Joyce's account of the Norwegian sailor (*F.W.*, Part II, Section 3). Joyce wrote to Frank Budgen that the latest instalment which he had been promised had been 'washed off by Anna Ohio out of pure jealousy.'[21] When a second set of proof took so long to arrive by boat, Joyce wrote Lord Carlow of the Corvinus Press who was also expecting a copy, '*transition* is still swimming bravely across the seven seas, a wave a week.'[22]

The passage not only draws together the earlier references and relates them to the flood, but also provides an evaluative comment. It is hygienic because of Jolas's first name, but it was also hygienic in another sense. Among little magazines *transition* was particularly healthy. Jolas had been able to keep publishing at just the time when many other magazines were going out of circulation. And despite complaints he made about it, *transition* was healthy for Joyce. He felt pressured by the need to meet deadlines, but he flagged when he no longer had to meet them. Certainly the task of finding and training readers for *Finnegans Wake* would have been more difficult, if not impossible, without *transition*. It was the barrel, the indispensable means of conveyance, that brought Joyce's work to his readers. Even after Joyce's death his former editors continued to defend and explain him.[23]

In light of his agreement with its basic principles and of the many advantages which Joyce gained from *transition*, it is difficult to see how his relationship to it can have been called into question. But this is typical of the misunderstanding that has surrounded *transition*. In their superficial reaction to Jolas's manifestos the critics of *transition* have missed the fact that the writers he published did share important new attitudes and that it was Jolas who recognized them and brought them together, when other editors dismissed them.

In the end the serious assessment which Joyce had given humorously in the *Wake* remains as fair and complete as any given by his contemporaries. To be involved with *transition* was to be marked as part of the zealous avant-garde and to invite misunderstanding and hostility. But it was also to enjoy the benefits of a congenial, uniquely perceptive editor, open to radical experimentation and willing to provide the kind of context and explanation which defined the new modes of writing. Most of all it was to be a part of a significant literary revolution which produced some of the best literature of the century.

Notes

1 V. F. Calverton, 'The Revolution-in-the-Wordists', *Modern Quarterly*, V (Fall, 1929), pp. 276–283.

2 F. R. Leavis, 'Joyce and the Revolution of the Word', *Scrutiny*, II, No. 2 (September, 1933), pp. 193–201.

3 Geoffrey Wagner, *Wyndham Lewis A Portrait of the Artist as the Enemy* (New Haven, 1957), p. 184.
4 Wyndham Lewis, *The Diabolical Principle and the Dithyrambic Spectator* (London, 1931), p. 3.
5 *Ibid.*, p. 7.
6 *Ibid.*, p. 7.
7 *Letters of James Joyce* III, p. 216.
8 *Ibid.*, p. 22.
9 *Ibid.*, p. 238.
10 Lewis, *The Diabolical Principle*, p. 42.
11 *Ibid.*, pp. 42–43.
12 *Ibid.*, p. 14.
13 Tristan Tzara, *Sept Manifestes Dada* (Paris, 1920), p. 77.
14 Lewis, *The Diabolical Principle*, p. 10.
15 Interview with Maria Jolas.
16 Lewis, *The Diabolical Principle*, p. 4.
17 Ellmann, *James Joyce*, p. 721.
18 Jolas, 'My Friend James Joyce', p. 8.
19 Robert McAlmon, *Being Geniuses Together: An Autobiography* (London, 1938).
20 Ellmann, *James Joyce*, p. 600.
21 *Letters of James Joyce* III, p. 394.
22 *Ibid.*, p. 397.
23 Maria Jolas, 'James Joyce as a Revolutionary: Letter in reply to Max Lerner', *New Republic*, CVII (November, 1942), 613; *A James Joyce Yearbook*, ed. Maria Jolas (Paris, 1949); Maria Jolas, 'Joyce's Friend Jolas', *A James Joyce Miscellany*, ed. Marvin Magalaner (New York, 1957), pp. 62–74; and Maria Jolas, 'The Little Known Paul Léon', *A James Joyce Miscellany*, ed. Marvin Magalaner, 2nd Series (Carbondale, Illinois, 1959), pp. 225–233.

APPENDICES

transition 1

TABLE OF CONTENTS

Reproductions of Paintings by MAX ERNST, L. TIHANYI, and PAVEL TSELITSIEFF.

Poems by HART CRANE, ROBERT DESNOS, PAUL ELDRIDGE, VIRGIL GEDDES, ANDRÉ GIDE, BRAVIG IMBS, R. ELLSWORTH LARSSON, ELSE LASKER-SCHULER, ARCHIBALD MAC LEISH, MARCEL NOLL, EVAN SHIPMAN, PHILIPPE SOUPAULT, GEORG TRAKL

Introduction by the EDITORS.
Book Reviews by KAY BOYLE and ROBERT SAGE.
" *Zukunftsmusik,* " *by* ELLIOT PAUL.

The May number of *Transition* will include contributions by JEAN-GEORGES AURIOL, ERNEST SUTHERLAND BATES, ALEXANDER BLOK,

Kay Boyle, Emilo Cecchi, Serge Essenin, Kenneth Fearing, André Gide, Eugene Jolas, James Joyce, René Schickele, Valery Larbaud, R. Ellsworth Larsson, Ludwig Lewisohn, Elliot Paul, Velko Petrovitch, Henri Poulaille, Burton Rascoe, Laura Riding (Gottschalk), Rainer Maria Rilke, P. Drieu La Rochelle, Robert Roe, Isidore Schneider, Gertrude Stein, William Carlos Williams, and others.

transition 2

TABLE OF CONTENTS

Reproductions of Paintings by Juan Gris, Yves Tanguy, Giorgio de Chirico, Max Ernst.

Poems by Paul Eluard, William Carlos Williams, John Gould Fletcher, Pierre Loving, Valery Larbaud, Robert Roe, Sidney Hunt, Bravig Imbs, Rainer Maria Rilke, Kenneth Fearing, René Schickele, Kay Boyle, Serge Essenin, Arno Holz, Léon-Paul Fargue

JEAN GEORGE AURIOL	*The Occident.*
ROBERT SAGE	*La Réalité.*
ELLIOT PAUL	*The New Nihilism.*
VICTOR LLONA	*Paris Letter.*

Extracts from an Interesting Correspondence.
Glossary.

Among the contributors to the June and July numbers of *transition* will be: CASIMIR EDSCHMID, GERTRUDE STEIN, RUTH JAMESON, PHILIPPE SOUPAULT, JAMES JOYCE, VELKO PETROVITCH, ANDRÉ GIDE, MARJORY LATIMER, ALEXANDER BLOK, ERNEST SUTHERLAND BATES, VALERY LARBAUD, KAY BOYLE, BURTON RASCOE, LAURA RIDING, BERNARD FAY, BORIS PILNIAK, JOHN MITCHELL, MICHAIL ZOSTCHENKO, ARCHIBALD MACLEISH, ALEXANDER NEVEROV, KURT SCHWITTERS, STUART DAVIS, PAUL ELUARD, CARL STERNHEIM, JEAN RICHARD BLOCH, ALLEN TATE, ERNEST BOYD, EDMUND WILSON, ROBERT SAGE, ROBERT MCALMON, EUGENE JOLAS, GEORGES RIBEMONT-DESSAIGNES, EVAN SHIPMAN, ERNEST STADLER, SOLITA SOLANO, NICOLA TIHINOFF, ALEXANDER PUSHKIN, RENÉ CREVEL, RHYS DAVIES, GUSTAV DAVIDSON, ISIDORE SCHNEIDER, HART CRANE, and others.

transition 3

TABLE OF CONTENTS

GERTRUDE STEIN	*As a Wife Has a Cow A Love Story.*
JOHN MITCHELL	*Portraits of Innocence.*
MORLEY CALLAGHAN	*Last Spring They Came Over.*
KAY BOYLE	*Portrait.*
JAMES JOYCE	*Continuation of a Work In Progress.*

238 *Appendix*

Margery Latimer	*Grotesque.*
Philippe Soupault	*The Silent House.*
Velko Petrovitch	*Sara's Lenka.*
Michail Zostchenko	*Foma, the Faithless.*
Elin Pelin	*Stoychko's Willow.*
Alexander Blok	*The Unknown Woman.*

Reproductions of paintings by Kurt Schwitters, André Masson and Pavel Tchelitcheff, *and a boule de neige by* Man Ray.

Poems by Laura Riding, Hart Crane, Eugene Jolas, Rhys Davies, Bryher, Gustav Davidson, Allen Tate, Kurt Schwitters, Georg Trakl, Georges Ribemont-Dessaignes, Berenice Abbott, *and* Georg Dobo.

Laura Riding	*The New Barbarism, and Gertrude Stein.*
Robert Sage	*Is 5.*

K. O. R. A. A.
Suggestions for a New Magic.
Glossary.

transition 4

TABLE OF CONTENTS

JAMES JOYCE	*Continuation of a Work In Progress.*
VSEVOLOD IVANOV	*The Old Timer.*
ELLIOT PAUL	*The Open Shop.*
RUTH JAMESON	*This Is No Conclusion.*
EMILIO CECCHI	*The Equine Express.*
VIRGIL GEDDES	*The Meddler.*
ALEXANDER BLOK	*The Unknown Woman.*

Reproductions of paintings by JUAN GRIS and KRISTIAN TONNY, *and an embroidery by* MARIE MONNIER.

Poems by H. D., JOHN HYDE PRESTON, ALEXANDER PUSHKIN (MAX EASTMAN), EUGENE JOLAS, E. GIMINEZ CABALLERO, ARCHIBALD CRAIG, YVOR WINTERS, CURTIS BRUEN, RAFAEL ALBERTI, ANTONIO ESPINA, R. ELLSWORTH LARSSON, GERTRUDE STEIN.

ROBERT SAGE	*Melodramadness.*
GERTRUDE STEIN	*The Life of Juan Gris.*
	The Life and Death
	Of Juan Gris.
ELLIOT PAUL	*A Master of Plastic Relations.*
GEORGE ANTHEIL	*Jacques Benoist-Méchin.*
KENNETH FEARING	*Cultural Notes.*
MURRAY GODWIN	*From Work On Sidetrack.*
F. T. MARINETTI	*Futurist Standards Of Measurement.*
	Glossary

transition 5

TABLE OF CONTENTS

Reproductions of paintings by PABLO PICASSO
and Aztec sculpture.

Poems by EUGENE JOLAS, BRAVIG IMBS, A. S. J. TESSIMOND, PAUL
ELUARD, EMILY HOLMES COLEMAN, KAY BOYLE, H. B. ARMITAGE,
HORACE GREGORY, JOSEF WITTLIN, ELSE LASKER-SCHULER, BLANCHE
MATTHIAS.

Glossary.

transition 6

TABLE OF CONTENTS

Reproductions of paintings by YVES TANGUY *and* JOAN MIRO, *an arping by* HANS ARP, *and a section of a new film by* MAN RAY.

Poems by ARCHIBALD MAC LEISH, LAURA RIDING, SERGE ESSENIN, ANDRÉ GAILLARD, LIOUBOMIR MITZITCH, EUGENE JOLAS, BRAVIG IMBS, GRACE HOFFMAN WHITE, LOTHAR MUNDAN, W. C. EMORY, LORINCZ SZABO, RAINER MARIA RILKE, CHARLES RECHT.

Glossary.

transition 7

TABLE OF CONTENTS

Photograph of a wire sculpture by ALEXANDER CALDER, *and reproductions of paintings by* POLELONEMA *and* MAX ERNEST.

Poems by the COMTE DE LAUTRÉAMONT (ISIDORE DUCASSE), (*translated by* JOHN RODKER), YVOR WINTERS, GIUSEPPE UNGARETTI, KAREL TOMAN, ALLEN TATE, HENRI SOLVEEN, PIERRE MINET, EMILY HOLMES COLEMAN, PIERRE REVERDY, HART CRANE, HANS ARP, ROBERT GRAVES, ELSA VON FREYTAG-LORINGHOVEN, IVAN GOLL.

Glossary.
Advertisement.

transition 8

TABLE OF CONTENTS

Reproductions of paintings by POLELONEMA *and* MA PE WE.

Poems by ANDRÉ GIDE, WALTER LOWENFELS, MICHAEL FRAENKEL, EUGENE JOLAS, GEORGE WHITSETT, VIT NEZVAL, VALERY LARBAUD, ROBERT WOLF, ALFRED KREYMBORG, TONY PALMER, THEO RUTRA.

GLOSSARY.

transition 9

TABLE OF CONTENTS

transition 10

TABLE OF CONTENTS

GERTRUDE STEIN	*If He Thinks.*
	A Novelette of Desertion.
GEORGES RIBEMONT-DESSAIGNES	*Confiteor.*
ELLIOT PAUL	*States of Sea.*
LYDIA SEIFOULINA	*The Golden Childhood.*
LAURA RIDING	*Fragment.*
WILLIAM CARLOS WILLIAMS	*Theessentialroar.*
MALCOLM COWLEY	*Race Between a Subway Local and the Subway Express.*
VIRGIL GEDDES	*Uncle James' Woman.*
ELIN PELIN	*Dreamers.*
I. M. VEISSENBERG	*Mazel-tof.*
PHILIPPE SOUPAULT	*Hymn to Liberty.*
EUGENE JOLAS	*Flight into Geography.*

Reproductions of paintings by GIORGIO DE CHIRICO, TONITA PENA *and* SIDNEY HUNT.

Poems by MALCOLM COWLEY, EMILY HOLMES COLEMAN, EUGENE JOLAS, H. B. ARMITAGE, JOHN HYDE PRESTON, VIRGIL GEDDES, HORACE GREGORY, KENNETH FEARING, JAMES YOUNG, GEORGE DANGERFIELD, CLAIRE GOLL, IVAN GOLL, PAULINE LEADER, YVOR WINTERS, KAY BOYLE, BRAVIG IMBS.

IN THE MANNER OF — — —	*The Fixer.*
MARIA MCDONALD JOLAS	*Black Thoughts.*
GEORGE ANTHEIL	*Music Tomorrow.*
ELLIOT PAUL *and* ROBERT SAGE	*Artistic improvements of the cinema.*
KAY BOYLE	*Mr. Crane and His Grandmother.*

transition 11

TABLE OF CONTENTS

Death mask of ELSA VON FREYTAG-LORINGHOVEN.

Reproductions of paintings by PABLO PICASSO
and YVES TANGUY.

Poems by ST-J. PERSE *and* COMTE DE LAUTREAMONT.

EUGENE JOLAS
YVOR WINTERS
ROBERT SAGE
THEO VAN DOESBURG

BERNARD FAY

The Revolution of Language and James Joyce.
The Indian in English.
Williams as the Crow Flies.
Avant-Garde Literature in Holland.
Travel and Flight.

GLOSSARY.

transition 12

TABLE OF CONTENTS

Reproductions of paintings by ANDRÉ MASSON, GIORGIO DE CHIRICO, MAN RAY *and* FRANCIS PICABIA.

Poems *by* PAUL ELUARD, PIERRE UNIK, JAMES DALY, JACQUES BARON,
STANLEY BURNSHAW, WALTER LOWENFELS, PAUL BOWLES, CARL
RAKOSI, M. G. SHELLEY, CHARLES NORMAN, GEORGETTE CAMILLE,
ALLEN TATE, RENE LAPORTE, ESTHER KAUFMAN, EDWARD ROBBIN,
EVAN SHIPMAN.

EUGENE JOLAS and ELLIOT PAUL	*A Review.*
ROGER VITRAC	*Raymond Roussel.*
MARCEL BRION	*The Idea of Time in the Work of James Joyce.*
A. LINCOLN GILLESPIE JR.	*Textighter Eye-Ploy or Hothouse Bromidick?*
SYD. S. SALT	*America and George Antheil*
JOHN HERRMANN	*And Then The (Bridge) Failed.*

GLOSSARY.
INDEX.

transition 13

TABLE OF CONTENTS

transition 14

TABLE OF CONTENTS

transition 15

TABLE OF CONTENTS

———

transition 16/17

TABLE OF CONTENTS

GLOSSARY

transition *18*

TABLE OF CONTENTS

———

EXPLORATIONS

THE REVOLUTION OF THE WORD

WORK IN PROGRESS

NARRATIVE

GLOSSARY

transition 19/20

TABLE OF CONTENTS

———

DREAM AND MYTHOS

EVOLUTION OF THE SENSES

CAMBRIDGE EXPERIMENT
A MANIFESTO OF YOUNG ENGLAND

REVOLUTION OF THE WORD

ANNOUNCEMENT by THE EDITOR

THE ATLANTIC WORLD

---

transition 21

TRANSITION 1932

THE VERTICAL AGE

METANTHROPOLOGICAL CRISIS: a manifesto   105—145
Gabriel Audisio, Gottfried Benn, Martin Buber, Whit Burnett,
Leo Frobenius, Stuart Gilbert, Richard Huelsenbeck, C. G. Jung,
H. L. Mencken, Georges Ribemont-Dessaignes, Camille Schu-
wer, David A. Siqueiros, Philippe Soupault, Gertrude Stein,
Ronald Symond, Roger Vitrac, Ewald Wasmuth.
    Alberto Giacometti, Sculptures.   t/o 146

POETRY IS VERTICAL: 147—188
Poems by: Hans Arp, Joë Bousquet, Kay Boyle, Emily Holmes
Coleman, Charles Henri Ford, Hoelderlin, Eugene Jolas, Thomas
McGreevy, Georges Pelorson, Paul Scheerbart, James J.
Sweeney.

THE MANTIC PERSONALITY: 189

HOMAGE TO JAMES JOYCE
James Joyce at the Half Century: Padraic Colum, Stuart Gilbert,
    Eugene Jolas, Thomas Mc Greevy, Philippe Soupault.

LABORATORY OF THE WORD

transition 22

THE VERTIGRAL AGE

Cover by Sophie H. Taeuber-Arp

VERTIGRAL DOCUMENTS:

JAMES JOYCE: WORK IN PROGRESS:

LABORATORY OF THE MYSTIC LOGOS:

transition 23

CONTENTS

VERTIGRAL

Cover: "Hope and Destruction" by *Paul Klee*

Paramyths: *Wayne Andrews, Dorothy Boillotat, Eugene Jolas, Franz Kafka, Jean Paul, Georges Pelorson, Hans Schiess, Margaret Shedd.*

Four Primitive Documents: *Gustavo Barroso, Alejo Carpentier, Leo Frobenius, Texte Enfantin.*

Little Mantic Almageste
F. M. Huebner, Possession
Lothar Mundan, Vertigral Poetry

Hypnologues: *Thérèse Aubray,* (note by *Marcel Brion*), *Arthur Cummins, Homer Jeffries, Eugene Jolas, John Frederick Means, Georges Pelorson, Camille Schuwer, James Johnson Sweeney, Theo Rutra.*

Three Romantic-Mystic Texts: *Franz von Baader, Hugo Ball, Franz Werfel.*
Stuart Gilbert, Algernon Blackwood: Novelist and Mystic.

Eugene Jolas: Workshop
Transmutation Vertigraliste

JAMES JOYCE AND HIS NEW WORK
James Joyce: Continuation of Work in Progress
Léon-Paul Fargue, The Alchemist
Armand M. Petitjean, Joyce and Mythology. Mythology and Joyce.

MUTATION IN LANGUAGE
Inquiry on the Malady of Language: Answered by: *Gottfried Benn, Joë Bousquet, Marcel Brion, H. S. Canby, Malcolm Cowley, Luc Durtain, Norman Foerster, Ivan Goll, Philippe Lamour, H. L. Mencken, Francis de Miomandre, Gorham Munson, Emmanuel Mounier, C. K. Ogden, A. R. Orage, P. D. Ouspensky, Georges Pelorson, Armand M. Petitjean, Léon-Pierre Quint, Raja Rao, Theo Rutra, Jack Sanford, Camille Schuwer, Philippe Soupault, Louis Untermeyer, Laurence Vail, Edmond Vandercammen, Lansing Warren, Jean Wahl.*

Malady of Language, an Almageste
Louis Lerman. I am Talking to You: You are Talking to Me.

Experiences in Language Mutation: *Michaux, Georges Pelorson, Eugene Jolas, Camille Schuwer.*

THE SUBOBJECT OF ART
Carola Giedion-Welcker: New Roads in Modern Sculpture, with photos of work by: *Hans Arp, Umberto Boccioni, Konstantin Brancusi, R. Duchamp-Villon, N. Gabo, Alberto Giacometti, G. Gonzales, H. Laurens, J. Lipschitz.*

SUPPLEMENT
Testimony Against Gertrude Stein by: *Henri Matisse, Tristan Tzara, Maria Jolas, Georges Braque, Eugene Jolas, André Salmon.*

transition 24

CONTENTS

COVER by *Fernand Léger*

transition 25

CONTENTS

COVER by *Joan Mirò*

transition 26

CONTENTS

COVER *Marcel Duchamp:* 3 ou 4 gouttes de hauteur n'ont rien à faire avec la sauvagerie

transition 27

CONTENTS

HOMAGE TO THE MYTHMAKER

James Joyce is completing the last pages of his protean book of the night. *Work in Progress*, eighteen fragments of which have been published by *Transition* during the last ten years, will appear in book-form in 1938, and doubtless attract the attention of the inter-continental world with the electric shock of the thunder-word that epitomizes poly-syllabically one of its leit-motifs.

Fifteen years of word-ecstatic labours are about to close.

To the very end, like one of the Celtic ornament-makers, the Irish writer has worked, in painstaking solitude, at the gigantic vision which has possessed him ever since he sent *Ulysses* on its world-migration. As his Nocturne reaches the ultimate note of a word mutilated in the nightmind, as a final challenge to the spirit and grammar of the sun, he accelerates the rhythm, suffers the ensemble of his highly charged pan-logos once more, organizes into one synoptical prose-poem the most tenuous threads of the three parts and postlude that compose his tale of humanity's progress through the abyss of the ages.

Soon our curiosity as to the mysterious and jealously guarded title of the book—a title that was first conceived fifteen years ago—will be satisfied.

What will the finished book be like?

This complex, this enigmatic work has challenged contemporary speculation as no other book has done for a long time. Its fragmentary appearance will probably have militated against an immediate acceptance, but the reader has doubtless now been prepared through *Transition* and the exegetical efforts of *Transition* writers. There have been a few indications in the past fifteen years sketching the ultimate silhouette.

We know that Mr Joyce's ambition has been to write a book dealing with the night-mind of man. We have already followed most of the purgatorial, multiple characters, blundering through their larval and anthropological transmigrations. We have had glimpses of that titanic city-mountain synthesis: Humphrey Chimpden Earwigger, and have watched his countless human metamorphoses. We have followed the pan-symbolic pattern in the creation of Anna Livia Plurabelle, the river-woman, magna mater. Shem and Shaun, the adopted daughter, the household slut, the topers and gossips of pre-history and history, have passed by, in their primordial drama; the contour of the conflict that dominates the conception on the nocturnal stage plays in a continuous mutation of locality, objects, happenings, language, characters. Examining with new eyes Mr Joyce's revolutionary conception of the paragraph, we have tried to keep in mind that the dramatic dynamis is based on the Bruno theory of knowledge through opposites, and on the Vico philosophy of cyclic recurrence.

We are once more in the ambience of Dublin, 'The Black Pool', yet there is a new topographical background the action of the 'story' being played in a suburb: Chapelizod. We are in the Valley of the Liffey. Phoenix Park, the Wellington Monument, the Magazine etc . . . are constantly before us. Chapelizod is said to have taken its name from Iseult, made famous in our day by Tennyson and Wagner. All these elements are constantly used in the structure of *Work in Progress*.

The 'story' deals with the outer and inner world of a lower middle-class family living in a hotel beside the prattling Liffey, in the vicinity of Phoenix Park. It is a sultry summer-night. Lightning rolling over the Dublin mountains strikes primal fear in the hearts of the inhabitants. A thunder-clap roars through the phantasmal dusk. The customers in the pub forget their gargantuan tales. Rain clears the atmosphere. The children play on the square. Then the house goes to sleep. We are in the abyss of time and space, in the world of phantoms, in the night-memory of the family—and of the human race.

Mr Joyce is now finishing the last pages. We may expect technical innovations that go beyond Marion Bloom's monologue in audacity.

For now the author deals with the dream-phantasies, with the hypno-gogic hallucinations, the inner scissions of an entire household, of mankind in general.

Nietzsche says somewhere: 'In sleep and dream we pass once more through the early phases of mankind.' Modern psychology has made enormous progress in delineating the *mythological* remnants of the un-conscious. Man, in his night-life, re-lives the phantasies that were those of the Magdalenean man, the dream-phantoms which produced the great myths of all the races.

In *Work in Progress*, the pre-logical or pre-conscious mind of the ancestors is continuously at work. Mr Joyce presents his phantasma-goric figures as passing back and forth from a mentality saturated with archetypal images to a contemporary kinesis, from the past of child-hood memories to a vision of future construction.

History being, in his earlier words, 'a nightmare' Mr Joyce gives us the multi-dimensional idea of Time in sleep. His conception of Time is born out of his deep sense of race parallelism. It has relations with the newest discoveries of physical science as well as with oneiromantic experiments. The Joycean idea is cosmic Time, a colossal vision that negatives Bergson's theory of *durée*.

Legend tells us that prehistoric man possessed a third eye, which was the 'seat of the soul' in the Cartesian philosophy. The pineal eye was said to have given ancestral man the natural intuitive faculties which modern man has apparently lost. The man with the third eye may come back again, according to certain modern palaeontologists, who foresee the eventual re-development of that anatomical organ.

Perse O'Reilly, hotelier at Chapelizod, Vico Road, is a man with the third eye.

One of the chief myths which *Work in Progress* treats exhaustively and with glacial objectivity is that of original sin. The myth of the fall of the angels: the idea of the 'diabolical principle': the gnostic-mystic idea of the demi-urge; the antithetical dynamism of good and evil.

It has always been diverting to me to see my Catholic co-religion-naires assail Mr Joyce's work because of its apparently heretic content. Is it necessary to point out to them the enormous role the concept of evil plays in Catholic theology? The Paschal acolyte does not hesitate to eulogize 'the sin of Adam' in a famous liturgical passage. St Augustine himself declared: 'Felix culpa! O fortunatissimum Adae peccatum!'. The obscene distortions of gargoyles on Gothic cathedrals show the very luxuriant imagination of the conformist architects. The satanic chimeras of the paintings of such believers as Mathias Grunewald and Hieronymus Bosch lead us into the abyss of the grotesque. And what of the book of Kels? Mr Joyce, who knows his fathers of the Church, assumes the right which the Catholic Church has always given to the artist, to present the carnal side of man's consciousness with all the mastery of his verbal art.

The opposition of Catholic puritans is not shared by the highest ecclesiastical authorities, and it might be of interest to hear what the *Osservatore Romano*, world-organ of the Vatican, has to say about James Joyce. In a recent issue of that famous newspaper (22 October 1937), we find the following reference to him in an essay on modern Irish literature:

'. . . . e infine James Joyce, di fama europea, iconoclasta e rebelle, che dopo aver cercato di ringiovanire il vecchio naturalismo, tenta nell' *Ulyxes* di tradurre plasticamente la realta interiore, e nell' *Opera in Corso* attraverse una esperienza onirica et insieme linguistica si sforza di aprire altre vie all' espressione del sentimento umane'.[1]

The Catholic Church is apparently far removed from the philistinism and hypocrisy of some of the orthodox literary critics of Dublin, London and New York.

It is now more than ten years since I read the first version of *Work in Progress*, then a comparatively small manuscript. I had the privilege of seeing it grow bit by bit, of watching its expansion at close range. In Mr Joyce's word-alchemical laboratory I have had the pleasure of glimpsing the amalgamations he made of his journeys into the unconscious of mankind.

The publishing of any one of the seventeen fragments in *Transition*

---

1 'And finally James Joyce, of European fame, iconoclast and rebel, who after having sought to renovate the old naturalism, attempted in *Ulysses*, to translate plastically the inner reality, and, who, in *Work in Progress*, in an experiment, both oneiric and linguistic, is seeking to open up new paths for the expression of human sentiments'.

has always been an event in the editorial life of the review. It was not the simple process of taking over from the author a completed manuscript, but required the active collaboration of members of the *Transition* staff, of friends and sympathizers. It was necessary to go through a number of note-books each of which had esoteric symbols indicating the reference to a given character, locality, event, or mood. Then the words accumulated over the years had to be placed in the segment for which they were intended.

It has been interesting to see Mr Joyce's very special method of working. His interest in the little events of every day, during a period filled with political upheavals, is a constant source of wonder. Rivers, and mountains, and children, and apparently insignificant occurrences in the streets, preoccupy him. He incorporates continually into his work the living folklore and mythology gathered in his travels through Europe and the British Isles. His verbs transmute the quotidian gesture, which Jousse and Paget tell us was man's primal language.

'This book', he sometimes says, 'is being written by the people I have met or known'. Sometimes he hardly seems to be listening to the conversation around him. Yet nothing escapes his prodigious memory, whether the dialogues be in English, French, German, or Italian. It may be a slip of the tongue, a phantasmatic verbal deformation, or just a tic of speech, but it usually turns up later in its proper place.

Only absolute indifference to the sociological habit of thought could make possible such a devotion to the purely creative *élan*. Joyce does not take sides. He tells the pessimistic story of mankind's internecine war with a smile of irony and sometimes pity. He presses seconds into interplanetary aeons by looking at everything from a 'funnominal' perspective. He has no 'ethical' axe to grind. Yet is it not a fact that all his characters—beginning with those in *Dubliners* and continuing through *Work in Progress*—are people of the lower social strata, the so-called proletarized lower middle-class, the poor white whose struggles in the never changing world of Cain and Abel, or Shem and Shaun, he presents with the detachment of a whimsical understanding? The martial antinomies of life are the elements with which he deals. In lowly puns, irrational junctions, cross-currents from more than forty languages, we see the child-play of '*The Mime of Mick, Nick and the Maggies*', the legend of the '*Mookse and the Gripes*', the myth of '*Anna Livia Plurabelle*', the fantasia of '*Shem and Shaun*', the grotesque of

'Haveth Childers Everywhere', the fable of 'The Ondt and the Gracehoper' —all of them folk of the common, human run, yet made sublime by the creative imagination of a poet.

Work in Progress is 'a compendium, an encyclopedia of the entire mental life of a man of genius', a definition which Wilhelm Schlegel posited, more than a hundred years ago, for the novel of the future.

Soon the Book of Proteus will appear in its entirety. We who have watched it grow, hope that there will be ears to hear and rejoice at the fabulous new harmonies of this All-World Symphony!

Eugene JOLAS.

BIBLIOGRAPHY

Afrikanische Legenden, ed. Carl Einstein. Berlin: Ernst Rowohlt, 1925.

Allen, Charles. 'American Little Magazines: Transition', *American Prefaces*, IV, viii (May 1939), 115.

Anderson, Margaret. *My Thirty Years War*. New York: Covici, Friede, 1930. London: A. A. Knopf, 1930.

Anthologie de la Nouvelle Poésie Américaine, ed. Eugene Jolas. Paris, 1928.

Arp, Hans, Richard Huelsenbeck, and Tristan Tzara. *Die Geburt des Dada*. Zurich, 1957.

Atherton, James S. *The Books at the Wake*. London: Faber and Faber, 1959.

Balakian, Anna. *The Literary Origins of Surrealism*. New York: NYU Press, Kings Crown Press, 1947.

The Basic Writings of Sigmund Freud, trans. and ed. A. A. Brill. New York: The Modern Library, 1938.

Baumgarth, Christa. *Geschichte des Futurismus*. Hamburg: Rowohlt-Taschenbuch-Verlag, 1966.

Beach, Sylvia. *Catalogue of a Collection Containing Manuscripts and Rare Editions of James Joyce, Etc.* Paris: Shakespeare, 1935.

Beckett, Samuel. *Echo's Bones and Other Precipitates*. Paris: Europa Press, 1935. In *Poems in English*. London: John Calder, 1961.

——. *How It Is*. New York: Grove Press, 1964. London: John Calder, 1964.

——. *More Pricks than Kicks*. London: Windus, 1934. Recent: London: Calder & Boyars, 1970.

——. *Murphy*. London: Routledge: 1938. Recent: London: Calder, 1963.

——. *Poems in English*. London: John Calder, 1961.

Beckett, Samuel, et al. *Our Exagmination Round His Factification for Incamination of Work in Progress.* Paris: Shakespeare, 1929 (Sylvia Beach). London, Chartres: Faber & Faber, 1936, 1962.

Belaval, Yvon. *Poèmes d'aujourd'hui.* Paris: Gallimard, 1964.

Bentley, Eric. *The Importance of Scrutiny.* New York: G. W. Stewart, 1948. New York University Press, 1964.

Blackmur, R. P. *Form and Value in Modern Poetry.* Garden City, New York: Doubleday & Co., 1957.

Boyle, Kay, and Robert McAlmon. *Being Geniuses Together.* New York: Doubleday, 1968. London: M. Joseph, 1970.

Briefe der Expressionisten, ed. Kasimir Edschmid. Frankfurt/M.: Ullstein, 1964.

Budgen, Frank. *James Joyce and the Making of Ulysses.* Bloomington: Indiana University Press, 1960. London: Oxford University Press, 1972.

Calverton, V. F. 'The Revolution-in-the-Wordists', *Modern Quarterly,* V (Fall, 1929), 276–83.

Campbell, Joseph, and Henry Morton Robinson. *A Skeleton Key to Finnegans Wake.* London: Faber and Faber, 1944.

Cazamian, L. *A History of French Literature.* London: Oxford University Press, 1963.

Coe, Richard N. *Samuel Beckett.* New York: Grove Press, 1964. Edinburgh and London: Oliver & Boyd, 1964 (*Beckett*).

The Collected Poems of Hart Crane, ed. Waldo Frank. New York: Liverwright, 1933. London: Boriswood, 1938.

Colum, Mary and Padraic. *Our Friend James Joyce.* New York: Doubleday, 1958. London: Victor Gollancz, 1959.

The Complete Poems and Selected Letters and Prose of Hart Crane, ed. Brom Weber. New York: Liverwright, 1966. London: Oxford University Press, 1968.

Connolly, Thomas E. *The Personal Library of James Joyce: Descriptive Bibliography* ('University of Buffalo Studies', Vol. XXII, I.). Buffalo, 1955.

Contempo, III, no. 13 (February 1934).

Contemporary German Poetry, ed. and trans. Babette Deutsch and Avram Yarmolinsky. London: John Lane, 1923 (Printed in U.S.).

Cowan, Louise. *The Fugitive Group.* Baton Rouge: Louisiana State University Press, 1959.

Cowley, Malcolm. *Exile's Return.* New York: Viking, 1951. London: Bodley Head, 1961.

The Critical Writings of James Joyce, ed. Ellsworth Mason and Richard Ellmann. New York: Viking, 1959. London: Faber & Faber, 1959.

Croce, Benedetto. *The Philosophy of Giambattista Vico,* trans. R. G. Collingwood. London: Macmillan (?) , 1913.

Dada Eine Literarische Dokumentation, ed. Richard Huelsenbeck. Hamburg: Rowohlt, 1964.

Dada Monographie einer Bewegung, ed. Willy Verkauf. St. Gallen: Tiranti, 1958. London: Tiranti, 1961.

The Diary of Anaïs Nin 1934–1939, ed. Gunther Stuhlmann. New York: Swallow Press, 1967. *Journals of Anaïs Nin*. London: Owen, 1966.

Deming, Robert H. *A Bibliography of James Joyce Studies*. Lawrence, Kansas: University of Kansas Press, 1964.

Deutsch, Babette. *Poetry in Our Time*. Garden City, New York: Doubleday & Co., 1963.

The Divine Comedy, trans. by Henry F. Cary in *Harvard Classics*, XX. New York: P. F. Collier, 1909. London: Popular Ed., 1903, also G. Bell, 1910.

Documents, I (March 1929).

Dujardin, Edouard. *Les lauriers sont coupés*. Paris: A. Messein, 1924.

Dupuy, M. *La Philosophie de Max Scheler*. Paris: Presses universitaires de France, 1959. II, 682.

Duwe, Wille. *Deutsche Dichtung Des 20. Jahrhunderts*. Zurich: Orell Füsseli, 1936.

Duwe, Wilhelm. *Ausdrucksformen Deutscher Dichtung*. Berlin: E. Schmidt, 1965.

Dylan Thomas A Collection of Critical Essays, ed. C. B. Cox. Englewood Cliffs, New Jersey: Prentice-Hall, 1966.

Edel, Leon. 'James Joyce: The Last Journey', *Story*, XXXII, No. 129 (Summer, 1948), 139–47.

Edschmid, Kasimir. *Lebendiger Expressionismus*. Munich: Wein, K. Desch, 1961.

Einstein, Carl. *Gesammelte Werke*, ed. Ernst Nef. Wiesbaden: Limes Verlag, 1962.

Eliot, T. S. *The Complete Poems and Plays 1909–1950*. New York: Harcourt Brace, 1958. *Collected Plays* and *Collected Poems 1909–1962*. London: Faber & Faber, 1962.

Ellmann, Richard. *James Joyce*. New York: Oxford University Press, 1959.

Emrich, Wilhelm. *Franz Kafka*. Bonn: Athenäum-Verlag, 1958.

Esslin, Martin. *The Theatre of the Absurd*. Garden City, New York: Doubleday, 1961. London: Spottiswode, 1962.

Expressionismus, ed. Paul Raabe. Freiburg: Olten, Walter-Verlag, 1965.

Federman, Raymond. *Journey to Chaos: Samuel Beckett's Early Fiction*. Berkeley: University of California Press, 1965.

Fitzgibbon, Constantine. *The Life of Dylan Thomas*. Boston: Little, Brown, 1965. London: J. M. Dent, 1965.

Fletcher, John. *The Novels of Samuel Beckett*. London: Chatto & Windus, 1964.

Flores, Angel. *Franz Kafka A Chronology and Bibliography*. Houlton, Me.: Bern Porter, 1944.

Freud, Sigmund. *The Ego and the Id*, in *The Standard Edition of the Complete Psychological Works of Sigmund Freud*, ed. James Strachey, XIX. London: Hogarth Press, 1961.

Gheerbrant, Bernard. *James Joyce: Sa Vie, Son Oeuvre, Son Rayonnenment*. Paris: La Hune, 1949.

Gilbert, Stuart. 'Why a Revolution of the Word?' *Modern Quarterly*, V (Fall, 1929), 284–5.

Gillet, Louis. *Claybook for James Joyce*, trans. Georges Markow-Totevy. London, New York: Abelard-Schuman, 1958.

Glasheen, Adaline. *A Census of Finnegans Wake*. London: Faber & Faber, 1957.

Gorman, Herbert. 'Experimentalism—and Experimentalists', *Modern Quarterly*, V (Fall, 1929), 292–3.

——. *James Joyce*. New York: Farrar & Rinehart, 1939. London: John Lane, 1941.

Gotham Book Mart. *We Moderns, 1920–1940*. New York, 1940.

Hamburger, Käte. *Philosophie der Dichter: Novalis, Schiller, Rilke*. Stuttgart, Berlin, Koln, Mainz, Kohlhammer, 1966.

Hardre, Jacques. 'Present State of Studies on Literary Surrealism'. *Yearbook of Comparative and General Literature*, No. 9, Chapel Hill, N.C.

Hart, Clive. *A Concordance to Finnegans Wake*. Minneapolis: University of Minnesota Press, 1963.

——. *Structure and Motif in Finnegans Wake*. London: Faber & Faber, 1962.

Harvey, Laurence. *Samuel Beckett; poet ad critic*. Princeton: Princeton University Press, 1970.

Hausmann, Raoul. *Courrier Dada*. Paris: Le Terrain vague, 1958.

Hayman, David. *Joyce et Mallarmé*. 2 Vols., Paris: Lettres modernes, 1956.

Heap, Jane. 'Lost: A Renaissance', *The Little Review*, XII (May 1929), 5.

Hemmerle, Rudolf. *Franz Kafka Eine Bibliographie*. Munich: R. Lerche, 1958.

The Henry Miller Reader, ed. Lawrence Durell. Norfolk, Conn: New Directions, 1969.

Higginson, Fred H. 'James Joyce, Linguist', *Word Study*, XXXI (May 1956) 1–3.

Hill, Archibald. 'A Philologist Looks at *Finnegans Wake*', *Virginia Quarterly Review*, XV (October 1939), 650–6.

Hoffman, Frederick, Charles Allen and Carolyn F. Ulrich. *The Little Magazine: a History and a Bibliography*. Princeton, N.J.: Princeton University Press, 1946.

Hoffman, Frederick J. *Samuel Beckett The Language of Self*. New York: E.P. Dutton, 1964.

Hoffman, Michael J. *The Development of Abstractionism in the Writings of Gertrude Stein*. Philadelphia: University of Pennsylvania Press, 1965.

Horton, Philip. *Hart Crane*. New York: W. W. Norton, 1937.

Hough, Graham. *The Last Romantics*. New York: Barnes & Noble, 1961. London: Methuen, 1961.

A James Joyce Miscellany, ed. Marvin Magalaner, 1st series. New York: James Joyce Society, 1957.

A James Joyce Miscellany, ed. Marvin Magalaner, 2nd series. Carbondale, Ill: So. Illinois University Press, 1959.

A James Joyce Miscellany, ed. Marvin Magalaner. 3rd series. Carbondale: So. Illinois University Press, 1962.

James Joyce's Scribbledehobble: The Ur-Workbook for Finnegans Wake, ed. Thomas E. Connolly. Evanston: Northwestern University Press, 1961.

James Joyce: Two Decades of Criticism, ed. Seon Givens. New York: Vanguard Press, 1963.

A James Joyce Yearbook, ed. Maria Jolas. Paris: Transition Workshop, 1949.

Järv, Harry. *Die Kafka-Literatur*. Malmö: Bö Cavefors, 1961.

Jeffers, Robinson. *Roan Stallion, Tamar and Other Poems*. New York: The Modern Library, 1935, ii. London: Hogarth Press, 1928 by Leo. and V. Woolf.

Jolas, Maria. 'James Joyce as a Revolutionary: Reply to Max Lerner', *New Republic*, CVII (November 1942), 613.

——. 'Joyce en 1939–1940', *Mercure de France*, CCCIX (May 1950), 45–58.

Jolas, Eugene. *Cinema*. New York: Adelphi, 1926.

——. *The Language of Night*. The Hague: Servire Press, 1932.

——. 'Man from Babel' unpublished autobiography in the possession of Mrs Eugene Jolas in Paris.

——. 'My Friend James Joyce', *Partisan Review*, VII (March–April, 1941), 82–93. Reprinted in *James Joyce: Two Decades of Criticism*, ed. Seon Givens. New York: Vanguard Press, 1948.

——. 'Prolegomenon of White Romanticism and Mythos of Ascension', unpublished essay in the possession of Mrs Eugene Jolas.

——. 'Rambles in Literary Paris', *Chicago Tribune*, Paris edition, 29 May 1927.

——. 'The Revolution of the Word' (A Symposium), *Modern Quarterly*, V (Fall, 1929), 273–92.

——. 'The Spirit and the Troglodytes', *Living Age*, CCCIX (May 1941), 255.

——. 'transition: An Epilogue', *American Mercury*, XXIII (1931), 184–91.

——. 'Verbirrupta For James Joyce', *Contempo*, III, no. 13 (February 1934), 3.

Josephson, Matthew. *Life Among the Surrealists*. New York: Holt, Rinehart, Winston, 1962.

Journey into the Self being the letters, papers & journals of Leo Stein, ed. Edmund Fuller. New York: Crown, 1950.

Jousse, Marcel. '*Les Lois psycho-physiologiques du Style oral vivant et leur Utilisa-tion philologique*', in *L'Ethnographie, bulletin semestriel*, new series no. 23, 15 April 1931, 23–40.

———. *Du Mimisme et la Musique chez l'Enfant*. Paris: Geuthner, 1935.

———. *Mimetisme humain et Psychologie de la Lecture*. Paris: Geuthner, 1935.

———. *Mimetisme humain et Style manuel*. Paris: Geuthner, 1936.

———. '*Le Style Oral*' in *Archives de Philosophy*. II, iv. 1925.

Joyce, James. 'From Work in Progress', in *Contact Collection of Contemporary Writers*, ed. Robert McAlmon. Paris: Three Mountains Press, 1925.

———. *A Portrait of the Artist as a Young Man* in *The Portable James Joyce*, ed. Harry Levin. New York: Viking, 1947. London: Cape (new ed.), 1968.

———. *Finnegans Wake*. New York: Viking, 1964. London: Faber and Faber, 1964 (third ed.).

———. *Ulysses*. New York: Random House, 1946. London: New Travellers Library, 1950.

Kenner, Hugh. *Dublin's Joyce*. Bloomington: Indiana University Press, 1956. London: Chatto and Windus, 1955.

———. *Wyndham Lewis*. Norfolk, Conn.: New Directions, 1954. London, Binghamton: Methuen & Co., 1954.

Kermode, Frank. *Romantic Image*. New York, and London: Routledge & Kegan Paul, 1957.

Leavis, F. R. 'Joyce and the Revolution of the Word', *Scrutiny*, II, No. 2 (September 1933), 193–201.

The Letters of Ezra Pound 1907–1941, ed. D.D. Paige. New York: Harcourt, Brace, 1950. London: Faber & Faber, 1951.

The Letters of Hart Crane, ed. Brom Weber. Berkeley: University of California Press, 1965.

Letters of James Joyce, ed. Richard Ellmann, II and III. New York: Viking, 1966. London: Faber & Faber, 1966.

Letters of James Joyce, ed. Stuart Gilbert, I. New York: Viking, 1957. London: Faber & Faber, 1957.

Levin, Harry. *James Joyce: A Critical Introduction*. Norfolk: New Directions 1941. London: Faber & Faber, 1944.

Lewis, R. W. B. *The Poetry of Hart Crane A Critical Study*. Princeton: Princeton University Press, 1967.

Lewis, Wyndham. *The Diabolical Principle and the Dithyrambic Spectator*. London: Chatto & Windus, 1931.

———. 'The Diabolical Principle', *The Enemy*, No. 3 (January 1929), 9–84.

———. 'The Revolutionary Simpleton', *The Enemy*, I (January 1927), 25–192.

———. *Time and Western Man*. London: Chatto & Windus, 1927.

Lichtenberger, Henri. *Novalis*. Paris: Bloud, 1912.

Lohner, Edgar. *Gottfried Benn Bibliographie* 1912–1956. Wiesbaden: Limes Verlag, 1958.

Magalaner, Marvin, and Richard M. Kain. *Joyce The Man, the Work, the Reputation*. London: John Calder, 1957 (printed in New York).

Marinetti, F. T. 'Futurist Manifesto', in *The Modern Tradition*, ed. Richard Ellmann and Charles Feidelson. New York: Oxford University Press, 1965.

——. 'Technical Manifesto of Futurist Literature', in Christa Baumgarth, *Geschichte des Futurismus*. Hamburg: Rowohlt, 1966.

McAlmon, Robert. *Being Geniuses Together: An Autobiography*. London: Secker & Warburg, 1938.

McMillan, Dougald. 'Influences of Gerhardt Hauptmann in Joyce's *Ulysses*', James Joyce Quarterly, IV (Winter, 1967), 107–119.

Miller, Henry. *Cosmological Eye*. Norfolk, Conn.: New Directions, 1939.

Miller, Rosalind S. *Gertrude Stein: Form and Intelligibility*. New York: Exposition Press, 1949.

Mizener, Arthur. *The Cornell Joyce Collection, given to Cornell University by William G. Mennen*, Ithaca, 1958.

The Modern Tradition, ed. Richard Ellmann and Charles Feidelson, Jr. New York: Oxford University Press, 1965.

Monroe, Harriet. 'A Discussion with Hart Crane', *Poetry*. October 1926.

——. *A Poet's Life*. New York: Macmillan & Co., 1938.

Muir, Edwin. *Transition*. London: L. and V. Woolf, 1926 (printed in USA).

Nadeau, Maurice. *The History of Surrealism*. New York: Macmillan & Co., 1965. London: J. Cape, 1968.

New Directions, ed. James Laughlin, IV, No. 1 (1936). Norfolk, Conn.: New Directions.

The New Science of Giambattista Vico, trans. from 3rd ed. (1744) by Thomas Goddard Bergin and Max Harold Fisch. Ithaca: Cornell University Press, 1948.

Noël, Lucy. *James Joyce and Paul Léon: the Story of a Friendship*. New York: Gotham Book Mart, 1950.

Noon, William T. *Joyce and Aquinas*. New Haven: Yale University Press, 1957.

Novalis. *Fragmente*, ed. Ernst Kamnitzer. Dresden: Wolfgang Jess verlag, 1929.

O'Faolain, Sean. 'Style and the Limitation of Speech', *Criterion*, VIII (1928), 67–87.

Ogden, C. K. and I. A. Richards. *The Meaning of Meaning*. London: Kegan Paul, 1944.

Paul, Elliot. 'Farthest North: a Study of James Joyce', *The Bookman*, LXXV (May 1932), 156–63.

Poètes a l'écart, ed. Carola Giedion-Welcker. Bern: Berteli, 1946.

Putnam, Samuel. 'If Dada Comes to America', *Contempo*, II, 25 July 1932.
——. *Paris was Our Mistress*. New York: Viking Press, 1947.
Radek, Karl. 'James Joyce or Socialist Realist?' in *Problems of Soviet Literature*, ed. A. Zhdanov et al. New York: International Publishers, 1935.
Raymond, Marcel. *From Baudelaire to Surrealism*. New York: Wittenborn, Schultz, 1950. London: Methuen, 1970.
R[ead,] H[erbert]. 'Foreign Periodicals', *Criterion*, V, iii (June 1927), 372–5.
La Révolution Surréaliste, N.2, 15 January 1925.
Ribemont-Dessaignes, G[eorges]. *Déja Jadis*. Paris: R. Julliard, 1958.
Richards, I. A, *Principles of Literary Criticism*. New York: Harcourt Brace, 1959 or 1961. London: Routledge & Kegan Paul, 1960.
Rosenthal, M. L. *The Modern Poets*. New York: Oxford University Press, 1965.
Rowe, H. D. *Hart Crane A Bibliography*. Denver: A. Swallow, 1955.
Salemson, Harold. 'James Joyce and the New Word', *Modern Quarterly*, V (Fall, 1929), 294–312.
Samuel Beckett. *A Collection of Critical Essays*, ed. Martin Esslin. Englewood Cliffs, N.J.: Prentice-Hall, 1965.
Scheler, Max. *Vom Ewigen im Menschen*, in *Gesammelte Werke*, Band V. Berne: Francke, 1954.
Scholes, Robert E. *The Cornell Joyce Collection: a Catalogue*. Ithaca: Cornell University Press, 1961.
Scott, Nathan A. *Samuel Beckett*. London: Bowes & Bowes, 1965.
Selected Letters of Dylan Thomas, ed. Constantine Fitzgibbon. New York: New Directions, 1966. London: Dent, 1966.
Simon, Heinrich. *Der magische Idealismus*. Heidelberg: Winter, 1906.
Sitwell, Edith. *Aspects of Modern Poetry*. London: Duckworth, 1934.
Sokel, Walter H. *Franz Kafka Tragik und Ironie*. Munich: A. Langer, 1964.
Sprigge, Elizabeth. *Gertrude Stein Her Life and Work*. London: Hamish & Hamilton, 1957.
Stead, C. K. *The New Poetic Yeats to Eliot*. New York: Harper & Row, 1964. London: Hutchinson, 1964.
Stein, Gertrude. *Autobiography of Alice B. Toklas*, ed. John Lane. London, Dublin: Arrow Books, 1933–4 (publisher: John Lane).
——. *Lectures in America*. New York: Random House, 1935.
——. *Portraits and Prayers*. New York: Random House, 1934.
Sutherland, Donald. *Gertrude Stein*. New Haven: Yale University Press, 1951.
Sweeney, James J. 'The Word was his Oyster', *Hudson Review*, V (Autumn, 1932), 404—8.
Thomas Dylan. *The Collected Poems of Dylan Thomas*. New York: New Directions, 1971, London: J. M. Dent, 1956.

Thompson, W. I. 'Language of *Finnegans Wake*', *The Sewanee Review*, LXXII, No. I (Winter, 1964), 78–90.

Transition Workshop, ed. Eugene Jolas. New York: Vanguard Press, 1949.

Tzara, Tristan. *Sept Manifestes Dada*. Paris: J. Budry, 1924.

Vogler, Thomas A. 'A new View of Hart Crane's Bridge', *The Sewanee Review*, LXXIII, No. 3 (Summer, 1965), 381–408.

Voyager: A Life of Hart Crane. New York: Farrar, Straus & Giroux, 1969(?). London: Bloud, 1970.

Wagenbach, Klaus. *Franz Kafka*. Hamburg: Rowohlt, 1964.

Wagner, Geoffrey. *Wyndham Lewis: A Portrait of the Artist as the Enemy*. New Haven: Yale University Press, 1957. London: Routledge & Kegan Paul, 1957 (printed in U.S.).

Waldberg, Patrick. *Surrealism*, London: Thames & Hudson, 1965.

Walser, Martin. *Beschreibung einer Form*. Munich: Hanser, 1961.

Wasserstrom, William. *The Time of the Dial*. Syracuse, N.Y.: Syracuse University Press, 1963.

Weber, Brom. *Hart Crane: A Biographical and Critical Study*. New York: Bodley Press, 1948.

Wilson, Edmund. *Axel's Castle*. New York and London: Scribner's Sons, 1931.

Yeats, W. B. *A Vision*. London: Macmillan & Co., 1937.

INDEX